GREAT
HISTORIC
PLACES
of
EUROPE

The Horizon Book of
GREAT HISTORIC PLACES *of* EUROPE

Marshall B. Davidson
and the Editors of *Horizon*

Published by
AMERICAN HERITAGE PUBLISHING CO., INC.
New York

Book Trade Distribution by
McGRAW-HILL BOOK COMPANY

STAFF FOR THIS BOOK

EDITOR
Marshall B. Davidson

ART DIRECTOR
Elaine Golt Gongora

ADDITIONAL TEXT BY
Margot Brill Higgins
Wendy Buehr Murphy
Bruce Bohle
Ormonde de Kay, Jr.
Walter Karp

ASSOCIATE EDITOR
Helen C. Dunn

PICTURE EDITOR
Mary Z. Jenkins

ASSISTANT PICTURE EDITOR
Ellen F. Zeifer

EDITORIAL ASSISTANT
Donna F. Whiteman

CONSULTANT LIBRARIAN
Laura L. Masters

EUROPEAN BUREAU
Gertrudis Feliu, *Chief*

American Heritage
Publishing Co., Inc.

PRESIDENT AND PUBLISHER
Paul Gottlieb

GENERAL MANAGER,
BOOK DIVISION
Kenneth W. Leish

EDITORIAL ART DIRECTOR
Murray Belsky

The editors appreciate the assistance provided by many individuals and institutions during the preparation of this book. They especially wish to thank the following:

British Tourist Authority
May Beth Fenton
Marilyn Marx

Jane Horton de Cabanyes,
Madrid

*Cooper-Hewitt Museum
of Design,
Smithsonian Institution*
Elaine Dee

*Danish Information Office,
Consulate General of
Denmark, New York*
Inge Winkelmann

*French Government
Tourist Office*
George Hern, Jr.,
Public Relations Director
Danielle Lecoq

Bianca Gabbrielli, Rome

*Greek National
Tourist Office*
Marjorie Bosch

Vasi Joannopoulos, Athens

Metropolitan Museum of Art
Margaret Bertin
Marcy McKee
Margaret Nolan
Nada Saporiti

*Norwegian National
Tourist Office*
Solveig Cordova

*Rhode Island School
of Design*
Catherine McCauley,
Assistant Curator

Spanish Heritage Association
Father M. J. Rodriguez

Christine Sutherland, London

*Swedish National
Tourist Office*
Louise Malmstrom

Time-Life Picture Agency
Phyllis Grygalin
Catherine Rhyden

Special Photography
Geoffrey Clements
Frank Lerner

Library of Congress Cataloging in Publication Data

Davidson, Marshall B
    The Horizon book of great historic places of Europe.

    Companion vol. to A Horizon guide: great historic places of Europe.
    1. Europe — Description and travel — 1971-   —
Views. 2. Historic sites — Europe — Pictorial works.
I. Horizon (New York, 1958-   ) II. Title.
III. Title: Great historic places of Europe.
D910.5.D38   914'.03'550222   74-11098
ISBN 0-07-015433-3   Nov. 26, 1974
ISBN 0-07-015434-1 (deluxe)

HALF-TITLE PAGE: *Mont Cenis Alpine pass between France and Italy*
BRITISH MUSEUM

TITLE PAGE: *Paris, seen from the Louvre, painted by V. J. Nicolle*
MUSEE CARNAVALET, PARIS

CONTENTS PAGE: *A painting of the Roman Forum by Antonio Canaletto*
BY GRACIOUS PERMISSION OF HER MAJESTY QUEEN ELIZABETH II

Introduction

When traveling, Dr. Samuel Johnson once observed, "a man must carry knowledge with him, if he would bring home knowledge." Although the way of the traveler has vastly changed in the meantime, that dictum still holds true. In Johnson's day, to journey through Europe—to make the Grand Tour—was an essential part of every English gentleman's education. On the Continent the tourist would acquire a firsthand understanding of foreign languages and manners, of ancient and modern art and architecture, of comparative history, and of cultural refinements and oddities in general that would enrich his life when he returned to his insular homeland. (Quite aside from the pursuit of such edifying experience, it was considered preferable for a young man inclined to adventures of another sort to sow his wild oats abroad rather than at home.)

Such expeditions were sometimes hazardous—bandits were a common threat on the road; often uncomfortable—verminous bedclothes and indigestible meals could be expected at ordinary inns; and usually lengthy—the most thorough of those tourists spent several years on their journeys. Affluent American colonists joined their British cousins on such travels. In 1763 young Samuel Powel, later a friend of and a host to George Washington, sailed from Philadelphia for London, where he was presented to George III. Proceeding to the Continent, he was received by the pope in Rome and by the king of Sardinia in Turin. Before returning home two years later, where he would be Philadelphia's last colonial mayor, Powel joined the parade of celebrated persons who journeyed to Ferney, near Lake Geneva, to visit with Voltaire.

The expenses of such expeditions ran high, of course. On almost any count the Grand Tour was nothing to be undertaken lightly, and the better part of those who took off across the English Channel from Dover to Calais to start their trip prepared themselves that they might the more richly benefit from the experience, as Johnson suggested. If only the wealthy could afford such a program, there were enough of them to make the Englishman a familiar sight in Europe throughout the eighteenth century. In the summer of 1785, Edward Gibbon was told, there were forty thousand of them on the Continent.

In our own time many hundreds of thousands from all over the globe swarm to Europe every year. Not all of them are wealthy by any means, nor are all of them bent on improving themselves, as were most of their eighteenth-century antecedents. Not only has getting about over long distances become easier and on the whole more comfortable, but with jet planes and auto routes as commonplace inducements, getting about speedily has become for many an end in itself. Indications of time zones appear like zebra stripes on the daily calendar. Under the circumstances, for those who travel with some intention of learning, Johnson's pronouncement is of even more practical interest than it was in his day. In any event, his words have been clearly in mind during the preparation of this book. It has also become much easier for the vicarious traveler to explore distant parts of the world to advantage. Thanks to the wide-ranging eye of the camera and the fidelity of modern photoreproduction, facilities unknown to much earlier generations, he can form a fair impression of faraway places without leaving his armchair.

Several generations ago the American expatriate Henry James judged that his fellow countrymen had "a superstitious valuation of Europe." That statement is not as patronizing as it may sound, or as James may have meant it to be, and there is still a measure of truth in it. As Thomas Paine pointed out almost two centuries ago when the American nation was a-borning, all Europe, not England alone, was its parent country. For all the nation's independent achievements, the roots of American history and culture remain widely spread throughout Europe. Aside from any other considerations, a natural curiosity and interest lead Americans back to the lands of their origins. Those works of man that have been either consciously or accidentally preserved in defiance of time have a compelling hold on the imagination, for they contain much of the meaning of history; they offer a material explanation of those adventures in civilization that led out of the past and into the present.

On a map of the globe Europe appears as a relatively small extension of the vast Asiatic land mass. In turn, the part of Europe covered by this book, the lands lying west of the bloc of Soviet nations, occupies less than half the area of the continent. Yet no comparable area on earth has such a dense concentration and such a diversity of sites, monuments, and locales that bear witness to human enterprise over the millenniums—to man's continuing aspirations and achievements, his follies and frustrations, from the prehistoric caves of Lascaux and the great menhirs at Stonehenge to those many cities of today that still harbor aspects of their more or less remote past amid their modern developments. In some of those cities—as in Rome and Paris, for example—we can trace almost the entire course of history from pre-Roman days to the present. Indoors and outdoors they are living museums of the long past.

That abundance of tangible evidence serves to remind us that European experience has generated forces which, for better or for worse, have reached about the globe and had an impact over the centuries out of all proportion to the size of the land itself. To visit, or even to be able to visualize, these historic places adds a dimension to our understanding of such matters that the written record alone cannot provide; it adds a fresh sense of reality to the pages of history.

History does not just happen, of course; people make it. Carlyle once wrote that the history of the world is but the biography of great men. Inevitably the places selected for illustration in the following pages are associated with men and women who have helped to shape the destiny of the Western world. It is hardly possible to stand on a site in Europe where such persons have performed their deeds or voiced their thoughts without sensing their presence. The list of characters is too long for rehearsal here, but a brief mention of a few of these notables suggests the wealth of such associations that await us as we travel from place to place. Athens would be a much lesser place in our mind's eye without recalling the roles in its history played by Pericles and Plato and Sophocles. It kindles the imagination to gaze at that spot in the Roman Forum where Caesar was slain by Brutus, ending a career of almost legendary accomplishment. The crosscurrents of history swirl about us at Monte Cassino, where Saint Benedict established the monastic order that played such a vital part in the cultural history of the Middle Ages—and where almost a thousand years later Allied troops, after a tragically bloody contest, blasted open the road to Rome and on to ultimate victory.

And so throughout the ages and across the face of Europe; it is not possible to take the road to Canterbury Cathedral, for example, without evoking Chaucer's pilgrims en route to the shrine of that redoubtable martyr Thomas à Becket. Or to visit Worms without bringing to mind the historic message of Martin Luther and the commanding importance it had for so many of his time. Everywhere we turn in Europe, it seems, some figure re-emerges from the past to enhance our interest in the landscape and the monuments we may see there. The historic places included in this book suggest the varieties of enriching experience that await the tourist who goes prepared "to bring home knowledge"—as well as gratification.

7

Greece

reece is a land with few natural advantages to lure permanent settlers. The face of the mainland is wrinkled with mountains. Much the same may be said of the islands—more than fourteen hundred of them, constituting one fifth of the land area of Greece—that lie scattered about the Aegean and Ionian seas. Hardly a fifth of this land area is arable. Speaking of the Attic landscape more than two millenniums ago, Plato said it resembled "the skeleton of a body wasted by disease." About the same time the great historian Herodotus observed that "Hellas has always had poverty as her companion." Yet this unpromising land was permanently settled more than a score of centuries before the time of Christ, and here in ancient times flourished rich cultures and brilliant civilizations that have left the world forever in their debt. As is the case in most other countries, the history of Greece can be read in its geography. The relatively inhospitable land could not easily support an increasing population; thus the Greeks early took to the sea—rarely more than thirty miles distant from any point in the mountainous interior—to settle near and distant colonies, to establish trading posts, to gather food and other supplies to supplement the meager yield of the homeland. Thereby also Greek thought and Greek values were widespread throughout the entire Mediterranean world. At home the scarcity of fertile soil led to the establishment of small rather than large communities. Without navigable rivers to provide lines of communication and with land travel made difficult by the mountainous terrain, these separate clusters of the population found little encouragement to unite in common causes. Rather, such circumstances fostered a spirit of individualism and of local independence that, when threatened, caused internecine strife among Greeks. Aside from its internal conflicts, throughout its long history Greece has suffered recurrent wars with and among alien powers, for it stands on the battle-scarred routes of Eastern conquerors and Western invaders. Out of its heroic struggle with Persia came the great upsurge of Greek civilization that culminated in the glorious age of Pericles. In later centuries long and often Greece knew the humiliation and harassment of foreign domination and occupation. Although the little country devised the idea of political democracy, which it passed on to posterity, it all too rarely has had the opportunity to make it work at home. However, tangible reminders of "the glory that was Greece," as well as of the country's more ancient past and of its later years of changing fortunes, abound in the land. The evidence presented in the following pages suggests why these historic places have increasingly attracted people about the world to come to Greece and pay them tribute in wonder and admiration. Here were once planted the roots of Western culture.

The cloud-capped summit of Mount Olympus, home of the gods, in Thessaly

The Isle
of Crete

A Minoan bronze (above) depicts an athlete performing the dangerous stunt of grasping a bull's horns and somersaulting over it. Griffins crouch among lilies in the fresco below in the throne room at Knossos Palace.

Crete, the mountainous island paradise in the southern Aegean described by Homer as a "rich and lovely land washed by waves on every side . . . and boasting ninety cities," was the cradle of Europe's earliest civilization and the seat of a brilliant and sophisticated culture. Settled as early as 3000 B.C. by nomadic groups of people from Asia Minor, Syria, Palestine, and perhaps Egypt, Crete within a millennium had developed into a prosperous maritime power that sent out colonies and traded with ports from Malta and Sicily to Syria and Egypt. Cretan civilization had reached its zenith by 1700 B.C., an age that saw great palaces arise at such cities as Knossos, Phaistos, and Mallia, which were ruled by potent chieftains. When the English scholar Sir Arthur Evans uncovered the remains of a multistoried, multiroomed structure at Knossos in 1900, he termed his findings "Minoan" after the mighty King Minos of Greek myth, a son of Zeus who ruled over an urban center and port of possibly one hundred thousand inhabitants from this princely residence; the palace's mazelike corridors, or labyrinth, imprisoned the bullheaded beast known as a Minotaur, which devoured the flower of Athenian youth annually until it was slain by the hero Theseus. Evans devoted some thirty years to excavating buildings, frescoes, and pottery at Knossos and interpreting the archaeological evidence in light of the legends. Covering three acres and capable of housing a retinue of several hundred people, the largest of Crete's palaces has now been restored. The entrance, with its portico of downward-tapering red-painted columns, the ancient throne room, with its alabaster throne guarded on either side by painted griffins, and chambers decorated with scenes of bull games—often depicted in Minoan art—that occurred at the palace on festival days recreate the wonders of Minoan civilization.

HARISSIADIS

The northern entrance at Knossos Palace, with a ramp leading to a courtyard and columned portico

11

A cult image of a goddess from Knossos

The Minoan temperament has been aptly described as a "curious mixture of religious formalism and a real *joie de vivre*." Unthreatened by foreign invasion on their isolated island and blessed with natural bounties, the sunny-dispositioned denizens of ancient Crete excelled, not in the art of war, but in creating beautiful palaces filled with fine pottery vases, delightful mural paintings, and exquisitely wrought ornaments. Frescoes uncovered and restored at Knossos portray in their variety elegant bearers parading down palace corridors or the fluid forms of dolphins cavorting in the Queen's Chamber. In the realm of religion, the Minoans were not unduly awed by the supernatural and worshiped at small shrines rather than in monumental temples. Although Zeus, king of the Greek pantheon, was born and buried on Crete, the principal Minoan deity was always a goddess or earth mother, who was commonly represented as a bare-breasted, wasp-waisted woman in a flounced skirt, as is the faience figurine with writhing snakes and a leopard excavated in the Central Sanctuary at Knossos Palace. At some cataclysmic moment about 1400 B.C., Minoan civilization came to an abrupt end. One theory is that a devastating earthquake, followed by a civil uprising, so weakened Crete that it fell prey to an armed invasion—quite possibly by the powerful and warlike Mycenaeans of the Greek mainland—that resulted in the looting and burning of its cities. The Minoans were unable to recover. By the time Homer composed his *Odyssey* in the eighth century B.C., Crete was an unimportant island, although legends of its glorious past persisted; the bard doubtless incorporated fragments in his description of the Phaeacians' island, where the fair Nausicaä says, "There is no man on earth . . . who would dare to set hostile feet on Phaeacian soil. The gods are too fond of us. . . . Remote in this sea-beaten home of ours, we are the outposts of mankind."

A fresco of dolphins (above) recalls Crete's dependence on the sea. Opposite is a fresco detail of bearers with a vase and rhyton.

ARCHAEOLOGICAL MUSEUM, HERAKLEION—HASSIA

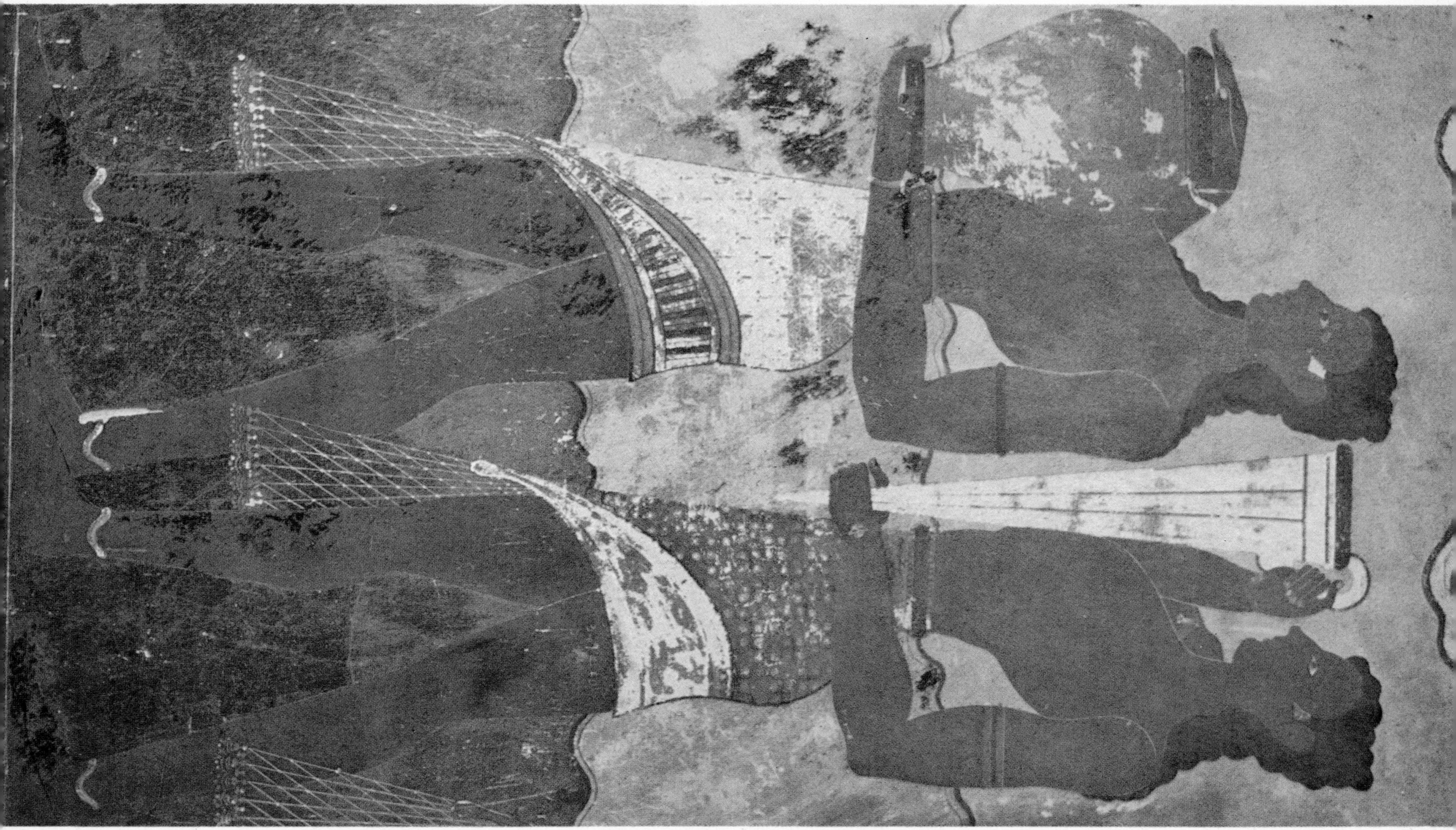

Mycenae

ALISON FRANTZ, ATHENS

The "golden mask of Agamemnon" (above) covered the face of a prince buried in a shaft grave at Mycenae. Below are ruins of a tholos tomb at Pylos. The Lion Gate (opposite), crowned by the oldest extant examples of monumental Greek sculpture, pierces the massive wall at Mycenae.

Unlike the peaceful Minoan islanders, Agamemnon, Achilles, Odysseus, Nestor, and other heroes of legend and history, whom Homer called Achaeans and we know as Mycenaeans, belonged to a warrior race that dwelt in fortified citadels on the Greek mainland. From approximately 2000 until 1700 B.C. the first Greek-speaking peoples, possibly from Anatolia in Asia Minor, settled in Greece. Initially within the cultural sphere of Minoan Crete, Mycenaean civilization burgeoned suddenly and dramatically about 1500 B.C., when cities that Homer wrote about—"Mycenae rich in gold," "Tiryns of the great walls," Pylos, home of the wise King Nestor, Thebes, and Athens—became powerful feudal kingdoms, which for the next two centuries dominated a vast commercial empire on the Aegean and in other parts of the Mediterranean. By the thirteenth century B.C. the princes and overlords of the Mycenaean aristocracy owed at least nominal allegiance to Agamemnon, Homer's "king of men," who ruled from Mycenae, the richest and most powerful of all citadels in Greece. Overlooking the fertile Argive plain, the ancient stronghold that once commanded the main highway to the Peloponnesus is now in ruins. Its massive stone walls were believed to have been built by the Cyclopes, fabled giants who were also credited with creating the proud lionesses that still guard the portal through which Agamemnon led his followers to besiege Troy about 1200. The Mycenaeans regarded their monarchs as gods, and upon their death accorded them divine honors and elaborate burials, as evidenced by the golden death masks and other funerary treasures recovered from the shaft graves and beehive-shaped *tholos* tombs of the royal families at Mycenae and Pylos.

Greece at Bay

The Trojan horse, depicted with Greek soldiers inside in a seventh-century-B.C. relief (left), was mistakenly admitted into Troy as a peace offering. Above is a Hellenistic head of Homer. Opposite, a Turk stands on the site of ancient Troy, with the Hellespont beyond.

Mycenaean power culminated in the ten-year siege and conquest of Troy, on the coast of Asia Minor, which began in the thirteenth century B.C. when King Agamemnon led an armada of 1,200 Greek ships across the Aegean. Although ostensibly fought to avenge the honor of Agamemnon's brother Menelaus, whose wife, Helen, had been abducted by a Trojan prince, the war occurred at a time when Mycenaean society was being rent by civil unrest as well as by incursions of uprooted tribes on its territory and may have represented a last desperate effort of the Mycenaeans to secure new lands and trade routes. Within a century of the final destruction of Troy, the Mycenaeans themselves suffered abject defeat at the hands of the Dorians, an illiterate people from the northwest, who invaded central Greece, burned their citadels, occupied the Peloponnesus, and thrust Greece into a Dark Age that lasted for more than four centuries.

This time as refugees, the Mycenaeans again crossed the Aegean and established on its eastern shore and nearby islands a new homeland, which came to be called Ionia. A native of the Ionian island of Chios, the poet Homer drew upon legend and history transmitted orally for generations in composing his epic chronicle of the Trojan War, the *Iliad,* between 750 and 700 B.C. Despite his obvious sympathies, which made the Mycenaeans "dear to Zeus," the blind bard portrayed with rare insight the struggles of the warriors who may have been his ancestors and who would just as soon fight among themselves as alongside one another in a common cause. Nowhere is rage more unrestrained than when Achilles directs his wrath at Agamemnon: "It was no quarrel with the Trojan spearmen that brought *me* here to fight. They have never done *me* any harm." Homer's tale was regarded mainly as myth until 1873, when the German Heinrich Schliemann discovered the site of Troy.

17

In an epic struggle between East and West that lasted for some twenty years, the allied Greek city-states cast off the yoke of Persian despotism and made their land safe for the development of democracy. Hostilities began early in the fifth century B.C., when Persia's Ionian subjects on the coast of Asia Minor, abetted by sympathetic Athenians and Eretrians from the island of Euboea, revolted and razed the town of Sardis. To chastise the Greek conspirators, the Persian king Darius in 490 B.C. dispatched westward a mighty force of thirty thousand men in six hundred ships that descended first upon the mid-Aegean island of Delos, which had been deserted by its fearful inhabitants and was shortly thereafter shaken by the only earthquake in its recorded history. This calamity, according to Herodotus, who chronicled the war in a lengthy narrative, was "an act of God to warn men of the troubles that were on the way." After destroying Eretria and enslaving its population, the Persians crossed to the Greek mainland and encamped at Marathon. Defending this approach to Athens, a small force of Greek spearmen inflicted a surprising defeat on the numerically superior Persian bowmen and forced the survivors to scramble aboard their ships and sail for Asia. A ten-year respite from a second enemy onslaught enabled the Athenians, upon the advice of Themistocles, a young politician who became their military commander, to modernize their fleet and fortify their harbors. The war machine was again set in motion in 480 B.C., when Darius' son Xerxes, the self-styled "Great King and King of Kings," unleashed a much vaster armament of nearly two million troops and twelve hundred ships upon Greece. This time the city-states suffered a tragic setback at Thermopylae.

TIME-LIFE PICTURE AGENCY — PHOTO EMILE

During the Battle of Salamis, shown in the painting at right, a Persian galley rams another in a ruse to make the Greeks think it an ally and allow it to escape unharmed. A Greek runner, opposite, top, falls in exhaustion. A glazed brick relief, opposite, bottom, depicts exotically attired Persian warriors.

The Persians intended to cross this precipitous pass between mountain and sea in their march to central Greece. Here the entire Persian host was met by the Spartan king Leonidas, who with only three hundred veteran soldiers fought valiantly to the death. The tide of the war turned during the naval battle off the island of Salamis, where the Athenians had taken refuge before the Persians captured their city. In "a narrow sea with few ships against many," the allied Greek fleet delivered a crushing blow to the invading armada before the eyes of Xerxes, who from a high ridge above the strait watched his ships and means of retreat reduced to broken timber. Thus humbled, the leader of the world's largest empire returned to Asia overland with most of his army. A last major engagement occurred in 479 B.C. at Plataea in Boeotia, where a remnant of Xerxes' army was routed by skilled Spartan warriors. The islands and Ionia won their freedom in another few years. In the wake of the war the playwright Aeschylus, who had fought at Marathon, celebrated the decisive Greek victory in a tragedy taking the Persian point of view. At the end the Persian chorus laments, "The word of power is not spoken/By the princes of Persia, their day is o'er/. . . . For the earth of Ajax is red/With the blood of Persia's noble dead."

Frederick Church painted the Parthenon (above) as seen from the Propylaea in 1871. A detail of horsemen from the Parthenon frieze (right) was taken to the British Museum by Lord Elgin in 1803-12. Opposite is a Roman copy of Phidias' statue of Athena.

NIKOS KONDOS

Athens' Glory

Following the victory of the Greek city-states over the Persian menace, Athens attained hegemony over its erstwhile allies and exacted tribute from them, which was used to rebuild monuments laid waste by the enemy. After restoring his city's walls and defenses, the Athenian leader Pericles, in the mid-fifth century B.C., appointed the sculptor Phidias to supervise the replacement of ruined shrines atop the Acropolis with a glitter of new temples. The Parthenon, crowning glory of that sacred eminence of rock, was dedicated to Athena, the city's patroness, and constructed from 447 to 432 B.C. by the architects Ictinus and Callicrates. The friezes, metopes, and pediments of the Doric structure were adorned with hundreds of carved figures, fragments of which survive *in situ* and in museums. Within the temple sanctuary loomed a colossal ivory and gold cult image of Athena, Phidias' masterpiece, which has long been lost. Embodying the classic Greek ideals of harmony, proportion, and nobility, the Parthenon, over the centuries, has occupied a very special place in the mind's eye for visitors to Athens, including the American landscape painter Frederick Church, who viewed its ruins in 1869 and recorded them on canvas.

21

PHOTO RESEARCHERS—F. B. GRUNZWEIG

The Temple of Athena Nike, with its graceful Ionic columns, is at right. Pericles (below) was master builder of Athens from about 460 to 430 B.C. Opposite is the caryatid porch of the Erechtheum, an Athenian favorite.

Of all the domestic reforms and civic improvements instituted during his three decades in power, none was as dear to Pericles as his beloved building program. Although political opponents denounced the statesman-philosopher's visions as excessively costly and vainglorious and accused him of "gilding and adorning our city like a wanton woman," Pericles persevered in making Athens not only the undisputed mistress of the Mediterranean, but the "school of Hellas" as well. A spirit of pride and even elation roused the citizenry to unleash great creative energies, embellishing the Acropolis with temples of incomparable beauty. Such a formidable achievement was recalled centuries later by the Greek biographer Plutarch, who wrote, "As the buildings rose stately in size and unsurpassed in form and grace, the workmen vied with each other that the quality of their work might be enhanced by its artistic beauty. Most wonderful of all was the rapidity of construction. . . . all [of the buildings] were completed in the heyday of a single administration." The Parthenon had been erected in fifteen years of intensive effort, and the imposing Propylaea, or Sacred Gateway, subsequently arose in five years under the direction of the architect Mnesicles. Perched on the brink of the cliff in front of the Propylaea, the tiny Ionic Temple of Athena Nike was finished next, in 424 B.C. And by the latter part of the fifth century the Erechtheum, originally raised on the legendary site of the duel between Athena and Poseidon for the patronage of Athens, had been reconstructed. This shrine is famous for its porch, supported by stone maidens known as caryatids, who maintain inscrutable expressions while balancing two and one half tons of Pentelic marble on their elegantly coiffed heads.

A *plan of the Acropolis (opposite) reveals the ease and naturalness with which architects of the fifth century* B.C. *plotted their structures. A view of the Acropolis' western slope (below) shows the Parthenon façade and Propylaea.*

Greek Architecture, BY A. W. LAWRENCE, THE PELICAN HISTORY OF ART

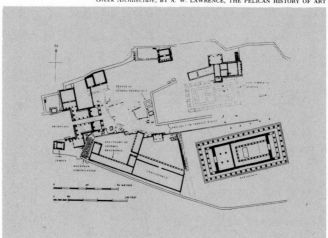

Most of the edifices built on the Acropolis during the Periclean age rose on the site of still older sanctuaries. In remote Mycenaean times this rocky limestone plateau—more than five hundred feet above sea level—served as a stronghold and place of refuge for the early Athenians and was enclosed by massive cyclopean ramparts. By the more peaceful period of the seventh century B.C. the hilltop citadel had also become a religious sanctuary thronged with tufa-stone temples and votive statues dedicated to Athena, who had won the contest with Poseidon for the guardianship of the city by causing an olive tree to spring forth from a rock. When the Athenians returned to their denuded Acropolis after the Persian Wars, they could not decide whether to remain faithful to a vow made on the eve of their victory that they would never rebuild the temples destroyed by the Persians in order to perpetuate the memory of their sacrilege. However, when the burnt stump of Athena's olive tree issued a green shoot, it was interpreted as a propitious omen to sweep away the debris of the past, bury the broken votive statues, and create everything anew. The resulting architectural masterpieces represented the happiest solution ever conceived to the problem of postwar reconstruction. Because the Acropolis was rebuilt within fifty years, the relation of the buildings to one another was well planned. Rather than adhering to the rigid symmetry of a central axis, the architects designed the complex to accommodate the wild, precipitous site, with its crags, grottoes, and other accidents of nature, and the winding processional path by which celebrants of the Panathenaea, a quadrennial festival, made their steep ascent to pay homage to Athena. The Acropolis itself may be viewed as a monumental piece of sculpture whose separate elements have never ceased to work with the sun, sky, sea, and mountains in a harmonious relationship. As Plutarch perceptively put it in the second century A.D., "There is a sort of bloom of newness upon these works . . . preserving them from the touch of time, as if they had some perennial spirit and undying vitality mingled in the composition of them."

25

An English print of 1787 (opposite) shows a mosque in the Parthenon shell. Opposite, bottom, is the well-preserved Monument of Lysicrates. Below is the Temple of Olympian Zeus.

Only a few battered and scattered relics of classical antiquity survive in modern Athens. When the Romans absorbed Greece into their growing empire in the second century B.C., Athens became a vast museum whose priceless treasures were appropriated by the Latin emperors to embellish their temples and palaces. The leafy Corinthian columns of the partially completed Temple of the Olympian Zeus, begun in 174 B.C., were spirited to Rome by the consul Sulla in 86 B.C. to adorn the Temple of Jupiter Capitolinus. Although Athens' last great pagan monument was spared further dismantlement by the philhellenic emperor Hadrian, who completed and dedicated the structure in A.D. 132, only ruins remain. The exquisite rotunda known as the Choragic Monument of Lysicrates, erected in 334 B.C. to commemorate the winner of a musical competition, for centuries escaped harm within the walls of a French Capuchin monastery, and it is one of the rare buildings to have been preserved nearly intact. On the Acropolis, the Parthenon and Erechtheum were converted into Byzantine, and later into Roman Catholic, churches. During the four centuries of Ottoman occupation, the Erechtheum housed a harem, the Propylaea was turned into a crenelated palace, the Temple of Athena Nike (now reconstructed) was dismembered to build Turkish defense works, and the Parthenon was transformed into a mosque with an attached minaret. Athena's former sanctuary finally became a Turkish gunpowder magazine and was severely damaged by the Venetians during their bombardment of Athens on September 26, 1687.

Grecian Apogee

Believing that the physically fit body was as important as a well-developed mind, all Greeks, from an early date, acclaimed the athletic ideal. As Socrates aptly expressed the Pan-Hellenic sentiment, "What a disgrace it is for a man to grow old without ever seeing the beauty and strength of which his body is capable." The differences and long distances that often divided the Greek city-states were forgotten, and a consciousness of a common race and civilization was fostered, at the quadrennial games dedicated to the god Zeus at his sanctuary at Olympia, which were played without interruption from 776 B.C. until they were suppressed by the emperor Theodosius in A.D. 383. Held for five days during a full moon between late June and early September, this sacred festival attracted Greek athletes and pilgrims from throughout the Mediterranean; participants were granted safe passage to Olympia even if they crossed enemy territory en route. And once the games commenced, all wars were temporarily suspended. Playing before a thronged stadium of some twenty thousand spectators, the best athletes from the various cities strove to excel one another in events that measured an individual's harmonious demonstration of beauty, skill, and strength. The most popular contest, known as the pentathlon, comprised running, jumping, discus throwing, javelin throwing, and wrestling, sports that depended as much on coordination as on brute power. Competition among the participants was so fierce that bribes to feign defeat, as well as other inducements to unsportsmanlike behavior, were not unknown. Only victors, who were awarded crowns of olive leaves, public honors, and sometimes money, were applauded, while losers were disgraced.

Opposite are ruins of the vaulted entrance to the stadium at Olympia. An Athenian vase painting (below) portrays nude athletes competing in a spirited foot race.

Religion was a major unifying force in the widespread Hellenic world. Early in their history the Greeks cast their gods in man's own image, and as time passed their deities became increasingly civilized and humane. Foremost in the Greek pantheon were the stately Olympians, who, despite occasional erratic, immoral, and selfish behavior, at their noblest possessed the wisdom, grace, beauty, and strength that man strove to attain. The reverence paid each god varied from place to place, and shrines came to be erected to the favorite deity of a particular locale. Apollo, god of light, truth, law and order, and healing, was worshiped from vertiginous Delphi, below the peak of Mount Parnassus, the most sacred and influential shrine in Greece. Here, according to myth, Apollo slew the dragon Python, which guarded Mother Earth's oracle, and appropriated it to use as an intermediary between gods and men. Over the centuries hundreds of thousands of petitioners journeyed to Delphi to pay obeisance to and seek the advice of the oracle.

The ruined 4th-century-B.C. Temple of Athena at Delphi

Remains from the Roman epoch stand on a terrace at Eleusis, above. The relief below depicts Demeter instructing an Eleusinian youth to teach cultivation to mankind.

The oracle's pronouncements and prophecies were considered essential to any person or city-state about to begin an important undertaking. Interpreted by an elderly virgin priestess known as a Pythia, the oracle could be deliberately ambiguous so as to seem right no matter what happened. However, since the priests of Apollo gathered and stored information about the outside world from pilgrims to the sanctuary—which from the seventh century B.C. served as the central archive of Greece—the oracle's prophecies may actually have been well-educated guesses. At any event, the numerous monuments built along the Sacred Way to Delphi and the costly gifts that filled its treasuries attest to the satisfaction of at least some of the suppliants. A more curious cult flourished at Eleusis, where the mysteries of Demeter, the patroness of agriculture, were performed. Legend has it that when Demeter's daughter Persephone was abducted to the nether world by Pluto, the goddess in her agonized search for her child visited Eleusis, whose inhabitants received her kindly. In gratitude Demeter taught them the secrets of growing things, which were celebrated in annual rites that eventually took the form of secret and inspired religious pageants. Initiates came to believe that they were Demeter's grandchildren, and thus immortal.

31

Tragic actors wore masks like the one above to evoke character and mood. The frieze at left depicts Orestes brandishing a knife to kill his mother, who weakly tries to restrain him.

In addition to providing entertainment, the theater of classical Greece acted as a moral monitor that uplifted and instructed a large cross section of the public. The stage play itself was a Greek invention that originated in magical and primitive rites performed by masked worshipers of the god Dionysus. As it evolved, the drama reflected a concern with the ever-changing and problematical condition of man. Tragedy was created when man, through his *hubris* (overweening pride), passions, or other frailties, broke the divine laws that governed the universe and suffered the inexorable consequences. In a lesser vein, comedy arose when man was pitted against man, and his vulgarities, vanities, and follies were exposed. Although the earliest playgoers watched performances unfold on simple threshing floors worn smooth by oxen, by the fifth century B.C. huge circular theaters carved out of hillsides accommodated thousands of spectators, who could see clearly the action taking place in the orchestra below. Recalling the ancient prototype is the majestic stone theater at Epidaurus, which was built about 350 B.C. and even in ruins boasts perfect acoustics. The finest flowering of Greek drama occurred in Periclean Athens when the unsurpassed masters of tragedy—Aeschylus, Sophocles, and Euripides—dominated the stage with their blood-drenched dramas based on myths familiar to all. Their profoundly human characters, brought to life by actors appearing larger than life in elevated boots and awesome masks, moved audiences to feel pity and fear, because, as Aristotle later explained, "pity is aroused by unmerited misfortune, fear by the misfortune of a man like ourselves." Greeks of every rank and region shared in the righteous wrath of Aeschylus' Orestes, who killed his mother to avenge her murder of his father.

Audiences still occupy the benches at Epidaurus, where ancient masterpieces are revived at annual festivals.

They felt compassion for Sophocles' Oedipus, who unwittingly committed parricide and married his mother; empathized with Euripides' Medea, who slew her children to wreak vengeance on a philandering husband; and were often unable to comprehend the seemingly harsh justice meted out to these miserable heroes. Despite the lawlessness and violence in their work, the great tragedians believed in an underlying moral order or design, however inscrutable, which they expressed in mighty cycles of action and reaction, of a crime and an avenging crime, as Aeschylus' somber trilogy illustrates. Orestes' unnatural act of matricide was inevitable in a course of events that saw his ancestors bring the curse of the gods upon themselves and cause horror to beget horror. When the ill-starred protagonist receives his deserts and is being pursued by the implacable Furies, who eventually drive him mad, the chorus ponders, "Where is the end? Where shall the fury of fate be stilled to sleep, be done with?"

After the Persian Wars a formidable Athenian fleet imposed on the Aegean a peace that made the sea safe for a vast resurgence of trade and commerce. Under Pericles' direction, the great marble temple to the sea god Poseidon, which had crowned the steep headland of Cape Sounion at the tip of Attica until it was destroyed by the Persians, was reconstructed. Once again mariners were able to rely on this prominently placed edifice — in effect a lofty lighthouse — to guide their cargoes safely through the treacherous straits off the bleak promontory. To prevent a renewed Persian assault, men from Attica to Ionia formed a defensive alliance that had its headquarters on the mid-Aegean island of Delos, and thus became known as the Delian League. The legendary birthplace of Apollo, Delos had become an important cult center early in Greek history. By the fifth century B.C. Delos — with its many shrines dedicated to Apollo and its votive offerings left by such visitors as the Naxians, who a century earlier had erected the slim marble lions that still lord over the terrain — was the scene of a Pan-Hellenic festival that annually attracted pilgrims from the entire Greek world. Although the federal treasury of the Delian League was relocated to Athens in 454 B.C. because, it was claimed, Delos lay in a vulnerable position, the island remained an Athenian province until it gained its independence in the power struggle following the death of Alexander the Great in 323 B.C. During the Hellenistic period the inhabitants encouraged Egyptians, Syrians, Persians, and other non-Greeks to settle and establish their own religious shrines on the island, and in the second century B.C., under the Romans, Delos developed into a free port that became the entrepôt of the whole Mediterranean. Wharves, warehouses, and marketplaces grew up around Apollo's sanctuary, and in the new theater and port districts bankers and traders raised sumptuous villas richly decorated with paintings and mosaics. Delos' prosperity ended abruptly in the first century B.C., when trade routes shifted toward Rome, and the island was laid waste by invading armies and pirates. Eventually abandoned, Delos never revived, but became a dead city whose surviving statues and monuments fed the lime kilns of a marble quarry.

The ruins of the Temple of Poseidon (opposite) stand in splendid isolation on their pedestal of rock at Cape Sounion. Created from Naxian marble in the sixth century B.C., well-preserved lions (top) line the way to Delos' port. The floor in the House of Dionysus at Delos contains a mosaic of the god on a leopard (above).

In 437 B.C. Athens commenced a long and suicidal struggle with Sparta that left Attica a shambles and all Greece in disarray. Athens' remarkable rise to power in the preceding decades under Pericles had provoked unquenchable fear and jealousy in other city-states, notably Corinth, Thebes, and Sparta, which formed a defensive alliance known as the Peloponnesian League that soon rivaled the Delian League, composed of Athens' satellites. An uneasy balance of power prevailed for years until it was upset by the maritime colony of Corcyra on the island of Corfu, which went to war with its mother city of Corinth and obtained Athenian support, thus binding Greece's two strongest fleets together. When Athens in 432 B.C. crushed a revolt on her island tributary of Potidaea, which had been founded by and was still under the sway of Corinth, the entire Peloponnesus was incited to take up arms. Athens rejected an ultimatum from Sparta demanding, in effect, that Athens dissolve its empire and humble itself, and the Greeks came out in full force against each other. Lasting for twenty-seven years, the Peloponnesian War was, according to Thucydides, who witnessed and survived the catastrophic collision, "the greatest disturbance in the history of the Hellenes, affecting also a large part of the whole of mankind."

Greeks versus Greeks

Comprised of a series of small conflicts interrupted by long stalemates and treaties that neither side honored, the war unfolded in a theater that eventually extended from Sicily to the Bosphorus. Pericles devised a strategy in which Athenians would keep a strictly defensive posture at home, not offering battle but withdrawing behind their extended and fortified walls. Offensively, Athens would try to preserve its command over the sea and its supply routes and send its navy on punitive raids along the Peloponnesian coast. Pericles did not live to implement his plans; he died in 429 B.C. in a plague that ravaged Athens and carried off one fourth of its populace. At the end of a decade, the struggle was still indecisive with no end in sight, and Athens concluded a fifty-year treaty with Sparta. The peace lasted only until 415 B.C., when the Athenians sent an expedition, described by Thucydides as "by far the most costly and splendid Hellenic force that had ever been sent out by a single city up to that time," to subjugate the independent colony of Syracuse in Sicily. The assault failed, and the flower of Athens' soldiery was either killed or enslaved. Worse was still to come. Sparta, now joined by Syracuse and aided financially by ever vengeful Persia, renewed hostilities. Despite years of combined onslaught, the defection of its allies, one by one, to the enemy, a depleted treasury, and civil strife between radical and conservative factions at home, Athens managed to survive for another decade. In 407 B.C., its remaining fleet defeated in an abortive effort to save the vital grain supply routes to the Bosphorus, Athens capitulated under siege. The surrender stipulated that it dissolve its empire, raze its walls, forfeit its warships, and submit to a puppet government allied to Sparta. Although Sparta's hegemony was short-lived, and Athens regained political autonomy within a year, Pericles' beautiful city-state never recovered its former prominence but vied for many years with lesser states in a power vacuum in which no one could prevail.

Rivalry between the fertile island colony of Corcyra (above) and Corinth precipitated the tragic Peloponnesian War. A bronze spearman (opposite, below) is portrayed attired in a Corinthian-type helmet. Ruins of a sixth-century-B.C. temple of Apollo at the ancient city of Corinth appear opposite, above.

Byzantine Greece

On an eminence above the fertile Eurotas plain is the stone and brick church of Pantanassa (left), with its mullioned windows and festooned domes. The awe-inspiring Pantocrator Christ, opposite, peers down from a celestial vault of gold mosaic at medieval Daphni.

For nearly a millennium after the collapse of Rome, Greece survived as a secondary power in the Byzantine Empire, which had its capital at Constantinople. Although enervated by barbarian invasions, constant power struggles, and the unsurpassed horrors inflicted by the Crusaders of Western Europe, Greece over the centuries remained a bastion of Christianity. And the Orthodox Church, which broke from Roman Catholicism in 1054, became the very embodiment of national sentiment. Unlike the ancients, who celebrated their pagan rites at open-air altars, Orthodox Greeks worshiped within sacred edifices that found their finest architectural expression in beautiful domed buildings like the eleventh-century church at Daphni in Attica. Glowering down from the lofty cupola is a mosaic of the fearsome Pantocrator Christ, which illustrates Orthodoxy's preoccupation with God the all powerful, in contrast to the humanized Christ of Western iconography. Churches also dominate the dead city of Mistra, near the former site of Sparta. Founded by Franks who occupied the Peloponnesus early in the 1200's, Mistra was recaptured in 1259 by the Greeks. Such monuments as the graceful church of Pantanassa recall this late flowering of Byzantine culture. Certain devout men of the same period avoided the vicissitudes that shook the empire. These hermits withdrew to such places as Meteora, in mountainous Thessaly, where they built monasteries atop strange, bleak peaks and passed their ascetic lives in virtual isolation, suspended between heaven and earth.

Overlooking the Gulf of Argolis, the tranquil town of Nauplia, above, preserves many relics of its martial past. At Methone, of former strategic importance in the southwestern Peloponnesus, are ruins of a Venetian fortress-castle, opposite.

Years of Conflict

In 1204 the Venetians diverted Crusaders en route to the Holy Land to Constantinople, which they captured, pillaged, and burned. The Latin nations then divided defeated Byzantium into a series of feudal fiefs. Frankish knights imposed their iron rule throughout much of Greece, which soon bristled with battlemented castles. Venetians also established a foothold on the Greek mainland with the fortified towns of Methone and nearby Korone, which arose on the Ionian coast of the Peloponnesus about 1206 and were known thereafter as the eyes of the republic. Methone flourished as a port until 1500, when it fell to the Turks, an event that may have been heralded by natives who under the less than benevolent Venetians had been forced to renounce their Orthodox faith and kneel to Roman Catholicism. Founded by the Byzantines on the site of the ancient port of Argos in the eastern Peloponnesus, Nauplia developed into an important commercial city that changed hands several times in the course of its history, as attested by its hybrid architecture. Begun by French Crusaders, the Palamidi fortress on Nauplia's rocky heights was enlarged by Venetians, who held the town from 1388 until 1540, and later by the Turks. In 1827, after the Greek War of Independence, Nauplia became the first capital of the newly liberated nation, whose first parliament met in a former mosque. The town's winding medieval streets became the scene of political intrigue and even ambushes. Ioannes Kapodistrias, Greece's first president, was felled by an assassin as he approached the church of Saint Spyridon one Sunday in 1831. His Bavarian successor, Otto, appointed first king of the Hellenes, resided in the Palamidi fortress until the capital was moved to Athens in 1834.

FPG—LUCAS A. BENAKI

Ramparts raised by the Order of Knights enclose the ancient acropolis at the strategically situated port of Lindos.

Rhodes, more than anywhere else in Greece, preserves a sense of its rich historic heritage. Nearly all the successive civilizations that flourished on the island have left behind a wealth of monuments that bring to life each epoch. Dorian adventurers from the Greek mainland first settled Rhodes, anchored like a ship off the Asiatic coast, and founded the towns of Lindos, Camirus, and Ialysus, which prospered and sent colonies of their own throughout the Mediterranean. By the end of the fifth century B.C. the capital city of Rhodes, which with Lindos possessed the island's only natural harbors, had become one of the most beautiful and best-fortified ports of antiquity. It was here that the populace celebrated the lifting of a Syrian siege in 305 B.C. by erecting a one-hundred-foot-tall bronze Colossus, dedicated to the sun god, which stood in the harbor and achieved almost instant renown as one of the Seven Wonders of the World. Toppled shortly thereafter by an earthquake, the statue was never rebuilt, and its bronze parts have long since disappeared. Rhodes became a formidable maritime power under the Romans, and during the centuries of Byzantine rule, sporadically interrupted by incursions of Arabs, Crusaders, Venetians, and Genoese, continued as a cosmopolitan center. In 1309 the military Order of Knights, the Hospitalers of Saint John of Jerusalem, who had left the Holy Land when it fell to the Moslems, purchased Rhodes from declining Byzantium.

The medieval architecture of the inns on the Street of the Knights, above, and the hospital, below, better evokes some corner of old Europe than sun-drenched Rhodes.

Divided into groups, or "Tongues," according to their country of origin, the knights built on the ruins of the ancient capital a strongly fortified city, surrounded by wide moats and tower-encased ramparts pierced by infrequent gateways. Within the battlements arose a hospital, the Grand Master's Palace, and inns of the various nationalities that lined the Street of the Knights. The ancient acropolis atop Lindos was similarly fortified with a crenelated castle. From their secure island base the knights pursued pirates in their galleys and even hunted the infidel-infested lands of Turkey and Syria. After the Turks took Constantinople in 1453, Rhodes remained an isolated outpost of Christianity in the ever westward tide of Moslem expansion. In 1522 Suleiman the Magnificent, with an armada of three hundred ships and one hundred thousand men, finally conquered the island. The knights, along with many Greek inhabitants who preferred exile to the Ottoman yoke, departed for Malta. The Turks soon planted mosques and minarets in the medieval city of the knights, which they kept locked at night as a safeguard, forcing their subjects to retire outside its walls. The Greeks on Rhodes were thus inhibited from participating in the 1821 War of Independence. Rhodes remained a Turkish possession until 1912, when it was occupied by the Italians; in 1945 the island was annexed to Greece.

*I*TALY displays such a wealth of marvels that, as Dr. Samuel Johnson once observed, a man who has not been there is always conscious of an inferiority. From the Alpine formations in the north to the panoramic sweep of the Bay of Naples and the verdant shores of Sicily in the south, the land abounds in natural wonders. But it is the rich variety of manmade treasures overlaying the countryside in such great depth that give Italy a unique importance among the nations of the Western world. Every corner of the land bears witness to the creative and constructive genius of the people who have made Italian history. The focal point of that history is, of course, Rome, a city whose explosive energies within a few centuries transformed the ancient world. In the course of those centuries Rome grew from a settlement of a few thousand persons to become the center of the greatest structure of political power the world has yet known—a structure that controlled a vast area ranging from Scotland to Arabia and from the Strait of Gibraltar to the Black Sea. Wherever they went and conquered, the early Romans learned and borrowed from the peoples they overran; and they amalgamated these lessons—in art, philosophy, literature, and religion—into their own concept of civilization. In these matters they learned much from the Greeks; and when a new conception of deity was born in Judea, that "good news" ultimately made its way into the emperor's palace and was accepted as a prescription that replaced the older and miscellaneous pagan beliefs with a faith in Christ. Wherever their authority reached, the Romans impressed upon their subjects a splendid body of laws in accordance with which the Mediterranean world was virtually at peace for some two hundred years. When the Roman Empire finally fell before barbarian invaders in the fifth century, many Roman traditions endured in new contexts. In a sense the empire continued to exist in principle for another millennium, until 1806, in the Holy Roman Empire; and in a sublimated form it still exists in the Holy Roman Catholic Church, whose language is Latin and whose central seat remains in Rome. Culturally, the influence of Rome has never died. However, the political structure that had for so long centered in Rome collapsed in A.D. 476, when Odoacer, king of an obscure German tribe, deposed the puppet emperor in the West, established the first kingdom of Italy, and placed it under the suzerainty of Byzantium, the recently established eastern capital of the empire. For long centuries to follow, Italy was despoiled by foreign rulers and divided by internal factions. Popes contended with emperors (and with other popes); princes fought with princes; city-states vied with other city-states and with alien powers. Yet from about 1300 to 1600 Italy experienced a Renaissance of art and learning with important repercussions that were to be felt in Europe, and then in America, down to our own day. Politically, however, it was only a little more than a century ago that Victor Emmanuel II assumed the crown of a united Italy and brought to birth the modern state.

Opposite, one of Rome's innumerable fountains sends up a lofty spray before St. Peter's.

Sicily

Sicily, the largest of Mediterranean islands, has been called the archaeological museum of Europe. The generally mountainous countryside is overlaid with rich deposits left by settlers and invaders from many lands over the course of many centuries — with Greek temples and theaters, Roman bridges and aqueducts, Byzantine churches and Saracen mosques, Norman fortresses and palaces, Renaissance and baroque cathedrals, and public buildings of Spanish and Italian inspiration, among still other evidences of the varied cultural strains that have contributed to Sicilian history. Like a many-faceted jewel, a pendant to the southwestern tip of the Italian mainland, Sicily glistens with reflected lights from the civilizations of north, east, south, and west. Displacing earlier Phoenician settlers, Greeks from Corinth established a colony on a small island at the easternmost extreme of this agreeable land in the eighth century B.C. Here and on the nearby main island (to which the smaller one was early united by a bridge) rose the city of Syracuse, which at the height of its glory three centuries later ruled all Sicily and challenged Athens for supremacy in Magna Graecia (Greater Greece).

The Greek theater at Syracuse (opposite) is one of the largest of the ancient world. When the Temple of Athena was converted into a Christian church, its Doric columns were retained as supports (below) in the structure (right).

Late in the fifth century B.C., to extend its power over Sicily, Athens dispatched what Thucydides termed the most splendid and most expensive armada ever to sail from a Greek city. The resulting assault finally centered on Syracuse, and it ended in the almost total destruction of the invading forces. According to Plutarch's account written years later, the few struggling Athenians who managed to make their way home had been freed because they could recite choruses of Euripides: "For the Sicilians, it seems, had a passion for his poetry," as Plutarch wrote, "greater than that of any other Hellenes outside Greece." Earlier in the same century Syracuse had won a great naval victory over invading Carthaginians; to commemorate that triumph a magnificent Doric temple to Athena was raised within the city. A number of its massive columns remain imbedded in the walls of the cathedral that was subsequently built on the site. It was during still another conflict, in the third century B.C., when the Romans attacked the city, that Archimedes destroyed their ships by setting them on fire with the rays of the sun reflected from a focused arrangement of mirrorlike shields.

Greek and Roman elements mingle in the ruins of the theater at Taormina.

On a high ledge overlooking the Ionian Sea and the curving coast of northeastern Sicily, with a distant view of the snow-capped slopes of Mount Etna, the theater at Taormina enjoyed the most spectacular site of any theater in the ancient world. (Goethe described the scene as "the most colossal work of nature and art.") The structure was originally built by Greek colonists but was remodeled by the Romans to serve as an amphitheater. During the First Punic War (264–241 B.C.) the Romans were engaged in repeated campaigns to dislodge the Carthaginians from bases they had established in western Sicily. The success of the Romans in that rivalry led to their taking over Sicily as one of their own colonies — a colony that they exploited to the hilt. When they brought home booty from these conquests, the eyes of their compatriots were for the first time opened to the glories of Greek art and civilization. The discovery sparked a revolutionary turn in the direction of Roman culture. Both figuratively and literally Rome was to go to school in Greece for centuries to come.

Like the city-states of the Greek homeland, the colonial Greek cities of Sicily had their differences and fought their wars. One of the ostensible objectives of the ill-fated Athenian expedition that ultimately foundered at the siege of Syracuse was to aid the city of Segesta in a dispute with its neighbor Selinus, or Selinunte, over questions of boundary—although the two communities were thirty miles apart in the western corner of the island—and over problems of mixed marriages. Whatever glory those two rival cities aspired to quickly dissolved with the passage of time. About the beginning of our era the Greek geographer Strabo referred to Selinus, once a bustling commercial center and a maritime power second only to Syracuse, as already an extinct city. Today the desolate ruins of its seven great temples, some of which were raised as early as the first half of the sixth century B.C., lie in jumbled piles of massive gray-white fragments. (Some sculptured elements now shown in the museum at nearby Palermo are among the finest surviving examples of the provincial Doric style.) These last remaining vestiges of Selinus are as vast as the destruction is complete; they rest in an otherwise solitary spot, within sight of the African coast, where the silence is total and the *selinon*, the wild celery or parsley that gave the city its name, continues to grow amid the ancient debris. Although it was never finished, the temple of Segesta still stands on an equally deserted and silent site among the mountains that overlook the Gulf of Castellammare. It remains remarkably well preserved, much as it was late in the fifth century B.C., when for reasons history has not disclosed, its construction was interrupted. These haunting reminders of the Sicilian past indicate that the architects and artisans of this western island had little to learn from the greatest masters of old Greece.

A *sixth-century-*B.C. *relief from the Greek temple at Selinus depicts Perseus, with Athena's blessing, beheading a Gorgon (above). The temple at nearby Segesta (below) was never completed.*

More than any other site in Sicily, Palermo, the capital and chief seaport, reveals the complex crosscurrents of history that have given the island its uniquely colorful character. The city was founded by Phoenicians, then invested by Carthaginians before it was conquered, first by Greeks and in turn by Romans. After the fall of Rome Palermo was invaded by northern barbarians, then overcome by forces from Byzantium. Saracens took over the city in the ninth century only to be vanquished by Normans about two centuries later. In subsequent years the Holy Roman Emperor, King Charles I of Anjou, Aragonese Spaniards, Savoyards, and Neapolitan Bourbons all ruled the city in succession until, in 1860, Giuseppe Garibaldi annexed the entire island to the Italian kingdom. During their tenure in the eleventh and twelfth centuries the Normans, with the help of Arab artisans and architects, transformed Palermo into one of the great cities of the world — a treasure house of structures and decoration of rare beauty gleaming amid luxurious, exotic gardens. The interior of the Capella Palatina (Royal Chapel), built from 1130 to 1140 by King Roger II in a fusion of Norman and Saracenic styles, has been termed the "most splendid of any ecclesiastical interior in Christendom." The curiously carved ceiling, with its Arabic inscriptions, recalls the Alhambra in Spain. Rare marbles and glistening mosaics, and carved and sculptured furbishings of stone, wood, and metal, create an impression of indescribable beauty. The nearby church of San Giovanni degli Eremiti (Saint John of the Hermits), with its three pink domes of Moorish inspiration, was built at about the same time, also at Roger's suggestion. These two structures introduced the great era of Norman-Sicilian architecture of the twelfth century. The thirteenth-century adjoining cloister of Saint John's has double pillars of white marble that rise from a garden of tropical flowers and greenery almost as though they were an organic part of that luxuriant growth. Roger was the grandson of a petty seigneur of Hauteville in French Normandy, several of whose sons left home to seek wealth and glory by strength of arms in southern Europe, as their forefathers had swept down on France from Scandinavia a century earlier. Two of these sons, Robert and Roger Guiscard d'Hauteville, waged the personal war that won them Sicily and passed on their authority to Roger II of the next generation, the first of the family to reign as king of Sicily. He was a man of culture as well as a dauntless warrior; he had Ptolemy's writings translated from Arabic into Latin and supervised the compilation of a geography of the world. Jongleurs and troubadours brought from France sang at his court, and "justice and peace were universally observed throughout his dominions."

A lion support (above) for Roger II's tomb was modeled after Oriental-inspired, ancient Roman bronzes. Roger's palace chapel (opposite) and the nearby church of San Giovanni and its cloister (below) have a distinctly Moorish air.

Campania

The area of Italy adjacent to and south of Rome is known as Campania. In the first century of our era, in southern Campania, close to the Bay of Naples, the shores of the Tyrrhenian Sea were dotted with sumptuous villas. The emperor Tiberius had his favorite residence on the island of Capri; before that the emperor Caligula had settled on the nearby island of Ischia; along the mainland coast others of the leisured classes of Rome found a pleasant haven from the noisy congestion of the capital. The cities of Pompeii and Herculaneum, just south of Naples, had achieved a reputation for gracious and prosperous living. In that setting courtiers, aristocrats, generals, and the aspiring nouveaux riches passed their idle hours and indulged their sensual promptings. The walls of their houses, as well as those of shops, brothels, temples, and other structures that served community needs, were covered with a remarkable display of paintings that reflected the abundance, the ease, and the pleasure of that life. Then, in A.D. 63, a violent earthquake shook the area. Sixteen years later nearby Mount Vesuvius, without warning, began to spew sulfurous fumes and volcanic ash. Before the populace could flee the disaster, many of them—at least sixteen thousand—were overcome and buried deep beneath the ash. Within forty-eight hours a flourishing city was transformed into a communal grave. Like prawns in aspic or flies in amber the wretched victims were preserved in their volcanic shroud, rigidly posed in their dying agony amid their wealth of possessions—to be all but forgotten until they were rediscovered more than sixteen hundred years later.

The writhing throes of a chained dog (above) were recorded in Vesuvius's volcanic downpour. The Stabian Baths, a lavish facility for men and women, was located on the Via di Stabia, a main thoroughfare of Pompeii, shown at left. Surrounded by the magnificent hunt mosaics in the triclinium of a Pompeian house (opposite), the reclining host and guests partook of sumptuous, many-course meals prepared and served by a huge staff.

Above, Naples meets the harbor. Alfonso I added the splendid arch (opposite) to the Castel Nuovo; it is visible in situ *between the two figures on the bridge (opposite, top left). Its high-relief frieze (opposite, bottom) shows Alfonso's triumphal entry into Naples after wresting it from Anjou. During his reign he induced such artists as Jan van Eyck to come to Naples, patronized literature, and made necessary administrative changes.*

Naples is the heart of Campania. Nestled in a huge natural amphitheater facing a spacious bay, and within sight of Mount Vesuvius, the city occupies one of the most beautiful locations of any community in the world. Famous for its songs, festivals, and gaiety, it has been called the permanent playhouse of Italy. Naples originated as a Greek colony but was taken over by the Romans in the fourth century B.C. However, until the end of the empire the city retained the Greek language and Greek customs. That fact, along with its benign climate, its scenic beauty, and its baths, endeared it to sophisticated Romans, many of whom wintered there and (as earlier noted) in the surrounding area. Virgil wrote some of his finest poetry in Naples, and he was buried there. The celebrated epicure Lucullus kept a villa in Naples, as did several Roman emperors, Augustus, Nero, and Hadrian among them. (More than a thousand years later Boccaccio referred to it as the "gay, peaceful, abundant, magnificent" city.) When, in 476, the barbarian chieftain Odoacer won control of Italy, he pensioned off the last of the Roman emperors, the young puppet Romulus Augustulus, with six thousand pieces of gold a year to live on and Lucullus's former villa at Naples to live in, and there he died. Thus, in a sense the city became the ultimate resort and the burial place of the ancient Roman Empire. In subsequent centuries Naples and its adjoining districts were subjected to as many different alien rulers as Sicily. (During the Middle Ages the name Two Sicilies referred to the kingdoms of Naples and Sicily, which, in the course of turbulent experience, were at various times united.) It was in 1282, during the rule of King Charles of Anjou, that construction began on the formidable Castel Nuovo (New Castle).

The Castel Nuovo, modeled on the great French fortress at Angers, was for more than three hundred years to serve as the home of the kings of Naples, the royal palace of Anjou and Aragon, and the residence of Spanish viceroys. Petrarch came to the castle in 1341 to be examined for his qualifications as poet laureate by King Robert (grandson of Charles of Anjou and dubbed "the Wise"), an occasion witnessed by Boccaccio and a test that Petrarch easily passed. During his sojourn the young poet joined the royal party that daily adjourned to the high-walled garden for crossbow contests. He had long talks with the king on historical and literary matters, and when Petrarch left, Robert placed his own robe about the young man's shoulders, requesting that he wear it when he was crowned with laurel at Rome, which he did. (During another visit to Naples Petrarch admired the frescoes by Giotto in the royal chapel of the Castel Nuovo, which have long since disappeared.) In 1443 the pope named Alfonso the Magnanimous of Aragon the king of Naples. During the reign of this brilliant ruler, scholar, and patron of letters, a remarkable triumphal arch was added to the Castel Nuovo; it remains one of the finest works of art in Naples.

St. Benedict's monastery, rebuilt after being bombed out in World War II (above), caps Monte Cassino, opposite. The illumination of the saint seated in front of the abbey, at top, is from one of the 10,000 manuscripts still housed there. Those and frescoes and mosaics created by the Benedictines in the 11th century influenced contemporary European art.

Almost at midpoint on the way northward from Naples to Rome, visible for miles atop a mountain that rises abruptly from the surrounding plains, stands the fortresslike Benedictine abbey of Monte Cassino. In its lofty isolation it remains a monument of special importance in the history of Western Christendom. It was here that in the year 529 Saint Benedict gave his rule for the conduct of a monk's life, a rule that for centuries to come would be observed in most Western monasteries and that was to have important consequences reaching far beyond the cloister. In the centuries that attended and followed the barbarian invasions, the monasteries of Europe helped to restore order to a shattered society and to preserve for later centuries the classical ideals that had been in danger of disappearing — and, indeed, to convert a pagan world to Christianity. During Europe's Dark Ages monasteries played the role in society that cities had fulfilled in other eras; and Saint Benedict, with his early base at Monte Cassino, was the patriarch of that widespreading movement. When Italy dissolved its monasteries in 1866, the abbey became a national monument, with the monks remaining as custodians of the physical structure and its vast library of priceless archives. Thus it was in 1943, during World War II, when German troops occupied the site as a quintessential observation post and artillery emplacement for stemming the advance of Allied forces, after helping the resident abbot remove the most precious relics and objects to Rome. (German troops were forbidden to enter the abbey itself, where the abbot, five monks, five lay brothers, and about one hundred fifty civilians remained until, as the Allies approached, most of them were removed.) After anguished and often discordant deliberations the Allied command decided that in spite of humanitarian, religious, and sentimental considerations, the monastery must be bombed out if the campaigns were to succeed. The venerable establishment was then reduced to rubble, and the Allies marched on to Rome. Almost immediately afterward plans were made to rebuild the abbey. Today, completely reconstructed, it again serenely commands its height, although it now overlooks a military cemetery where lie the bodies of those, many of them Poles, who died in the heroic assault.

Circular mounds mark the tombs of a necropolis at Cerveteri, once a great Etruscan city.

The Etruscans

Before the Romans rose to power, a large part of the Italian peninsula had become dominated by the Etruscans, a people whose origins remain an enigma. Their heartland, ancient Etruria, is now known as Tuscany, the area in central Italy west of the Apennines between the Tiber and Arno rivers. From that base, subduing such local Italic tribes as hindered their way, they asserted their authority in a loose federation of city-states that ranged from the plain of the Po River in the north to Campania in the south. For a short time, also, Etruscan fleets dominated the Western seas as the Mycenaeans had earlier dominated the Aegean. Many of the sites they occupied during the seventh and sixth centuries B.C. ultimately developed into such important Italian cities as Bologna, Pisa, Siena, Assisi, Orvieto, and still others. It was they who made Rome a city in the beginning; according to Plutarch, Romulus brought in the Etruscans to provide plans for the urban development of the site that, Tyrrhenian soothsayers truly predicted, would one day be "the head of all Italy." Others of their once-thriving communities all but vanished after the Roman takeover of the land, until in fairly recent times archaeologists and plunderers rediscovered the rich evidence of this ancient culture that for the most part remained buried in underground necropolises. Cerveteri, the ancient Caere, was once a great Etruscan maritime center as well as the center of a refined culture. For almost a century it was ruled by the Tarquin dynasty, which provided the last kings of nearby Rome before the republic was founded. Today the site of Cerveteri consists of acres of circular mounds—some of them almost two hundred feet in diameter—the tombs of aristocratic families, where charming and enigmatic sculptured effigies of the deceased and walls painted with scenes of daily activities have been found, mute reminders of a people who loved life and celebrated death.

The Etruscans believed that their dead, as illustrated by the affectionate sixth-century-B.C. couple at right, were not likely to haunt their living relatives if they were shown in happy circumstances. The reliefs in the tomb below provided its occupants with useful utensils for the other world.

ITALIAN GOVERNMENT TOURIST OFFICE

The Etruscan bronze wolf below was provided with Romulus and Remus by a Renaissance sculptor. Early Roman Christians, reviled as degenerates and lunatics, dug miles of catacombs near the Appian Way (right) and decorated them with symbols and pictures, as in the Jordani tomb, shown opposite.

RAPHO-GUILLUMETTE PICTURES—VON MATT

As the ancient center of the Roman republic and empire, as the headquarters of the Western Christian Church, and as a repository of artistic treasures from all ages, Rome is uniquely important among the cities of the world. A pleasant and enduring fiction tells that the city was founded about 8 A.M. on April 21, 753 B.C., by a mighty chieftain named Romulus. As babes, the story goes, he and his twin brother, Remus, were abandoned on the banks of the Tiber River, where they were suckled by a she-wolf and fed by a woodpecker that nested in a sacred fig tree. Subsequently, in a fratricidal altercation, Romulus slew Remus and proceeded to become the legendary first king of Rome. Actually, the beginnings of the city remain dark, although it is certain that there was a settlement on the Palatine Hill shortly before the end of the second millennium B.C. By about 500 B.C. that community had developed into the Roman Republic, and well before the beginning of our era the phrase "all roads lead to Rome" was almost literally true. The Appian Way, main line of communication with southern Italy, with connections to Greece and the East, was begun about 312 B.C.—the first strand in what became a vast web of paved highways that reached from the capital to the ultimate limits of the Mediterranean world and far into northern Europe. Along the Appian Way, just outside Rome, Christians buried their dead in catacombs (burials were forbidden within the city), on whose walls they created the earliest examples of Christian art. There are more than sixty miles of galleries in these underground labyrinths; in these more than half a million tombs have been excavated. In the early days of the faith, such chambers incidentally also served for refuge from persecution and for religious services.

Rome

A detail from the Arch of Titus, above, depicts exultant Romans bearing away sacred booty, including the seven-branched candelabrum from the Temple in Jerusalem. The commanding view of the Colosseum framed by the arch is just as irresistible today (opposite) as it was in 1869, when the artists huddled in the foreground (below) portrayed Henry Wadsworth Longfellow and his daughter there.

The conversion of Rome from a republic to an empire followed Julius Caesar's conquests of Gaul and Britain, and his subsequent elimination of Pompey as a rival for power, in the first century B.C. With the rule of Augustus, Caesar's nephew, ward, and heir, the empire entered a period of unparalleled growth. The physical transformation of Rome that had been begun by Caesar was but one phase of a spectacular flowering of architecture and engineering encouraged by emperors of the next several hundred years. Far and near, the Mediterranean world sprouted in a dense growth of arenas and temples, of highways and aqueducts, of theaters and public baths and halls, whose vast and ubiquitous remains still astonish the traveler to Europe and the Near East. Triumphal arches, raised to celebrate the processions of victorious generals and emperors or to commemorate their accomplishments, were among Rome's unique contributions to architecture, and they proliferated throughout the empire. More or less typically, the Arch of Titus, built in A.D. 81, is adorned with scenes from the life of that emperor, including a triumphal procession bearing spoils from the Temple of Solomon following Titus's capture of Jerusalem eleven years earlier in a campaign that had brought the Jewish state to an end. The Romans were the first to create a concrete that could sustain outward thrust without much additional buttressing. They could thus construct larger buildings than had before been possible, such as the huge amphitheater known as the Colosseum, which covers about six acres of ground; its external wall rose to a height of more than a hundred fifty feet, and it could seat about forty-five thousand spectators. Titus opened the great structure in A.D. 80 with magnificent gladiatorial games and with naval contests for which the arena was flooded. Immense awnings that sheltered spectators from the sun were handled by seamen from the imperial fleet.

Although its surroundings have changed considerably, the Castel Sant' Angelo (top) has suffered only minor changes since the sketch above was made in 1491. The old Roman bridge was extended by one arch on each end in 1893; the third old arch is hidden behind medieval buildings.

The Castel Sant' Angelo is one of the most continuously used of Roman monuments. It all but summarizes the history of Rome in its own history. When it was built, between A.D. 135 and 139, to serve as a mausoleum for the emperor Hadrian and the succeeding caesars of his line, the massive structure was sheathed in white marble and surmounted by statues and a bronze imperial chariot drawn by four sculptured horses. Subsequently it served as a fortress-stronghold for whatever Roman party held power, and as both a palace and prison for popes, as well as a sanctuary when their lives were in peril (it was connected by a tunnel with the Vatican). Here, too, during the Renaissance, the Borgias incarcerated their enemies and killed the worst of them. Early in the present century this ancient tomb, which had also been put to use as a barracks and a storehouse for gunpowder, finally became a museum. In contrast to the castle, whose bold profile has dominated the east bank of the Tiber for almost twenty centuries, the very site of the ancient Forum, once the busiest place in Rome, for a time became neglected and all but forgotten. For more than five hundred years this great open area, lined with markets, temples, and government buildings, was the teeming center of Rome's public life. As early as Caesar's day it was often so congested with merchants, buyers, speculators, politicians, and sightseers that additional forums had to be planned to accommodate the overflow. It was here that Marc Antony read Caesar's will to the Romans over the body of the murdered emperor; and here remain the vestiges of the altar before the temple that was dedicated to mark the spot where Caesar's body was reverently burned in 44 B.C. By the Middle Ages this hub of intense activity had become a cow pasture; its ancient fallen monuments, half buried in centuries of slow decay, served as quarries for the construction of humbler buildings.

The ruins of the Forum (below) strongly evoke days when it was the hub of Roman life. As republicans and later emperors added temples and public buildings, the Forum evolved from the main entrepôt of the city to a resplendent religious and cultural center. Columns of the Temple of Saturn in the foreground seem to point to the Colosseum (left) and Palatine Hill (right) in the distance.

67

In the year 410 Visigoths from the north sacked the city of Rome. It was the first time in eight hundred years that a foreign army had forced its way into the capital—a clear indication of the fading strength and spirit of Romans. For centuries to come Rome was to know troubled times. A citizen of Caesar's day would scarcely have recognized the shattered capital of 1500: with cattle grazing about the half-buried ruins of the Forum, with the Colosseum housing a miscellany of squalid shops and taverns, and with thieves infesting the ancient baths and murderers lurking in filthy alleys. Then, with the Renaissance, Rome began a marvelous recovery. Princes of the Church lavishly patronized architecture and the arts, aiming to make Rome the most beautiful of Christian cities "for the greater glory of God and the Church." Giovanni Lorenzo Bernini (1598–1680), the greatest sculptor-architect of his day, who enjoyed large commissions from various popes and cardinals, produced one of his masterworks in the Piazza Navona, a public space he designed on the site of the ancient circus of Domitian.

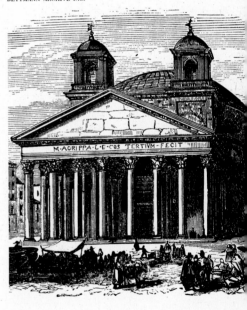

The dramatic exuberance of Bernini's Piazza Navona (shown opposite with Domitian's obelisk highlighted behind the Fontana del Moro) contrasts sharply with the symmetrical elegance of the Pantheon, shown in an engraving below. The 18th-century painting at left pictures the interior of the magnificent structure more eloquently than even the most sophisticated photography could.

The Pantheon, built for Hadrian about A.D. 125, represents Roman architectural genius at its apogee. It is not only the best preserved ancient monument in the capital; it is also the earliest existing building to be composed, with rare perfection, primarily as an interior space. Its great dome is more than one hundred forty feet in diameter and soars precisely that same distance above the marble pavement. Windowless, it is lighted by a single central eye that is thirty feet across and open to the sky and the weather. "It is, as it were, the visible image of the universe," wrote Percy Bysshe Shelley in 1819; "in the perfection of its proportions, as when you regard the unmeasured dome of heaven, the idea of magnitude is swallowed up and lost." As a pagan temple the structure was dedicated to the seven gods of the planets; then, in A.D. 609, it was consecrated as a Christian church, and bones of martyrs were transferred here from the catacombs. Added fame came to the Pantheon as the burial place for artists, notably Raphael, and in later years for kings and queens of United Italy.

69

In the rebirth of Rome's ancient glory, pope after pope strove to outdo his predecessor. Resplendent palaces were built amid the decaying ruins; churches rose in pagan baths; handsome gardens, spacious plazas, and wide avenues swept over and about crumbling temples and arches. The greatest artists and architects of the Renaissance were called upon to beautify public and private buildings with frescoes, statuary, and decorative art of endless variety and rare perfection. In 1506 Pope Julius II laid the cornerstone of a new church designed by Bramante, one of the most brilliant architects of the sixteenth century, to replace the old basilica of Saint Peter, which had risen on the site of Nero's circus (and over the spot where Saint Peter was martyred) and had long been in precarious condition. Over the years that followed, a succession of popes commissioned a series of architects, including Raphael and Michelangelo, to expedite the slow progress of the construction. Although he died before his work was completed, Michelangelo added the vast dome, a crowning achievement of the Roman Renaissance. When the building was finally dedicated by Pope Urban VIII in 1626 it was (and still is) the largest and most majestic edifice in Christendom. The Vatican City, within which it stands, is on the other hand the smallest state in the world, covering a mere one hundred nine acres. But in its various museums it holds a concentration of artistic treasures without parallel on earth.

Stately saints keep vigil over St. Peter's; Bernini's colossal colonnade encircles his vast piazza to suggest the Church's embracing arms.

TIME-LIFE PICTURE AGENCY—DMITRI KESSEL

Left, Bernini's canopy for St. Peter's tomb. Below, The Liberation of St. Peter, detail of a Raphael fresco in the Vatican Palace

Hadrian was one of the most enterprising of Roman emperors. He was not only a builder of empire (he extended the borders of Rome to their farthest limits); he was also a builder of great and enduring monuments, such as the Pantheon, the Castel Sant' Angelo, the great wall in Britain that was named after him, and, of course, his triumphal arch in Rome. Late in his career, when his extensive travels throughout the empire were over, he built for himself an extraordinary country house at Tivoli, the ancient Tibur, about sixteen miles east of Rome. This immense architectural complex covered one hundred sixty acres and was one of the most imaginative structures in the world. To help him recall the places in Greece and Egypt that had impressed him, he built miniature reproductions of the monuments he had particularly admired there on his imperial visits. These included a Greek theater; the Poecile, a peristyle — whose twenty-eight-foot-high wall still stands — reminiscent of a famous stoa in Athens; an academy, a reminder of Plato's academy, also in Athens; the Canopus, which copied the Egyptian canal leading to the Temple of Serapis; large and small baths; and so on in endlessly fascinating variety. There was also, to be sure, a magnificent imperial palace. Later emperors added to the villa before it was sacked by the barbarians. Aside from being a monumental extravaganza, this fantastic display of architectural forms, even in ruined condition, suggests how remarkably flexible the Roman combination of brick and concrete was as a building material.

The calm ruins of Hadrian's copy of the sanctuary of Canopus at his villa, top, contrast with a Villa d'Este fountain (above), with a super-endowed goddess.

Two of the 500 fountains at the Villa d'Este: at top, a hydraulic mechanism in the Water Organ played a tune; above, water pours from nostrils of a gargantuan face

Roughly fourteen centuries after Hadrian's death in A.D. 138, at the height of the Italian Renaissance, Cardinal Ippolito II d'Este also moved to Tivoli and created another spectacular residential complex. He chose Tivoli for his residence because he had been appointed papal governor of the town. Having failed in his attempts to be elected pope, he decided nevertheless to live in pontifical splendor. The gardens of his estate, occupying a terraced hillside, were designed in an orchestrated fantasy of vegetation, scenic views, sculpture, and fountains—fountains of the richest invention. No photograph can capture the spell created by the vision of this abundance of water in constant movement in myriad directions: spouting, spraying, cascading, spilling, running, and tumbling from some five hundred fountains. Some were operated by hydraulic devices that imitated bird song. There was the Alley of the Hundred Fountains (today there are ninety-two), an arrangment in three levels of jets, sprays, and spillovers now overgrown with maidenhair fern. Most spectacular of all was the Fountain of the Water Organ, with jets of varying heights to simulate organ pipes and a concealed organ that played a tune. At its inauguration the epic poet Torquato Tasso accompanied the spectacle by reading from his works. A number of these contrivances have been neglected over the years, but their ruins provide romantic compensation for their lost functions. The villa itself once contained a famous collection of classical sculpture.

Central Cities

Perched high on the rugged slopes of Mount Titano, with views of the Adriatic Sea and the Apennines, San Marino remains the capital of another tiny sovereign entity within Italy's boundaries. Covering barely twenty-three square miles, with parts of its ancient battlements still standing, this miniature republic has been a free state almost continuously for more than a thousand years. Directly across the peninsula, close to the shores of the Ligurian Sea, the city of Pisa, in spite of heavy damage suffered during World War II, still retains monuments that recall the days of the twelfth and thirteenth centuries when it was a powerful maritime republic. In 1063 Pisans won a great naval battle against the Saracens, returning home laden with rich booty. They also played an important part in the capture of Jerusalem in 1099, during the First Crusade. Pisa was the first city in Italy after ancient times to take pride in architectural magnificence, a point amply illustrated by the extraordinary cluster of buildings made of gleaming marble — the baptistery, cathedral, and campanile (the Leaning Tower) — illustrated above, dating from about 1053 to about 1350. As a teen-ager, it is said, Galileo timed the oscillations of a swinging lamp in the cathedral with his pulse beats and thus discovered the isochronism of the pendulum. It is also said that he later determined the laws of gravity by using the Leaning Tower to observe the velocity and acceleration of falling objects.

The famous Piazza del Duomo at Pisa, top, is said to have served as a laboratory for Galileo Galilei, portrayed above at age 70 by Justus Sustermans. San Marino, across the peninsula, was probably established by a Christian fleeing persecution. Each of its three prominent peaks is topped by a view-commanding tower like that opposite.

Serenely crowning its Umbrian hilltop site some sixty miles northeast of Rome, Assisi remains an enduring monument to the gentle Saint Francis, who was born in that city in 1182. Evidences of great antiquity surround the place —Etruscan tombs, remains of Roman temples, medieval castles, churches, and convents. The city itself has changed little since the Middle Ages; its great monument remains the basilica of Saint Francis, built over the tomb of the saint shortly after his early death in 1226. As a youth Francis was a dapper and adventuresome gallant. He took up arms in Assisi's wars with neighboring cities, and at one point he was imprisoned in nearby Perugia. However, as a result of serious illness, he underwent a psychological change that led him to renounce his worldly ways and to devote himself to a life of poverty and self-denial. His joyous religious fervor was infectious: his followers grew in numbers and devotion; and such was the odor of his sanctity that he was canonized within two years of his death. The church at Assisi is a measure of the veneration paid to his memory. Its walls display a rare wealth of frescoes by some of the greatest masters of the early Renaissance, among them Giovanni Cimabue, Giotto, Simone Martini, and their predecessors and followers. Giotto belonged to a Franciscan order, founded with permission of the pope, whose members were supposed to contribute their talents and efforts, and their wealth, to further Francis's teachings. It was Giotto or someone closely related to him who, about 1300, completed one famous cycle of these paintings depicting the life of Saint Francis in more than a score of scenes with a revolutionary degree of realism, which set the direction that Western art has followed ever since. In their paintings, Giotto and his followers revealed a new interest in the world about them, as though Francis had opened their eyes to the beauties of nature, the direct reflection of God's divine ordinance. In Giotto's cycle the saint is shown performing his miracles, in his ecstasy rising from the ground surrounded by a shining cloud, reconciling feuds between cities, preaching to the sparrows, who bend their heads in attending his words, and so on, until his dead body is pictured being carried to Assisi for burial. The most celebrated event of his life occurred when, it is recorded, fervently meditating on the Passion of Christ, Francis was afflicted with the wounds of the Crucifixion—the stigmata.

The monastery and church of St. Francis, located at the extreme left of the panoramic view of Assisi, left, are repositories of such priceless art treasures as Giotto's frescoes in the Upper Church. One, below, shows Fra Sylvester invoking the saint's name to drive seditious demons from disrupted Arezzo.

Ambrogio Lorenzetti's painting Blessings of Good Government, *below, is a fresco from the Hall of Peace of the Palazzo Pubblico, fronting on the Piazza del Campo (left). Siena appears as a thriving 14th-century city with an engaged, industrious populace; towered buildings line streets bustling with tradesmen, playing children, laborers, gossiping women, and mounted cavaliers; farmers thresh and gather grain on the outskirts of the town.*

The old ramparts that still surround Siena seem too extensive for a city whose population today is only about one third that of its heyday in the fourteenth century, when it was an independent republic that flourished on trade and banking. In the fierce rivalry between Italian cities at the time, each strove to reflect its power and wealth through its achievements in art and architecture. The great Piazza del Campo at Siena, a focal point from which the city radiates, is one of the most unusual public plazas in Italy. (Dante mentions it as a place of importance.) From time out of mind, in war and peace, it has been a gathering place for the Sienese. Shaped like half a saucer, the area has served over the centuries for assemblies, festivals, and tournaments. (The dangerous horse race known as the Palio has taken place here every summer for well over three hundred years.) At its lower edge rises the huge and graceful Gothic town hall, the Palazzo Pubblico, and the adjoining lofty tower, two of the noblest public structures in Italy, both completed in the fourteenth century. The fame of Siena was celebrated in its school of painters, including Duccio di Buoninsegna, Simone Martini, Ambrogio Lorenzetti, and others, in whose work the late medieval spirit came to full flower during that same century.

Sculptors and architects as well as painters were called upon in the late Middle Ages to fashion Siena into an urban masterpiece. The republic was prosperous and proud, and it was determined to realize on its earth-red base (the term "burnt sienna" is derived from the color of the local soil) an ideal of city planning that would in itself constitute a surpassing work of art—a single, balanced composition in which the cathedral would have a commanding role. In 1316 the city authorities decided to enlarge the scheme of the old Gothic church, begun in 1065 but not yet completed, to provide Siena with a structure that would outdo the great cathedrals of Pisa and Orvieto and the superb example then rising in Florence. At considerable risk—for the steep slopes of the site afforded only a precarious foundation—the chancel was enormously lengthened. Some years later plans were made to expand the structure even further, but these were halted when the Black Death struck in 1348. However, the vast nave of the cathedral as it stands today—with its clustered columns of alternately colored marble and with carved busts of the popes, shown larger than life, over its main arches—clearly suggests the exalted vision that inspired the Sienese more than five centuries ago. The unique pavement, added in the fifteenth and sixteenth centuries, covers nearly three thousand square yards and displays more than fifty pictorial designs in inlaid marble.

Below, the interior of Siena's cathedral; above, a detail from one of its many floor mosaics

BOTH: SCALA—ALINARI

Trade rivalry between cities had other beneficial aspects. At least partly because education paid off in business returns, a number of Italian cities sponsored universities. Helping poor students was a favorite benefaction of affluent merchants. The university at Bologna, as a conspicuous example, was founded in the eleventh century and at one early point in its development boasted an enrollment of ten thousand. During the Middle Ages Bologna was indeed one of the greatest centers of learning in Europe. Dante and Plutarch attended classes there, as later did Tasso. Among the numerous women professors, it is recorded that one was so beautiful she was obliged to deliver her lectures from behind curtains lest her manifest charms distract her pupils. The study of Roman law was an important part of the curriculum, since it helped to regularize and sanctify corporate practices. Study of the sciences was also fostered. As early as the fourteenth century anatomy was taught there, with fresh corpses for demonstration when they were available. In much later years Guglielmo Marconi worked on the development of wireless telegraphy at Bologna, and an atomic research center is now located there. The city was heavily bombed during World War II, but many of its centuries-old buildings remain in use, integrated into the tissue of modern city life. With its twenty-one miles of arcaded streets, Bologna has a fair claim to being the most civilized of urban places.

Above, Bologna's leaning towers seem to attract each other. At right, the convenient street-level arcades that line the Piazza Maggiore are characteristic of walkways throughout the city.

80

Bologna retains two of its curious tall towers, which served as individual citadels during the intense struggles of medieval civic life, both of them now leaning perceptibly (because of their great bulk they had a tendency to tip or tumble when not well founded). Once there were almost two hundred such structures in the city. There were a thousand in Pisa, it is somewhat extravagantly claimed, some of them ten or fifteen stories high. In San Gimignano thirteen survive, giving the town the appearance of a strange little medieval Manhattan. Florence once had scores of them, and the rich merchants and bankers who lived in them and also had their offices there were called towered men. From the high loopholes of such private fortifications, rival business families could take pot shots at neighboring competitors. As in modern America, these "skyscrapers" signalized a relentless competition among embattled interests. The municipal patriotisms that attended the rise of Italian cities led to hostilities as well as emulation. No sooner did a city achieve power than it turned upon its competitors. Within individual cities separate factions struggled for control, and the wealth that went with it. That sort of intramural strife was for centuries intensified by differences between those who supported papal authority (the Guelphs) and those who looked rather to the Holy Roman Emperor (the Ghibellines). In any case the way to power was often violent and bloody. Even at relatively peaceful Bologna, in 1445 the populace, enraged by the slaughter of its favorite family, the Bentivoglio, hunted down their enemies and nailed their steaming hearts to the doors of the Bentivoglio's palace—as a token of their love.

Towered Cities

Towers stripe the skyline of San Gimignano, the most typically medieval town in modern Italy.

Florence

Ghiberti's culminating work, the "gate to Paradise," included the self-portrait above in the border and ten Old Testament scenes. The panel below tells of events from the creation of Adam to the expulsion.

In the quiet splendor of Florence as captured by the American painter Thomas Cole in 1837 (opposite, top), the graceful tower of the Palazzo Vecchio (middle) and the cathedral guarded by Giotto's campanile watch over the city even as they do to-day (opposite, bottom). And traffic still crosses the Arno via the old Ponte Vecchio (at left in painting).

When Michelangelo planned the great dome of Saint Peter's in Rome he modestly observed that it was "larger but not more beautiful" than the one Filippo Brunelleschi had designed some years earlier for the cathedral of Florence. Like that city's vaulting ambitions, Brunelleschi's magnificent construction was based on examples of the ancient Romans, whose classic virtues Florentines believed had been reborn in their city. "The Florentine Republic," a typically Florentine proclamation announced, "soaring even above the conception of the most competent judges, deserves that an edifice should be constructed so magnificent . . . that it shall surpass anything of the kind produced in the time of their greatest power by the Greeks and Romans." With Brunelleschi's crowning architectural triumph, the Duomo at Florence did in fact seem to surpass anything yet achieved by mortal man, ancient or contemporary. The merchant guilds of the city—that is, the businessmen—not only financed the construction of the great building but also formed committees to pass upon designs. For long years wax effigies of leading traders, clothed in rich garments and sometimes appearing on horseback, were on display in the interior (much like an exhibit by Mme. Tussaud). Giotto's gleaming multicolored marble campanile stands beside the cathedral like a splendidly groomed sentinel. Together with the Gothic bell tower of the nearby Palazzo Vecchio, with its embattlements and crenelations, these lofty and highly disparate structures give Florence a distinctive skyline that as seen from neighboring heights has for long centuries been an inspiration for artists from around the world. The octagonal baptistery that faces the cathedral is the oldest building in Florence. It was dedicated to Saint John the Baptist in 1128 and served as a cathedral until the larger structure was built. Here Dante was baptized. Michelangelo referred to its celebrated bronze doors by Lorenzo Ghiberti as "the gate to Paradise." Artists from all parts of Italy, including such great masters as Brunelleschi, Donatello, Jacopo della Quercia, and Ghiberti himself, had been invited to prepare designs for these doors. "I had surpassed everyone," Ghiberti gloated when he won the final award. His pride was such that he twice included a self-portrait in the decorative borders surrounding the Old Testament scenes of the doors.

Bronze statues of Medici grand dukes line the ornate octagonal Chapel of the Princes (left) in the fifteenth-century church of San Lorenzo. Michelangelo seemingly designed the Medici Chapel there as a showcase for his overwhelming tomb figures; opposite, Lorenzo, deep in meditation, sits above male Twilight and female Dawn, representing states between action and repose.

Florence has been called the jewel of the Renaissance and the cradle of humanism, and it was magnificently both those things. Actually, the city was of no great importance before the Renaissance, and little enough happened there afterward to add significantly to its historic role. During its subsequent growth, largely in the nineteenth century, most of the new building went up in the outskirts, leaving the Renaissance city more or less intact. That part of the city, as it may be seen today, was to a considerable degree the accomplishment of the Medici. This extraordinary family, except for brief periods when its principal members were banished because of political feuds, directed the destinies of Florence for more than three centuries. Besides acquiring the title "grand dukes of Tuscany," three of the Medici became popes, two were queens of France, and several won a cardinal's hat. Endowed with great wealth derived from banking and trading enterprise, many members of the house could afford to be and passionately were lavish patrons of art, literature, and learning. During the days of their flourishing activity Florence became the greatest repository of cultural achievement since Pericles' Athens. As a promising youthful sculptor Michelangelo was taken into the home of Lorenzo de' Medici ("the Magnificent"); as an older man he was commissioned to design the sepulchral chapel of the Medici in the sacristy of San Lorenzo. The tomb statues he completed for this mausoleum after ten years of incessant work achieve a mysterious and almost superhuman grandeur. Forty-nine members of the family—grand dukes, their wives, and their children—were buried in the neighboring Chapel of the Princes, begun by Grand Duke Ferdinand I in 1604. With its walls of various rare marbles, its mosaics of marbles and precious stones, and its huge porphyry sarcophagi surmounted by gilded statues, this extravagantly costly memorial was still not finished when the last of the grand dukes died in 1737.

*As they have since the 16th century, gold- and silversmiths' shops
line the Ponte Vecchio, the only medieval bridge left in Florence.*

Renaissance Florence was a manufacturing city. The most picturesque reminder of its traditional artisanship is in the goldsmiths' and silversmiths' shops that still line the sides of the Ponte Vecchio, the oldest bridge in Florence. The Ponte Vecchio was designed in 1334 by Taddeo Gaddi, favorite pupil and godson of the renowned Giotto. In accord with the prevailing mercantile spirit of Florence, Giotto, "painter of divine Madonnas," was himself a businessman as well as an artist. A member of the wool guild, he rented looms to poor craftsmen who could not afford to buy such equipment outright—and charged them exorbitant rates for the usage. This, too, was in the Florentine tradition. The city's merchant-bankers were notorious throughout Europe for their usury. In the Hundred Years' War between France and England the Bardi family of Florence gave financial aid to both sides indiscriminately, profiting enormously in doing so. At one point, to help Henry III of England meet his running expenses, the Peruzzi family lent money to the king at 120 per cent interest, then charged an additional 60 per cent when repayment was not prompt.

Verrocchio's unsparing bust of Lorenzo the Magnificent (above) bespeaks the man's strength. Below is a serene fountain in the Boboli Gardens, built by Cosimo I, another of the great Medicis.

As international merchants, industrialists, and bankers the Medici were incomparable. Late in the 1400's the ruling Medici annually reviewed the books of his far-flung branches, including twenty-four reports from France, fifty from Turkey, and thirty-seven from Naples. Cosimo I, who became head of the family in 1537 as an almost unknown teen-ager and who thereupon became incontestable chief of the Florentine state, enhanced his fortune by marrying a Neapolitan heiress. Secure in his ducal authority and in his affluence, he set about building a new palace that would do full justice to his eminence. As a site he chose a slope of the Boboli hill on the southern bank of the Arno, near the Ponte Vecchio, where a rich merchant named Luca Pitti had eighty years earlier begun to construct a great residence but had quickly run out of funds for his ambitious undertaking. When it was finally completed, Cosimo's building became the most monumental of Florentine palaces. It is still known as the Pitti Palace, although it was never occupied by the Pitti family and was rather the home of the Medici for two hundred years. Today its galleries and royal apartments that serve as a museum house an extraordinary collection of paintings and art objects. Extending up the slope behind his new palace and covering a vast area overlooking Florence, Cosimo had laid out superb terraced gardens—the famous Boboli Gardens—ornamented with antique and Renaissance statuary and planted with long avenues of cypress, ilex, and stone pine, with roses and azaleas, with citrus trees and fountains.

Jutting sharply from the earth, Orvieto, opposite, crowned with a magnificent cathedral, reigns over the countryside. At left, the façade of the church glows in the sunlight; above, one of its delicately carved holy water basins is shown.

Orvieto

Orvieto crowns a huge volcanic rock that rises abruptly like an island rampart from the plains. Here the Etruscans had built one of their twelve capitals. In the Middle Ages it became a papal stronghold. It remains one of the most remarkable towns in Italy. Most of its buildings date from the 1600's or earlier, but even so, it has its own "old quarter." Although it was deeply involved in the factional warring of medieval and Renaissance Italy, it is apparently the only Italian hill town that had no walled fortifications; stationed in breathtakingly dramatic isolation on its high butte it hardly needed further protection. Seen from a neighboring height at sunset, its colorful buildings clustered about its extraordinary cathedral, the town resembles a glowing set from some enchanted theater. The cathedral itself presents a dazzling encrustation of mosaics, reliefs, stained glass, bronze and carved embellishments, and a variety of columns and tracery, like some intricately designed altarpiece brought outdoors to sparkle in the sunlight.

A miracle was responsible for the building of the cathedral. In the year 1263 a young Bohemian priest was celebrating Mass at the town of Bolsena, twenty miles southwest of Orvieto. The youthful priest had doubts about the doctrine of transubstantiation, according to which the Eucharistic bread and wine proffered at Mass are actually transformed into the flesh and blood of Jesus Christ. During this particular ceremony, however, real blood began spouting from the Host, and the celebrant's doubts were at once and finally laid to rest. Pope Urban IV heard of the miracle, which he decided to commemorate by building a splendid cathedral at Orvieto. Construction was started in 1290 and with the help of 33 architects, 152 sculptors, 68 painters, and 90 mosaicists was completed in the following century. At one early point the master architect Lorenzo Maitani was summoned from Siena to oversee the work. He was told that the growing structure must have a "wall figured with beauty . . . on the front part, and with all the other masteries and ornaments appropriate to this same fabric," which was clearly and wonderfully accomplished by Lorenzo and his successors. The interior of the cathedral was elaborately finished with, among other marvels, paintings by Fra Angelico, Benozzo Gozzoli, and—most impressively—by Luca Signorelli. For more than five centuries the series of powerful frescoes by Signorelli, the *"famosissimus pictor in tota Italia,"* has proclaimed the end of the world and the Last Judgment. These apocalyptic visions remain one of the crowning achievements of the early Renaissance. Michelangelo is said to have trudged his way up to the town to see them, and one eminent art historian concluded that no one is quite the same after having seen them.

The splendid "Army of Martyrs" marches down the aisles of Sant' Apollinare Nuovo, built by the barbarian king Theodoric (far right). The mausoleum of the ruler (right) was erected by his daughter in 526, also when Justinian gave San Vitale to the city. Among the brilliant mosaics that cover the church's interior is one of Empress Theodosia, below.

SCALA—ALINARI

SCALA

Ravenna

In A.D. 402, faced by the mounting threat of barbarian invasions, the emperor Honorius chose Ravenna as the new capital of the western part of the divided Roman Empire. Situated in the marshes formed by the rivers flowing into the Adriatic and close to the large naval base at Classis, Ravenna seemed a safe enough retreat. When Honorius died, his half sister Galla Placidia, an adventurous woman of dazzling beauty, for a time continued to rule as regent for her infant son. However, the barbarians were not to be denied. In 410 the Goths under Alaric sacked Rome, and not long afterward Gothic kings were reigning in Ravenna. For several vital centuries the coastal city felt the strong influence of Byzantium, renamed Constantinople when it was established as capital of the Eastern Roman Empire. Honorius and Galla Placidia were the children of the eastern emperor Theodosius the Great. Theodoric, king of the Ostrogoths (and a Christian), who governed the West from Ravenna between 493 and 526, had spent part of his youth as a hostage in Byzantium, and was, at least nominally, considered a vassal of the eastern emperor. Following Theodoric's death, Justinian the Great did actually govern Italy from Constantinople through his officials in Ravenna. As one consequence of these developments, and of lavish patronage, Ravenna became a unique repository of early Byzantine art. To this day the richest array of monuments in this style remains not in Istanbul, where much has been destroyed, but on Italian soil, in Ravenna. In the tomb of Galla Placidia, the basilica of Sant' Apollinare Nuovo, built by Theodoric, and the church of San Vitale, erected during Justinian's reign, is displayed a wealth of mosaics that are of unsurpassed magnificence and beauty. Dante, who went to Ravenna as an exile from Florence and died there in 1321, described their extraordinary quality in his *Divine Comedy*. By Dante's time Byzantine power in Italy had long since been broken, and the land was becoming an intermittent battleground for local and foreign rivals. In 1512 Gaston de Foix, most redoubtable of warriors, conquered Ravenna in the name of France—and was killed there at the moment of his victory.

The column above marks where Gaston de Foix fell in battle.

91

Queen of the Seas

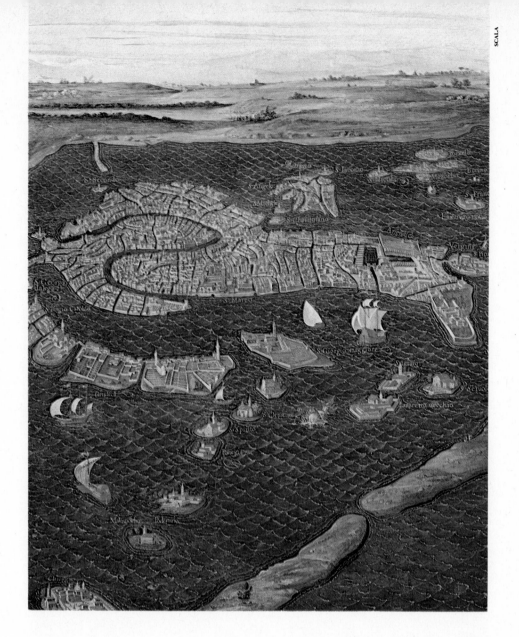

Like Ravenna, Venice served as a place of refuge from the barbarian invasions and was also under the direct sway of Byzantium during its early history. As early as the fifth century refugees from mainland Italy were seeking sanctuary on its alluvial islets, which, the secretary to Theodoric the Great observed a century later, lay scattered like sea-birds' nests on the face of the waters. From these hasty and elementary beginnings rose the city that more than any other in Europe has captured the imagination of poets and artists and romantics of all lands, from Petrarch and Shakespeare to Keats and Byron, from Turner to Monet and a host of others over the years. (This is not to mention the native Venetian artists — Giorgione, Titian, Veronese, and still many others — whose international reputation added luster to the city's fame.) In the eyes of the world Venice has long seemed an all but legendary city. Fittingly, we are told that in A.D. 811 refugees from nearby Malamocco swarmed to Venice, guided by pigeons carrying little crosses, and that this event marked the real founding of the city. It was also said that as a result of a shipwreck Saint Mark had visited the spot and had a vision there. To do the evangelist honor, in 828 Venetians stole his bones from Alexandria and brought them triumphantly home. Mark was nominated protector of the city, and his symbol, the winged lion, became the ubiquitous emblem of Venice.

Canaletto's painting below captures the excitement of an 18th-century Ascension Day celebration before the Piazza San Marco. At right is the fabulous—if no longer golden—Ca' d'Oro.

Venice's liquid streets are spanned by some 400 bridges, 5 of which appear at left. The highest one is the Bridge of Sighs, so named because condemned prisoners were led across it to their execution.

By the fourteenth century Venice, so magically risen from the waves, had become the indisputable "queen of the seas." Strategically placed at the junction of sea lanes from East and West, it gathered its large wealth from both. In 1362 Petrarch was lured to Venice, the noblest of cities, as he called it. Proud as any Venetian of the city's worldwide commerce, he wrote: "Our wine goes to bubble in British cups, our honey goes to tickle the taste of the Scythians, the lumber from our forests is carried to the Egyptians and the Greeks. Thence our oil, linen, and saffron are borne to the Syrians, Armenians, Arabs, and Persians, and in turn their goods come to us." To celebrate its mastery of the seas and the rich harvests gleaned from its seaborne trade, on Ascension Day every year from 1173 to 1797 Venice held an extravagant ceremony on the Grand Canal. The ruling doge, dressed in cloth of gold, boarded his gilded state galley, from which he threw a ring into the waters as he announced: "We wed the sea, in token of our perpetual rule." Meanwhile, on its 117 islands, separated by 160 canals and joined by 400 bridges, buildings of sumptuous beauty were erected. In 1421 the wealthy banker, cloth merchant, and patrician Marino Contarini undertook to build the celebrated Ca' d'Oro (Golden House) in the Venetian-Byzantine style. Made of Greek marbles, green cipolin from Carrara, and red marble from Verona, originally gilded all over, and embellished with the work of the finest artists and artisans of the time, it is the lightest and loveliest of the palaces reflected in the waters of the Grand Canal.

Shortly after the remains of Saint Mark were brought to Venice a church was built to serve as a reliquary for them—and to serve also as a private chapel for the ruling doge. In 1063 Doge Domenico Contarini decided that this early structure was too modest either for the growing republic of Venice or for his own eminence. Work was forthwith begun on the present basilica, one of the most ornamental monuments of Christendom. Early in the thirteenth century one chronicler pronounced it "the most beautiful church that there is." During the Fourth Crusade the Venetians diverted the European forces from their planned assault against the infidel Saracens—who were good customers of the Venetian merchants—and persuaded them rather to sack the great Christian city of Constantinople. A fair share of the fabulous spoils from this shameful expedition went to the Venetians themselves. Saint Mark's is a mixture of Byzantine, Romanesque, and Gothic styles, overlaid with a magpie accretion of surface detail added willy-nilly over the years as Venetians plundered the East of its treasures. The four great horses of gilded bronze that surmount the central doorway are ancient sculptures stolen from Constantinople's hippodrome during the Fourth Crusade. The porphyry group of "Four Tetrarchs" that stands at the right of the façade and that is one of Saint Mark's most cherished ornaments was probably also brought from Constantinople at the same time. Gradually the plain brick construction of the building was covered with a cosmetic overlay of glittering mosaics, translucent veneers of jasper and alabaster, varicolored inlays, and gem-encrusted goldwork. Yet in spite of the superficial clutter the church managed to achieve an unusual unity. John Ruskin proclaimed that the basilica was "in its proportions, and as a piece of rich and fantastic color, as lovely a dream as ever filled human imagination." With its surrounding and adjoining buildings the chapel frames a great marble piazza—Saint Mark's Square—ever the center of Venetian life and one of the most fascinating public places in the world.

The campanile of St. Mark's (shown opposite beside the basilica) was rebuilt with funds from around the world after it collapsed in 1902. One of four bronze horses (above) over the central entrance watches two giant clock-striking automatons. At left, the "Four Tetrarchs" occupy one corner of the church's façade.

Above the Porta della Carta (below) Doge Francesco Foscari kneels before the winged lion. Foscari chose the warrior Bartolommeo Colleoni, superbly portrayed above by Verrocchio, to command the Venetian army.

As he was banqueting at the Doge's Palace on a ceremonial visit, Henry III, son of Catherine de Médicis, remarked that had he not been king of France he would wish to be a Venetian. To this pleasure-loving monarch, as to so many others, the pageantry of Venetian life in its heyday, played against a background of extravagant and exotic luxury, had an almost unworldly brilliance. The Doge's Palace, directly adjoining Saint Mark's, was a symbol of the power and the glory of Venice, as audacious in its design as it was sumptuous in its embellishments. That power and glory reached an apogee in the fifteenth century. Venice had become one of the most formidable states of Europe, a challenge to both emperor and pope, on the mainland as well as on the seas. Under the able Doge Francesco Foscari work was undertaken to complete the palace. In 1443 the elaborate gateway known as the Porta della Carta was completed—a Venetian version of a triumphal arch; above its opening Foscari is shown kneeling before the lion of Saint Mark, flanked by statues representing Fortitude, Prudence, Hope, and Charity. (Aside from its carved and gilded decorations, the interior of the palace is virtually lined with allegorical and other paintings celebrating the wonders and triumphs of Venice by such masters of the Italian Renaissance as Tintoretto, Paolo Veronese, and others. The military fortunes of Venice under Foscari were advanced when in 1454 the redoubtable mercenary Bartolommeo Colleoni was hired as generalissimo of the republic's army. It was a profitable occupation for the *condottiere.* Upon his death in 1475 he bequeathed a large part of his immense wealth to the republic on condition that a large bronze equestrian statue be erected to his memory. Andrea del Verrocchio, the greatest sculptor of his day, was commissioned to create the memorial, and with it he produced the crowning achievement of his career. With his lip contemptuously curved, his legs rigidly straight in the stirrups, and his shoulder thrust arrogantly forward, Colleoni radiates a frightening impression of militant prowess.

Veronese's Triumph of Venice *and its elaborately carved surroundings (opposite) adorn a room in the Doge's Palace.*

Despite the delights of living in cosmopolitan Venice, the nearby mainland countryside held its separate attractions. In this rural setting, observed one Renaissance Venetian gentleman, the sun shone brighter, the sky was bluer, the stars were clearer, and bellyache was unknown. Here the patrician merchant could find a retreat from the pressures of the marketplace and devote his leisure to hunting, concerts, and playing, and to reading the Latin poets who more than a millennium earlier had inspired the fashion for country living. In the sixteenth century that agreeable area blossomed with handsome villas that followed designs by the famous architect Andrea Palladio of Vicenza, a city some forty miles inland from Venice. Like the bulk of his professional contemporaries, Palladio turned for his inspiration to the remaining structures and ruins of ancient Rome, and to the great ten-volume treatise compiled by Vitruvius in the first century B.C.—the only writing on architecture to survive from antiquity. Guided by such sources, in his turn Palladio issued his own treatise describing, explaining, and illustrating his "modern" interpretations of classical styles. First published in Venice in 1570, it was thereafter reissued in every country in Europe. Palladianism spread like a rash throughout most of the Western world, from Russia to the mountains of Virginia—and above all, to England. The Villa Capra, a few miles outside Vicenza, remains one of Palladio's most famous creations, one whose basic principles of design were clearly reflected in such distant structures as Lord Burlington's Chiswick in England, Thomas Jefferson's Monticello, and the Château de Marly on the outskirts of Paris. The so-called Palladian window, with three openings, the central one arched and wider than the flanking ones, was used by George Washington at Mount Vernon and still serves as a hallmark of elegance. The stage of Palladio's Teatro Olimpico in Vicenza—a building modeled on ancient theaters—is painted in false perspective that gives a completely illusory impression of great depth.

Palladio's World

Palladio's famous Villa Capra is shown at top. The "Palladian motif," which the architect used in the loggia of Vicenza's municipal hall (above), has long been a

popular design for windows. The trompe l'oeil *Roman street above, painted by Palla-dio as a permanent stage set, seems infinitely long but in fact is only 20 feet deep.*

The Scaligers of Verona

Early in the fifteenth century, during the course of its martial progress, the republic of Venice had conquered the ancient and neighboring city of Verona. Located on the main route leading toward the Brenner Pass and on to Austria and Germany, the site of that city had since Roman days been recognized as a strategic point, a key to northern Italy. It was earlier established as a stronghold by the Celts and taken over as such by the Romans. From about 1260 to 1387, under the princes of the della Scala, or Scaliger, family, Verona reached the zenith of its power as an independent city-state. The Gothic tombs of leading members of this dynasty, encircled by marble balustrades and wrought-iron grilles, still stand in the center of the city. During the reign of these nobles Verona was torn by strife between Guelphs and Ghibellines, papists and imperialists—strife immortalized by Shakespeare in *Romeo and Juliet*. Romeo's family, the Montagues, were Guelphs; Juliet's, the Capulets, were Ghibellines. According to Shakespeare's version of this old Italian romance, only the tragic results of their enmity—the needless death of the young lovers—could effect a reconciliation between the families.

In spite of heavy damage suffered during World War II Verona retains other outstanding reminders of its near and distant past, including the substantial remains of an ancient amphitheater second in size only to the Colosseum in Rome. In the fourth century Zeno, an African by birth, came to Verona as bishop. Although very little is known about him, his historical presence is memorialized in the twelfth-century church of San Zeno Maggiore, whose beautifully sculptured bronze doors depicting scenes from the Old and New Testament open on one of the finest Romanesque interiors in northern Italy. In 1354 the Ghibelline Cane Grande II della Scala, lord of Verona, erected an imposing castle overlooking the Adige River, which winds through the city. At the same time a fortified bridge was built connecting the castle with the north bank of the river. That picturesque, battlemented complex, now restored close to its early appearance, suggests the uneasy security that eight successive Scaliger despots, benevolent as they were, provided Verona from 1262 to 1387, before the city succumbed first to Milan and then to Venice.

A bronze panel from the eleventh-century doors of the church of San Zeno shows the creation of Eve from Adam's rib.

Like the Gothic celebration of Mastino II della Scala at top, opposite, monuments to other Scaliger princes are topped with equestrian sculptures. The self-satisfied grin of Cane Grande I (bottom, opposite), from another such statue, symbolizes fearless power. The bridge and fortresslike Scaliger Castle, shown below in a 1930's photograph, were bombed in World War II but have been rebuilt.

More than 200 statues grace the exterior of the cathedral of Milan.

The acoustically perfect La Scala opera house (above) seats 3,000.

Milan

Situated on the fertile Lombard plain at the intersection of a number of main European lines of communication, Milan has been a place of international importance since the Middle Ages. Because of its strategic position it has also been subjected to repeated sieges and assaults over the centuries, and many of its oldest monuments were destroyed in the course of such events. In the early centuries of our era, Milan all but rivaled Rome in size and grandeur; but nothing remains of this thriving ancient metropolis. In spite of a strife-torn history, during the Middle Ages Milan became a formidable power in Italy. From 1277 to 1447 the city was ruled by the Visconti family, whose most important member, Gian Galeazzo, was so rich that he married the daughter of the king of France. By 1400 he had extended his dominion to include Verona, Padua, Pisa, and Siena. After the Visconti, a new family of despots took over—the Sforza. The most famous figure in that dynasty was Lodovico il Moro, who through his power, his wit, and his enterprise gave Milan new glories and succeeded in making it a latter-day Athens. Leonardo da Vinci came to his court and painted his incomparable *Last Supper* on the walls of the church of Santa Maria delle Grazie. (He also installed a pump for the duchess's bath, devised unheard-of war machines, and mounted colorful spectacles for the diversion of the court.) Milan's great architectural monument, its unique Gothic cathedral, was started under Gian Galeazzo Visconti in 1386 and was continued more than four centuries later by order of Napoleon Bonaparte. This extraordinary masterpiece, bristling with belfries, gables, pinnacles, and statues, "as though with a forest of lances," was completed—entirely of marble—by a succession of master masons and architects from various European countries. The eminent historian Jakob Burckhardt described it as "a transparent marble mountain, hewn from the quarries of Ornavasso and Gandoglia, resplendent by day and fabulous by moonlight." It created an effect, Burckhardt continued, that could not "be matched elsewhere in the world." Not far from the cathedral, the La Scala Theater, built two centuries ago, still serves as the world's most celebrated opera house.

105

Lakes and Mountains

The northern part of Italy spreads out like an open fan, facing—east to west—Yugoslavia, Austria, Switzerland, and France. An extensive portion of the boundaries between Italy and those neighboring countries is formed by Alpine mountains pierced by deep passes that for long centuries have served as conduits for people, things, and ideas moving from north to south and back again in war and in peace. As the terrain slopes southward down from mountainous heights to the broad, low valley of the Po River, it embraces a cluster of glacial lakes of almost legendary beauty, sparkling introductions to the southern scene that lies beyond—Lake Como, Lake Lugano, Lake Maggiore, Lake Garda, and others whose names evoke visions of splendid villas with terraced gardens, of blue waters, clear skies, and a benign climate, of picturesque fishing villages and sheening olive groves. For two millenniums or more this enchanting lake district has served as a welcome retreat for the world-weary. The elder and younger Pliny, Virgil, and Catullus; Berengar, king of the Lombards; the Visconti and the Scaligers; Queen Victoria, Percy Bysshe Shelley, Lord Byron, and Alfred Lord Tennyson; Goethe, Gabriele D'Annunzio, and Benito Mussolini are but a few of those distinguished in one or another way who found haven and inspiration in this landscape. Sirmione, at the southern tip of Lake Garda, the largest of the Italian lakes, was a favorite resort of the Romans. It is still a delightful spot, situated on a thin tongue of rock that juts out into the water for several miles from the mainland. Visiting it today is like walking back through the Middle Ages into ancient Rome. The slender spit of land is commanded by a massive fortified castle, built for the pleasure and the security of the mighty Scaligers from nearby Verona. Inside there are some Roman ruins. At the extreme northern end of the little peninsula are other, crumbled ruins that the natives have named the "grottoes of Catullus," in memory of the poet who lived beside the lake and wrote of it in rhapsodic verse. Actually these are not grottoes and did not belong to Catullus; they are rather the ruins of a huge and sumptuous palace probably built some years after that poet died—remains of the largest such mansion yet to be discovered in northern Italy.

The Scaliger Castle (above) is the focal point of the ancient village of Sirmione, on a promontory in Lake Garda; just beyond lie the stately ruins of the "grottoes of Catullus" (left). Opposite, Courmayeur, a resort, huddles at the foot of Mont Blanc.

Over large areas of Italy one is rarely out of sight of mountains. Like a gigantic backbone the Apennines reach the whole length of the peninsula, at one point attaining a height of almost ten thousand feet. From Verona, Vicenza, Milan, and other northern cities the rising Alps are within clear view. In a farewell poem to his unfaithful promiscuous lady love, Catullus mentions in passing those Alpine passes that led "toward the new won triumphs of mighty Caesar, Rhine, the Gaul's frontier, and the terrifying outermost British." Almost two millenniums later, in 1800, at the command of Napoleon Bonaparte, an army of forty thousand French troops, including field artillery and baggage trains, descended on Milan by way of the Great Saint Bernard Pass, which leads from Switzerland to the northwest border of Italy, skirting the towering majesty of Mont Blanc, tallest of European mountain peaks. The Great Saint Bernard Road was completed only in 1905. To cross the pass with such an expedition in 1800 was an achievement comparable to Hannibal's historic crossing of the Alps with his elephants and cumbersome gear in the third century B.C.

Iberia

Iberia" is a name used in ancient times to refer to the massive peninsula that thrusts out of the southwestern corner of Europe, the land area that includes Spain and Portugal. Separated from the African continent by a scant eight miles, it all but seals off the Atlantic Ocean from the Mediterranean Sea. The peninsula is in turn virtually locked in from the north by the towering ranges of the Pyrenees, along which runs Spain's border with France. Aside from Switzerland, Spain is the highest and most mountainous country of Europe—a country fragmented into diverse regional pockets by the nature of the terrain. It was the wealth of metals imbedded in those mountains—the gold and silver, copper and tin, lead and iron—that lured the Phoenicians, the Carthaginians, the Greeks, and then the Romans to this rugged land, to mingle and trade with the more primitive Iberians and Celts who had earlier settled there. In 206 B.C. the Romans took over the peninsula as a colony. It was one of the earliest provinces to be acquired by the Romans under the republic. Thanks to the fiercely independent natives it was also one of the last Roman provinces to be truly pacified. The imprint of Roman occupation is still clearly visible throughout much of Spain and in parts of Portugal. By the end of the fifth century A.D., following the decline of Rome, Visigoths from beyond the Pyrenees had assumed control of the land. Roman Catholicism was established as the state religion of Spain in 598, although Jews formed an influential segment of the population then and for centuries to come. A crucial turning point in Iberian history came in 711, when an invading force of Berbers (commonly called Moors) from North Africa crossed the Strait of Gibraltar and quickly swarmed over the whole peninsula—and beyond. The occupation by those people of alien culture and religion had enduring and important consequences, most conspicuously apparent in the architecture of such cities as Seville, Córdoba, and Granada. It took almost eight centuries of intermittent warfare to win all Spain back from the infidels. The Reconquista was finally completed only when Granada, the last Moorish stronghold, was retaken by their majesties Ferdinand and Isabella in the fateful year of 1492. Then, fortified by the resources of its New World colonies, Spain became the greatest power in Europe. For more than a century it dominated Continental politics, and at the same time created a culture of magnificent achievement. However, within one hundred fifty years that glory was rapidly declining; the country entered a long period of political, economic, and educational backwardness that culminated just a generation ago in a tragic, large-scale civil war. The wounds from that bitter contest have not yet healed. In Portugal, which won its independence from Spain in 1143, the Reconquest was a matter of only a century and a half. Facing the open sea for its entire length, the country had its days of great glory in the fifteenth century, when its navigators found their way to the Orient, with its fabled treasure. Then it, too, suffered a decline in worldly importance.

The ruins of the great 11th-century castle of Loarre, near Huesca in northeastern Spain

PHOTO HORIZONS DE FRANCE

Above, a trudging pilgrim displays the cockleshell of St. James, emblem of his trek to Santiago. Below, the saint's remains arrive in Spain and are removed to Compostela.

PRADO, MADRID

Santiago

The Moslem conquest of Spain early in the eighth century was almost absurdly quick and easy. Within a brief seven years the entire peninsula was won over in the name of Mohammed, except for a pocket of Spanish resistance in the northwest (held, according to Moslem chronicles, by a handful of "savage asses"). To recover from the depths of almost total defeat and to win the land back in the name of Christ required little short of a miracle — and so one came to pass. During the early, dark days of the Moslem occupation, it was reported that the remains of Saint James the Greater had been discovered under miraculous circumstances in that remote area of Galicia where the few Christians still held out. Following his martyrdom in Jerusalem, it was told, the Apostle's body had been wafted to Galicia by divine guidance in a vessel without sail or rudder. That James, the most ardent of Christ's Apostles, he whom the Lord termed a "son of thunder" because of his fiery zeal, had chosen his last resting place in remote Spain was a sensational revelation that electrified Europe as the wondrous news spread, and that led to extraordinary consequences far beyond the borders of Spain. Spain, it could be claimed, was his special protectorate, which he would never abandon to unbelieving invaders. The "son of thunder" became Santiago Mata-moros, "Saint James the Moorslayer," who at critical points thereafter during the Reconquest could be seen in the heavens astride a white charger, brandishing a flashing sword. Reports of the saint's miraculous interventions, in peace as in war, set in motion a vast movement of people who swarmed to Spain from all quarters of the Western world to pray at the shrine that was built over his remains at Santiago de Compostela and to fight in his cause. Pious monks, kings and queens, saints and sinners, artists and architects, thieves and merchants, and above all, ordinary folk in countless hordes found their way to Spain from France and Italy, England and Germany, Hungary, Switzerland, Poland, and Sweden. Even curious Moslems came to ponder those saintly relics that seemed to rival the wonder-working bones of Mohammed, which, it was said, were enshrined at Toledo. Dante likened the numbers of such pilgrims to the galaxy of stars that form the Milky Way. In addition, from the eleventh to the thirteenth centuries no less than thirty-five chivalric expeditions came from France to do battle with the infidels.

Opposite is the resplendent façade of the Santiago cathedral.

MARTIN HURLIMANN, ATLANTIS VERLAG, ZURICH

Spain Divided

The cross above stands in the much-traversed Roncesvalles Pass as a signpost for pilgrims on the holy journey to Compostela.

The long-drawn-out Reconquest of Spain was not from the beginning nor was it consistently an inspired Christian crusade, although legend has tended to make it appear such. In 718 at Covadonga, in the far north of the land, a band of mountaineers turned back a small force of marauding Moors because these aliens threatened to intrude on their pastureland, not because they were infidels. Bypassing such a hornets' nest, the Moors pushed on into France, where they were finally repulsed within a hundred miles of Paris. (Had it not been for that turning point in history, wrote Edward Gibbon in the eighteenth century, scholars at Oxford would then have been expounding the Koran to a circumcised Europe.) In Spain during the course of turbulent times to come Christians fought against Christians as well as Moors; Moors fought against Moors as well as Christians; and Christians allied with Moors to fight against other alliances of Christians and Moors. Loyalties were obviously not neatly decided by religious faith or by ethnic distinctions. Thus in 778 Charlemagne led his Frankish hosts across the Pyrenees to relieve the city of Saragossa, not so much to push back the Moslem aggressors in the name of Christianity as to support the cause of one Islamic faction against another. Unable to win a decisive victory, he soon retreated across the Pyrenees. There, at the famous Roncesvalles Pass, his rear guard was cut to pieces, not by Moslem troops (although some may have participated) but by a vengeful band of Christian Basque guerrillas incensed by Charlemagne's raid—a misadventure that grew in legend and story until, as described in the *Chanson de Roland*, it became one of the most popular epic tragedies of all history. The gallant Roland died not for his faith but in retribution for the destruction the Franks had wrought on Spanish soil in their passage through its northern sector. In our own generation that area has known unspeakable violence. On April 26, 1937, during the Spanish Civil War, German bombers, for no conceivable strategic reason, pulverized the little town of Guernica, the historical home of Basque liberties—a senseless catastrophe mordantly recorded by Pablo Picasso in his painting *Guernica*.

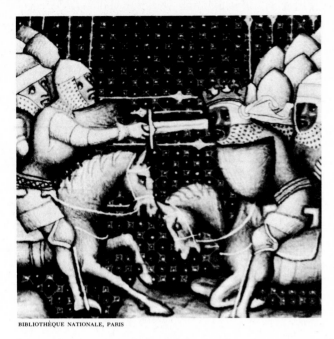

The ruins of an 11th-century pilgrimage church seem eerily out of place in a desolate mountainous pass between Spain and France (below). Early and late the north of Spain has been visited with violence: in the 14th-century illumination at left, Roland charges the Moors. In Guernica, opposite, Picasso immortalized his revulsion toward the wanton German destruction of the little town.

The Cid

The confusion that often attended the slow and erratic course of the Reconquest is suggested by the fact that the Cid, most celebrated and all but legendary warrior of Spanish history, fought against Christians and Moors alike. However, as the hero of Spain's earliest surviving epic poem he is remembered as the champion of the cross against the crescent, the personification of chivalrous knighthood, and the embodiment of the national destiny of his native Castile, then a separate Christian kingdom in north-central Spain. His crowning military exploit, conducted in the name of the king of Castile in 1094, was the reconquest of Valencia, a city he ruled until his death five years later. The Cid was born Rodrigo Díaz de Bivar near Burgos, capital city of Old Castile. There, early in the thirteenth century, was built a Gothic cathedral that one reporter described as "one of the largest, handsomest, and richest monuments of Christianity. . . . On whatever side you turn your eyes, you meet eyes that are gazing at you, hands that are beckoning to you, cherub heads that are peeping at you, scarves that seem to wave, clouds that appear to rise, crystal suns that seem to tremble; an infinite variety of forms, colors and reflections that dazzle your eyes and confuse your brain." With its groups of pinnacles and pale yellow spires that reach into the blue sky, the cathedral seemed to another observer of our own times like "a fairy building from lands of romance and chivalry." Amid this wealth of architectural and sculptural construction and adornment, after a series of misadventures, some of the Cid's bones were brought to rest in 1921. An effigy of the Cid is among the sculptured figures on the façade of the Arco de Santa María, through which one passes in approaching the cathedral from the south. This remarkable structure, flanked by two semicircular towers and surmounted by four turrets, was begun in 1536 in honor of Charles I, king of Spain and then, as Charles V, Holy Roman Emperor—whose statue also appears on the façade of the arch. Under Charles, a Flemish-born youth who inherited an enormous empire, the several kingdoms in Spain were finally united. However, his unpopular policies led Burgos and other Castilian cities to revolt in a brief war of the *comunidades* (commoners). Charles prevailed, and the Arco was raised to appease his wrath.

The cautious embrace of a Christian and Moslem (right) from a 13th-century miniature symbolizes the fitful alliances between the sects. The engraving at top shows an ornate staircase in Burgos Cathedral. Opposite, the cathedral rises behind the arch erected for Charles V.

Salamanca stands near the western edge of the spacious tableland of central Spain. In the third century B.C. the Carthaginians under Hannibal took over the site from the ancient Iberians. The Romans conquered the town in their turn, to be followed by the Visigoths. Then came the Moors, who occupied the place for about three centuries until they were ousted by Christian forces in 1085. In their retreat the Moors all but demolished the city. Salamanca's days of glory dawned with the opening of its university in the thirteenth century. For four hundred years this seat of learning was among the greatest in Europe, vying with those at Paris, Bologna, and Oxford. Throughout most of the Middle Ages and the Renaissance it attracted to its faculty the finest intellects of the time. Through its agencies Arabic philosophy was made available to the Western world. The sons of kings were sent there for instruction, and they sat in the drafty halls on the same hard benches occupied by the rest of the students. Christopher Columbus's proposals for exploring the oceans of the West were submitted to the judgment of Salamanca's professors. And in time, the first universities in Spanish America were modeled on its statutes. During those centuries, almost within the shadow of the university, a group of noble buildings arose, most of them still standing in their venerable splendor. One of the most celebrated of these, the House of Shells, was built in the fifteenth century for a prominent Salamanca sage. Its walls are covered with carved scallop shells, its windows guarded by elaborate wrought-iron grilles of Moorish design or embellished with panels and tracery in the Gothic style.

Salamanca

The scallop-shell motif adds its own shadowy decoration to a wall of the famous House of Shells (left). Alfonso X, "the Wise," shown in a contemporary illumination (opposite, top), was a major patron of the university that brought Salamanca renown throughout Europe. At bottom, the city's Gothic cathedral rises just behind the Romanesque church above the Tormes.

The university at Salamanca was founded only a few years after Christian Spaniards had won a great victory over the Moslems in the Battle of Las Navas de Tolosa in July, 1212 — a year as famous in Spanish history as 1066 and 1776 are in English and American history — and while the militant king of Castile, Ferdinand III, was winning still other important victories under the banner of Santiago. Ferdinand was the very embodiment of the thirteenth-century crusading spirit. His son, Alfonso X, called "the Wise," was rather a man of scholarly passions who gave powerful impetus to the revival of learning that took place at Salamanca and other Spanish universities — learning that was deeply indebted to Arabic thought and scientific practice and to Jewish enterprise and wisdom. The great days of Salamanca, "Mother of the Virtues, the Sciences, and the Arts," are long over, but a poignant sense of its varied and illustrious past endures. The old Roman bridge still spans the Tormes River, leading from the undulating red countryside on the east bank to the crowded houses of the city across the way. Two cathedrals crown the cluster of buildings that constitute the central city. The older of the two, built in the Romanesque style in the twelfth century, is overpowered by the Gothic cathedral raised directly beside it some four centuries later.

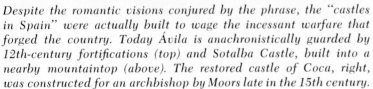

Despite the romantic visions conjured by the phrase, the "castles in Spain" were actually built to wage the incessant warfare that forged the country. Today Ávila is anachronistically guarded by 12th-century fortifications (top) and Sotalba Castle, built into a nearby mountaintop (above). The restored castle of Coca, right, was constructed for an archbishop by Moors late in the 15th century.

118

Embattled Spain

In Spain one is rarely out of sight of castles and fortifications or their ruins, reminders that the nation was forged in many battles. The name of the early Christian kingdom of Castile, whose history is inseparable from that of the entire country, was derived from *castillos*, the frontier defenses erected during the Middle Ages to guard that realm from the Moors. Century after century during the expulsion of the Moors, castles proliferated as Spanish kings moved their capitals from one front to another. Ávila, standing on the flat summit of a rocky hill arising from the *meseta* (tableland) midway between Salamanca and Madrid, was a city of Old Castile. It still retains its eleventh-century castellated walls, which with their eighty-six towers and nine fortified gates form a massive, remarkably well preserved barrier one and a half miles long about the ancient section of the city. Lofty snow-capped mountains ringing the plateau look down on this picturesque citadel, which has long since outlived any need of its mighty ramparts. Ávila was a mystic place as well as an enceinte. Within its fortifications, four centuries after they were built, Saint Theresa was born and educated. Theresa was one of the most remarkable women in history. Her ecstatic visions, transcribed in writings of rich but simple imagery, not only had a profound effect on timely reforms within the Catholic Church during her own life, but have come down to the present as a major source of modern mysticism. Endowed with a firm sense of practical affairs, she was the most robust of mystics, wishing that in a warring world she too could do battle in the Christian cause. Long after her death, during the Civil War of the 1930's, the battlemented city of Ávila fell to the Nationalists without bloodshed.

EUROPA VERLAG A. G. ZÜRICH — MICHAEL WOLGENSINGER

Segovia

Segovia lies within forty miles northeast of Ávila, but in mood it is a world apart. Its history is rich and colorful and can be clearly read in the city as it stands today. Against strong Iberian resistance, the Romans occupied the site and made it one of the chief cities of the peninsula. The immense and graceful Roman aqueduct, built of uncemented stones and more than half a mile long, still carries water to Segovia. For more than three centuries before it was finally delivered by Alfonso VI in 1083, Segovia was repeatedly taken and lost by the Moors, and for many years it was a Moorish capital. At Segovia in 1474, upon the death of her half brother Henry IV, Isabella was acknowledged as queen of Castile, with her husband Ferdinand as consort. Isabella was a sovereign of great ability and tireless zeal. She was ever ready to take to her horse and travel anywhere and everywhere in pursuit of her queenly duties. Even repeated pregnancies did not deter her from making such rounds, and as one result of those energetic expeditions, each of her five children was born in a different city. Her rule over Castile was at first challenged by various factions within and without the state, but in 1479 she became undisputed monarch. That same year Ferdinand succeeded to the throne of Aragon, and between them they sought to unify the entire peninsula, a project that was virtually completed when Granada, the last remaining Moslem stronghold, fell to their Christian majesties in 1492. (By coincidence, the Genoese adventurer Christopher Columbus was witness to the surrender; he had been summoned to discuss with the royal couple his scheme to cross the western ocean.) Isabella's favorite castle was the alcazar in Segovia, a fairytale-like structure, perched on a high cliff, that had been begun in the eleventh century but built largely just before her residence there.

*The 163 arches of a first-century-*A.D.* aqueduct transect the modern city of Segovia.*

Two magnificent edifices dominate Segovia. The alcazar (left), soaring above the western end of town, was the scene of many stirring events. Supposedly Alfonso X, while sitting in a room in the castle, speculated that the earth revolved around the sun and was warned of his heresy by a near-miss thunderbolt, after which he became a Franciscan. Segovia's 16th-century cathedral (below) was one of the last Gothic churches to be erected in Spain.

Looming on the harsh Castilian plain a few miles northwest of Madrid, the Escorial (literally, "slag-heap") remains one of Europe's most extraordinary structures. When they saw this gray, gaunt, and huge barracks of a building rising in the sixteenth century, contemporaries referred to it as the eighth wonder of the world. Its correct title is "the Royal Monastery of San Lorenzo (Saint Lawrence) of the Escorial," and it was built under the direction of King Philip II of Spain, at the time the greatest king in Christendom, as a monument to the glory of God and as a tomb for the body of his father, Holy Roman Emperor Charles V. The idea for this construction came to Philip when, on August 10, 1557, the day of the Feast of Saint Lawrence, his armies won a signal battle against the French. Almost immediately thereafter, news arrived that Charles had died, having spent his last days in a monastery in central Spain, constantly *a misa y a mesa* ("at Mass and at table"), preoccupied with his devotions and with gigantic meals, sometimes practicing his own funeral services in anticipation of his death, and abdicating all imperial responsibilities in favor of his son. To help him choose a site for the memorial to this pious and eccentric soul, Philip set up a commission of architects, master builders, physicians, and philosophers, finally settling on the miserable little village of Escorial on the wooded side of the Sierra de Guadarrama, within easy reach of Madrid, which Philip had nominated as the permanent capital of Spain. All the rest of his life Philip worked on the completion of this strange edifice, preparing it as a monastery in which he played the part of a regal monk, and as a sepulcher for the royal dead. To save his father's soul, he maintained there a veritable army of monks who could send up an irresistible volume of prayer in perpetuity: the Escorial has indeed been called the king's prayer factory. It also housed a great library, one of the world's greatest (most of the books are still there as he placed them), and a collection of paintings by the finest artists of the time, many of which may still be seen there. At the Escorial in 1588 Philip made his fateful decision to dispatch against England the Spanish Armada—a fleet fortified by a crescendo of prayers, processions, and other religious observances that God might be pleased and victory thus assured. Later, anticipating his own death, he ordained that "thirty thousand masses be said for the repose of my soul"—enough, as one historian has exclaimed, to do violence to Heaven.

Philip II was a collector of relics; he had saintly bones from all over Europe and the remains of Spanish relatives transferred to the Escorial. He lies in the chamber below along with many of his royal successors.

PHOTO RESEARCHERS – BRADLEY SMITH

The Prayer Factory

To honor St. Lawrence, who was martyred by being roasted on a grate, Philip chose a gridiron plan for his grim construction, the Escorial (below). Above, Philip and some of his family are shown at eternal prayer in his sepulcher.

Although El Greco's mystical view of the world seems not to have pleased the puritanical Philip II, the artist was immediately accepted in Toledo; seen from the same prospect today, Toledo is not greatly different from his view and plan below, commissioned by city officials. El Greco's house and garden (opposite) are well restored.

Toledo

In 1577 the Greek artist Kyriakos Theotokopoulos, better known as El Greco, arrived in Toledo, to stay there the rest of his life. That city, historically and culturally perhaps the most interesting one in Spain, had by then passed the peak of its commercial importance. Charles V had established Toledo as the capital of his empire—"on which the sun never set," stretching as it did from the Indies to the Americas. In 1561 Philip II moved the capital to nearby Madrid. However, the belated rediscovery of El Greco's unique genius has given Toledo new interest in our own day; many of his finest paintings may be seen in and about the city. In its general aspects Toledo has not changed significantly since El Greco painted his visionary panoramas of it more than three hundred fifty years ago, and the larger part of it is still medieval in character. In post-Roman times, for two hundred years before the Moslem take-over, Toledo was the capital of the Christian Visigothic kingdom in Spain. A number of important early church councils were held at Toledo, and it was there in 589 that Spanish Catholicism after a long contest with Arianism finally triumphed to become the state religion. The city remains the center of Spanish Christianity, and its archbishop is termed (ex officio) "primate of all the Spains." When they won Toledo in 712, there as elsewhere the Moslems observed a policy of religious toleration. Christians who chose to remain were subject to a poll tax, but they were free to observe their own faith. These Mozarabs, as they were called, spoke Arabic as well as their own language and in some respects followed Islamic ways of life. Living apart from the mainstream of Christianity, they developed a separate art, culture, and poetry, as well as a religious ritual that was distinctively their own. To this day the Mozarabic rite is celebrated in a chapel of the cathedral at Toledo. The large Jewish community there was also allowed to follow its own creed. Toledo thus became an important center of Arab, Christian, and Hebrew culture, a rich and prosperous amalgam given over to the Spanish when they reconquered the town in 1085.

As city after city was retaken by the Spanish—Córdoba in 1236, Valencia in 1238, Seville in 1248—the new rulers of the Reconquest were faced with a large problem. These cities had been occupied by the Moors for more than five hundred years. Arab culture, so long established in so much of Spain, was in many ways far superior to that of the Spanish Christians. Whereas thousands of Christians had lived under the Moors for centuries, now thousands of Moors and Islamized Christians and Jews were living in Spanish Christendom. To absorb this old and rich culture and to form a Spanish culture from disparate, long-established traditions became an urgent matter. Talented Moors and Jews had earlier been held in high esteem at the court of Castile. Now, under Alfonso the Wise, that court at Toledo became a flourishing center for the brightest minds of the time, regardless of their faith. In this revival of learning, Jews played a vital role, among other things by translating into Latin those Greek texts that had survived in Arabic versions. Jews were also valued financiers and traders. In 1365 Samuel Levi, a wealthy and powerful Jew, treasurer and finance minister to King Peter the Cruel, had built by Moorish workmen a proud synagogue, which contains some of the finest interior architecture and decoration in Toledo. However, in 1492, as the Reconquest was finally completed, the Jews were expelled from Spain. The next year the great Gothic cathedral at Toledo was finished, to remain the city's largest, most sumptuous and representative monument.

The wall of the Tránsito Synagogue (left) exemplifies the mingling cultures in Toledo. The cloisters of San Juan de los Reyes (above) exhibit Moorish influence. Opposite, the cathedral's setting for the Eucharist, the "Transparente," is very rococo.

Madrid

About forty miles northeast of Toledo, Madrid stands on a high plateau within sight of the Sierra de Guadarrama and close to the geographical center of the Iberian peninsula. The Moors had established a sort of stronghold there, overlooking the Manzanares River, which runs through the city, as an outer defense for Toledo. When that outpost fell to the Spaniards in 1083, the conquest of Toledo followed almost immediately. In view of Toledo's venerable Christian tradition, and the fact that it was the first great city held by the Moors to be taken back, its recapture was an event of enormous symbolic significance. Before and after the Reconquest Madrid, like Toledo, had a heterogeneous population of Moors, Jews, and Christians. However, until under Philip II it became the capital of the land in 1561, it remained a struggling and unimportant country town, with neither significant traditions nor imposing monuments to impede Philip's vision of a new city, which his kingly presence and power would shape into a dominant political center for his vast empire. Virtually nothing remains of medieval Madrid, and the city, grown large and sprawling in more modern times, is still surrounded by barren countryside. Even in its beginnings as a capital city, Madrid was deprived of any major constructive effort because of Philip's obsession with the building of the Escorial nearby.

OVERLEAF: *The Royal Palace, completed in 1764, after the original alcazar was destroyed in the reign of Charles V, remains the most magnificent of Madrid's public buildings.*

RAPHO-GUILLUMETTE PICTURES — J. ALLAN CASH

KINDEL, MADRID

Madrid's Plaza Mayor, ruled by an equestrian statue of Philip III, has been the stage for countless public happenings—among them autos-da-fé and executions.

SCALA—JOSEPH MARTIN

Philip's court overlooked two hemispheres. The new seat of the monarchy governed, beyond Spain itself, Flanders, Milan, Naples, Mexico, Peru, and the Antilles. Madrid's rise to political prominence was so sudden that the drab town had little time to transform itself materially into a city of grand pretension, befitting its lofty estate. And the moment of Spanish imperial glory was a brief one. Philip's role as ardent defender of the faith soon involved him in the wars of religion that would sear the face of Europe—and in the programs of the Inquisition, which struck at the roots of Spain's cultural progress. Philip declared that he "would rather not rule than rule over heretics." But he failed in his self-appointed mission, which his most Catholic majesty pursued with such fanatical zeal. The turning point in Spain's imperial destiny came with the humiliating defeat of the "Invincible Armada" in 1588. Under such circumstances the development of Madrid became somewhat casual for a national capital. The city, as one journalist wrote, is "a mansion, with its public squares for living rooms and its streets for vestibules." Only one of those public squares, the Plaza Mayor, was actually conceived as such; the others were developed more or less by chance, from crossroads, commons, and the like. The most important buildings in the city are the majestic Royal Palace and the Prado Museum, with its great art treasures.

129

La Mancha

The rigidity with which the Counter Reformation sought to control creative thought led to careful surveillance of the publication and importation of books. This denied to Spaniards knowledge of many new developments in learning and empirical science, and in general led to a cultural backwardness from which the country was long to suffer. Nevertheless, in spite of repressive measures and in spite of the sharp downturn of the nation's prestige in international circles, in the sixteenth and seventeenth centuries Spain produced a bright galaxy of poets, novelists, and dramatists. The outstanding luminary among these men and women, who were figures of world stature, was Miguel de Cervantes. It has been said that a nation is the creation of its novelists, and to the degree that this is true Spain may be considered the creation of the man from La Mancha, that desolate plain stretching across the heart of Spain—a land of wide vistas and of windmills. No novel is more national than Cervantes' *Don Quixote de la Mancha*, published in two parts in 1605 and 1615. The book is of its time and place. It reflects the conflict between past aspirations and growing pessimism that was then the mood of Spain, and the tension between hope and despair. It contrasts the touching idealism of the tall tilter at windmills Don Quixote with the shrewd, rustic realism of the squat and burly Sancho Panza. Beyond that, the book presents a brilliant panorama of Spanish society in the sixteenth century, and a universal, sympathetic criticism of the human condition as seen through the wealth of characters that people its story— nobles, knights, poets, and courtly gentlemen; priests, traders, farmers, and bakers; muleteers, scullions, and convicts; elegant ladies, impassioned maidens, and Moorish beauties; simplehearted country girls and blowzy kitchen wenches.

Don Quixote *has inspired countless works of art; opposite is Honoré Daumier's 19th-century vision of the knight, followed by Sancho Panza, on his quest. Windmills, long a familiar sight in La Mancha (top), were almost new to Spain when Cervantes, in a contemporary portrait above, wrote his epic.*

132

PHOTO RESEARCHERS—JOHN LEWIS STAGE

In effect Spain is an assemblage of diverse regional parts, separated one from another by the mountainous pattern of the land. Even when they united the country politically, the Castilian monarchs called themselves kings of the Spains, using the plural. Each region has its own social and linguistic character. None is more fiercely proud of its distinctive ancient traditions than Catalonia, beyond the Iberian Mountains from Castile, in the extreme northeast of the country. Catalan civilization antedates that of Castile, and pride in its cultural identity has led Catalonia more than once to political autonomy—the last time as recently as the 1930's. The Benedictine monastery at Montserrat, tucked in on a narrow ledge among fantastic rock formations halfway to the summit of towering crags, remains a citadel of Catalan culture; it has been called the emblem of Catalonia. It is one of the great religious shrines of Spain—a magnet for throngs of pilgrims. (It was said that the massive rocks of the mountain were rent at the time of the Crucifixion.) The present buildings at Montserrat are relatively recent constructions or restorations among the ruins of much earlier ones. Here, however, is displayed a wooden image of the Virgin, blackened by age and candle smoke, which is said to have been carved by Saint Luke and brought to Spain by Saint Peter in A.D. 30, there to be hidden in a cave during the Moorish occupation. In medieval times Montserrat was thought to have been the site of the castle of the Holy Grail. (That association inspired Richard Wagner in composing his opera *Parsifal*.) Here, too, in 1522, Saint Ignatius of Loyola laid down his sword, and, turning from his military career, dedicated himself to a religious vocation just before the founding of the Society of Jesus.

Medieval castles, rugged mountains, and beautiful harbors make Tossa de Mar (above), north of Barcelona on the Costa Brava, a favorite of tourists. Three-quarter-mile-high Montserrat's monastery (opposite) occupies its unusual position because, it is said, the still-extant statue of the Virgin, being moved by a bishop, refused to go another inch.

135

Barcelona

The bustling seaport of Barcelona, Spain's second largest city, is the historic capital of Catalan culture. According to tradition, this site was first occupied by the Carthaginian general Hamilcar Barca about 235 B.C. Then came the Romans, Visigoths, and Moors. In 801, swooping down from the north, Charlemagne took the city, incorporating it into what was called the Spanish March. Although in much later years it was off and on occupied by French forces, the city has remained a focus of the Catalan spirit of separatism. For centuries Catalonia had strangely little contact with the rest of Christian Spain. Its language, its arts, and its courts developed separately and distinctively. Thanks to its geographic situation on the seacoast and its many interests beyond the Pyrenees (at one point Catalonia's sovereignty extended over half a dozen counties in France reaching from Toulouse to Nice), it had outlooks to the north and east that landlocked Castile did not enjoy. Barcelona became an entrepôt of Mediterranean trade. The conquest of the Balearic Islands in 1229 was a Catalan enterprise, and in the fourteenth century those bold and formidable buccaneers who constituted the Grand Catalan Company, a band of adventurers, even seized and held Athens for a period of eighty years.

Barcelona's excellent harbor, opening to the east into the Mediterranean (below), has made the city Spain's largest port. Opposite, right, are the towers of the church atop Tibidabo. The old quarter of the city retains some picturesque examples of late Gothic architecture, opposite, left.

Facing the sea, with its back to the mountains, Barcelona presents a lively picture of a city as aware of its present importance as it is conscious of its colorful past. The tree-lined avenues that constitute the Rambla run like a broad, verdant river from the waterfront to the heart of the city, as can clearly be seen in the illustration opposite. The Rambla was in fact once a river bed down which sand and boulders descended from the hills behind the city. Today, with its all but incessant parade of strollers and its bright and fragrant flower stalls, the Rambla is one of the principal attractions of the modern city. From Roman ruins to the art nouveau constructions of Antonio Gaudí, Barcelona abounds in monuments and places that recall the wide range of its history. The old quarter of the city, neighboring its graceful Gothic cathedral—one of the finest in Spain—is threaded by narrow streets where medieval houses and shops with overhanging upper stories and pillared arcades jostle one another in a picturesque medley. Only the great hall remains of the Exchange, built in the fourteenth century when Barcelona ships vied with those of Genoa, Venice, and Ragusa along the Mediterranean sea routes and as far as the North Sea. Here merchants of the city have met daily for six hundred years. The fact that the Moors occupied Barcelona for less than one hundred years, and the fact that many of its interests early turned to the north and to the sea, explain much that distinguishes the character and culture of the city—and of Catalonia—from those of the rest of Spain. It has traditionally tended to go its own independent way and has emerged as the busiest and most modern city in Spain. From the hill of Tibidabo beyond the city limits, crowned by the modern church of the Sacred Heart, one can see the Pyrenees to the north, and on exceptionally clear days, the distant Balearic Islands to the southeast. In the closer distance lie the entire city of Barcelona and the magnificent harbor that was its birthright, with its incessant traffic of pleasure craft and seagoing vessels.

137

ARCHIVE MAS, BARCELONA

The vigor and distinctive quality of Catalan culture are brilliantly reflected in the early religious arts that flowered with remarkable suddenness toward the beginning of the eleventh century. It is a primitive art that expresses intense emotional experience and strong personal vision. The monumental Romanesque image of Christ in Majesty, part of a wall painting from the church of San Clemente at Tahull, a village in the Pyrenees, is one of a large number of examples of such art now happily preserved in Barcelona's museum of Catalan art. Catalonia never has ceased to produce great individualistic artists, as the works of Juan Gris, Joan Miró, and Salvador Dali—Catalans all—continue to remind us. During the early Middle Ages Catalan literature also flourished. As in Provence to the north, the rhymed songs of the troubadours developed into a gracious and courtly art form. In spite of the latter-day persecution of writers in the Catalan language, authors either underground or in exile have continued to produce memorable literature. One of the most original—and the most bizarre—architects of recent history, Antonio Gaudí, worked principally in Barcelona. He has been called an inspired freak, and he has also been judged the father of an organic, emotional style of architecture that is just coming into its own. His church of the Sagrada Familia remains unfinished some eighty years after it was started, but it leaves an indelible impression of some strange medieval cathedral half melted by the sun over Barcelona. (Strangely enough, he affected a deep scorn for the Gothic architects and rather expressed admiration for the classical Greeks.) Appropriately, Gaudí was an ardent Catalan separatist who refused to speak Spanish, the language in which he had been educated. The friend of artists, musicians, and poets, he was a witty and mordant conversationalist in his chosen tongue.

Although Gaudí's Sagrada Familia (left) is unfinished after 80 years, work is going forward on it again. Barcelona is dotted with his structures, for wealthy turn-of-the-century Catalans were proud of the unique architecture, a form of art nouveau, they called Modernismo. Opposite is a Romanesque Catalan image of Christ.

Andalusia

Andalusia is the southernmost region of Spain, a land of soaring mountains, hot sunshine, and the fabled cities of Seville, Granada, and Córdoba. This was where the Moors first triumphed in Spain and where their traditions remained strongest. According to an old Andalusian saying, *Quien no ha visto Sevilla, no ha visto maravilla* ("Who has not seen Seville, has not seen a wonder"). So it must have appeared to the Christians from the stark and windswept northern uplands when, after a bitter siege of sixteen months, they took over that beautiful southern city from the Moors in 1248. They were dazzled by the Oriental sensuality of the place (as visitors still are), so beloved by the Moors in their occupancy of more than five hundred years. It was the warrior king Ferdinand III of Castile, conqueror of Salamanca, who won the city. A few years later his son, the learned Alfonso X, drew up a chronicle describing the wonders of Seville. To northern eyes those wonders were breathtaking—the blossoming, perfumed gardens; the tiled and sunlit patios; the Tower of Gold, built to protect Seville's famous palace, the Alcazar (both still standing); the great Giralda, once the minaret of an adjoining mosque, now the campanile of the cathedral that replaced the mosque; and, as the chronicler continued, "many other great and marvelous things besides these we have mentioned." Alfonso concluded that "no place so wealthy or so beautifully adorned had ever been seen before, nor any so populous, or so powerful, or so filled with noble and marvelous sights." Here too, he observed, ocean ships came from down river to anchor, laden with precious freights from the most distant places. Seville could provide anything and everything. "If one were to ask for bird's milk in Seville," went one proverb, "he would be able to get it." By 1401 age and earthquakes had so damaged the cathedral that a new one was planned—to be "so great and of such a kind that those who see it finished shall think we are mad." And it became, in fact, the largest Gothic building in the world and the largest, highest, and richest in Spain. Christopher Columbus lies buried in the cathedral, and in 1519 another great mariner, Ferdinand Magellan, took off from Seville on his epoch-making voyage around the world.

The graceful Giralda, gliding into the air at the left of Seville's massive cathedral (opposite), was a Moslem minaret before it was converted into a belfry. Below, splendid polychrome tilework adorns the Salon of Ambassadors in the Alcazar. At left is a formal walk in the Alcazar garden, a charming place filled with botanical delights, beautiful mosaics, and a large variety of waterworks.

From its hilltop site the central city of Granada, the last refuge of the Moors in Spain, looks in one direction toward the snow-capped summits of the Sierra Nevada and in the other over a rich plain that is flowery in spring, green in summer, and golden in autumn and winter. Granada's period of splendor followed that of Seville—from about 1248 to 1492. During those two and a half centuries of the city's heyday, Moorish kings ruled their surrounding realm from what was for that time the most elegant, sophisticated, and beautiful residence in the whole Western world, the royal palace of the Alhambra. The palace formed but part of a fortress, whose tower-studded walls ring the enclave. Seen from the higher vantage of its neighboring pleasure dome, the Generalife (whose gardens were unsurpassed), those exterior walls of the Alhambra give no promise of the grace and delicate beauty of the palace interiors. "Hail, thou welcome, joyful fabric," extolled one Arab poet addressing the Alhambra. "All men are in awe of thy filigreed tissue, like the tissue of Spring when rain falls." In 1829 Washington Irving was invited to stay in the Alhambra, and he spent several enchanted months in this "Moslem Elysium" before he reluctantly returned to the "bustle and business of the dusty world" to record his memories in *Tales of the Alhambra*.

A royal portrait from a mural in the Alhambra appears above. Sultans and harems sported in the Lion Court there, below.

EVELYN HOFER

Granada remains today perhaps the most beautiful city in Spain. So their Christian majesties Ferdinand and Isabella must have thought of it as they entered the city in January, 1492, to receive its keys from Boabdil, the last Moslem ruler; and so must Boabdil have thought of it as he paused for one tearful backward look at his lost capital, at a point on the southward road ever since known as the Last Sigh of the Moor. During the victorious Spanish campaign Isabella had served as financier and quartermaster while Ferdinand led their armies. It was the first time in Spain's history that men from every region had fought under a single rule as a united force. Christopher Columbus was present to cheer the triumphal entry into Granada, and, flushed with the success of this national and Christian crusade, Isabella thereupon underwrote his enterprise of the Indies. The next year Columbus returned to Spain accompanied by six native Indians and laid at the feet of the royal couple pearls, gold masks, strange fruits, and exotic parrots — tokens from a vast new Western empire whose huge resources would for a time help make Spain master of Europe.

The gardens at the Generalife abound with fountains like those above and offer commanding views of Granada; below, the Alhambra from that vantage.

GIRAUDON

HERSCHEL LEVIT

The flowering house (right) is typical of most in the old quarter. The tenth-century ivory box above is unusual, for Moslems rarely portrayed people. Opposite is the march of arches in the cathedral.

The neighboring city of Córdoba became subject to Seville in 1078, before the latter reached the peak of its glory. For most of the preceding three centuries Córdoba had enjoyed the reputation of being the largest, wealthiest, and most civilized city in Western Europe. Arab historians acclaimed it as the jewel of the world. In the tenth century, it has been said, the city could boast 700 mosques and oratorios, 900 assiduously used public baths, and 50,000 imposing mansions; its main streets were paved and lighted; an abundant supply of water was brought to the city by a long aqueduct and distributed about the community, which literally flowered as a consequence; its royal library alone claimed 400,000 volumes of manuscripts. Córdoba was the scientific center of Europe. Christian kings and princes came to Cordovan physicians for treatment and operations. The accomplishments of Cordovan craftsmen in silver and gold, ivory and leather, and in weaving fine cottons and silk brocades were almost legendary. Through Córdoba and other centers the Moors introduced Europe to Arabic numerals, to the decimal point, and to the concept of zero, revolutionizing European mathematical and astronomical practices. Although only its ruins can now be seen, Medina Azahara, the palace city built just outside Córdoba, once housed the most luxurious court in Western Europe. Palace apartments, the principal ones lined with imported green and rose marble, housed 14,000 male domestics, and the harem held 6,000 women. The gigantic mosque in Córdoba still stands, long since converted into a cathedral. Started in the eighth century and several times enlarged, it became one of the largest and most beautiful buildings in Islam, with its 19 baroque gateways, its 4,000 lamps that burned perfumed oils, and its blazing forest of 800 pillars of porphyry, jasper, and many-colored marbles (most of them taken from various ancient structures), which support a double tier of horseshoe arches of white stone and red brick. Pilgrims from all over Europe came to this immense shrine to venerate some bones of the prophet Mohammed that, it was claimed, had been brought there.

145

The medieval citadel of Bragança (above) dominates a dazzling, whitewashed town. Opposite is the chapel-lined ascent to Bom Jesus in Braga, designed by the celebrated Cruz Amarante in the 1700's.

146

Portugal

In the extreme northeast of Portugal, in the rugged countryside close to the Spanish border, the village of Bragança occupies what was once the site of a Roman settlement. On a height overlooking the modern town, a medieval city still stands behind its long and tall ramparts—a picturesque reminder that, like most frontier citadels, Bragança has been involved in many of its country's past wars. From within those fortifications looms a massive, four-square castle, built in 1187, with its corner watch towers. In the fifteenth century an illegitimate son of the Portuguese king John I, taking the title of duke of Bragança, founded a family line that in 1640 became the royal house of Portugal. The passing of the throne to the house of Bragança marked the climax of an uprising against the Spanish, who for the past sixty years had subjugated Portugal to their rule. The estates of the new king, whose country home remained at Bragança, amounted to about one third of the kingdom. He was the wealthiest noble of the land. In 1662 Catherine of Bragança, daughter of that first king of the line, married the voluptuary Charles II, the "merry monarch" of England, bringing with her from her native Portugal the richest dowry in Europe. The Braganças ruled Portugal until 1910, and Brazil from 1822 to 1889. Across the country, in the northwest corner of the land, near the ancient city of Braga, stands the celebrated sanctuary of Bom Jesus do Monte, visited at Whitsuntide by thousands of pilgrims who do public penance as they ascend to the baroque shrine. The church is reached by way of three flights of stairs, separated by landings, leading to seven terraces, on each of which are tiny chapels.

147

The Greek historian Strabo wrote that Portugal was ". . . inhabited by the most powerful Iberian peoples, who resisted the arms of Rome for the longest period." Rome prevailed, however, molding the fierce tribes into a unit and imposing its Roman culture, as evidenced by the ruins near Coimbra (right). Below is Coimbra's perfect Romanesque church. The clock tower (opposite) symbolizes the venerability of Coimbra's university.

Almost halfway down the length of Portugal, close to the site of present-day Coimbra, bordering the road from Lisbon to Braga, a handsome Roman city once flourished. Today its ruins—its well-preserved pictorial mosaic pavements, the foundations of its dining rooms, baths, and other palatial accommodations, and the remains of its elaborate heating system—are among the most impressive witnesses to the classical age of the Iberian peninsula. In its heyday the community was served by an aqueduct two miles long. Nearby Coimbra has for centuries been celebrated for its university, founded in 1290 at Lisbon but subsequently transferred to Coimbra. The fame of that institution attracted teachers from such other great seats of learning as Oxford, Paris, and Salamanca; Coimbra became one of the most prominent humanist centers of the Renaissance period. Early in the sixteenth century the city also attracted a number of French sculptors under whose influence, along with that of native talents, a school of decoration emerged and then evolved into an architectural style that spread throughout the country. Much earlier, in 1162, other Frenchmen, Masters Robert and Bernard, had been called to Coimbra from Lisbon to undertake the building of a cathedral. Modeling their structure in good part on the smaller, fortified sanctuaries that lined the pilgrimage routes from France to Santiago de Compostela, they raised the most beautiful Romanesque church in Portugal. (Here, in 1355, was murdered Inés de Castro, Castilian mistress to Pedro I, heir to the throne of Portugal, by order of the young prince's father, who feared any threat of Spanish influence in his realm. That tragic romance has inspired innumerable plays and novels.) While the cathedral was a-building, Coimbra served as the capital city for Portugal's first monarch, Alfonso I, who had proclaimed himself king of the land in 1139. When the capital was removed to Lisbon in the thirteenth century, Coimbra remained a favorite royal residence.

The importance of the sea to the Portuguese probably caused Diego d'Arruda to choose a nautical motif for his famous convent window (left) in Tomar. The azulejo, or tile picture, on the arch in Óbidos (opposite) is one of thousands placed in and on buildings during the 17th and 18th centuries, when such decoration was immensely popular in Portugal.

It was during the reign of Manuel I (1495–1521) that Portuguese navigators discovered Brazil and the sea routes to India and the Orient. Suddenly Portuguese possessions girdled the globe. Gold, diamonds, silks and porcelain, and other exotic treasures from distant lands poured into the little country, and Manuel became one of Europe's wealthiest sovereigns. Under his lavish patronage the arts flourished. A style of architecture developed that was distinctively Portuguese in its play of naturalistic and sometimes fantastic forms used in a robust fashion. For want of a better name it is called the Manueline style. It is seen at its best in the great window of the conventual church of the Military Order of Christ at Tomar, about midway between Coimbra and Lisbon. This extraordinary creation was sculpted in 1510 as part of an addition to an octagonal twelfth-century church with a circular nave characteristic of the Templars, virtually the only example of its kind in Europe. Patterned and pictorial tiles are so ubiquitous in Portugal that they constitute a truly national form of decoration. The concept of using these colorful, gleaming forms to cover walls, floors, and even ceilings goes back to the culture of the Moors. At the little city of Óbidos, near the coast north of Lisbon, the narrow main street leads under a pointed arch with a facing of tiles above, and on between very white houses to Saint James's Church, located at the foot of the fortified walls originally raised by the Moors, by whom Óbidos had been occupied until it was liberated in 1148 by Alfonso I.

When he reached India by rounding Africa in 1498, Vasco da Gama (a contemporary portrait appears above) achieved a feat envisioned and put in motion some 80 years earlier by Prince Henry the Navigator.

An old legend has it that Lisbon was founded by Ulysses. More likely Phoenicians first settled at the site about 1200 B.C.—a site they referred to as their "serene harbor." More than two and a half millenniums later, when Portuguese navigators were opening up the wide world beyond the horizon, the poet Luiz Vaz de Camões referred to the city as the "princess of the world . . . before whom even the ocean bows." Between 1515 and 1520 a fortress, designed by the brother of the designer of the Tomar window, was built at Belém ("Bethlehem"), in the extreme west of Lisbon, to guard the harbor. It once stood on an island in the river, but as a result of silting it now stands on the mainland. Just below the top story of the structure is displayed a row of shields bearing the cross of the Military Order of Christ—an order established to provide a Portuguese home for the disbanded Knights Templar, who had helped rid the country of the Moors. That cross became the chief emblem of the great maritime discoverers and was borne on the sails of Portuguese ships that undertook those adventures.

In 1255, slightly more than a century after the city was retaken from the Moors (with the aid of Crusaders on their way to the East), Lisbon replaced Coimbra as capital of Portugal, the westernmost capital in Europe. Vasco da Gama's fleet sailed to India from the magnificent harbor where Manuel's robust fortress was to be built a bit later. Near that site, shortly after the return of the historic expedition, the king founded the royal monastery of Belém to commemorate the success of that undertaking—and to testify to the new-found wealth in the royal coffers. The buildings, completed over years by a number of architects, are among Portugal's finest monuments. They are built of the local marblelike stone, which gives Lisbon a glittering appearance resembling that of Venice. Within those structures are the tombs of Manuel I, Catherine of Bragança, and others of royal rank; and the remains of Vasco da Gama and Camões, those two great figures in Portuguese history, were interred there in 1880. The cloisters, a fabric of unusual beauty, are covered with a profusion of exquisite sculptures and graced by the lacelike tracery of Gothic arches arranged in two tiers. It is one of the most monumental cloisters in Europe. The monks housed amid these elaborate surroundings were of the Hieronymite order (as were those of the Escorial), which was established in Spain near Toledo in 1374. Members of this group possessed great influence at the Portuguese court and played an important part in the conversion of the Indians in Portuguese holdings in the New World.

Opposite is Manuel I's Belém fortress. The cloister above graces the Hieronymite monastery (below).

Like Rome, Lisbon was built on seven hills. Saint George's Castle, dominating one of the heights, is the cradle of the city. The earlier constructions were the work of the Visigoths in the fifth century and of the Moors in the ninth century, modified in later years by Alfonso I. Its ten towers are connected by massive crenelated walls. At the southwest corner of this pile, the Arabic palace was for several centuries the residence of the Portuguese royal families. The fortress itself has long since abandoned its original warlike purposes, and its grounds have been converted to peaceful gardens and pleasant terraces that command a fascinating view of the city and the Tagus estuary. In its heyday Lisbon, with its unsurpassed harbor, was the center of a worldwide trade. Portuguese discoveries of new ocean routes had altered the destinies of Western Europe. But the far-flung empire was of a size out of all proportion to that of the mother country, and as other nations contested the sea lanes and robbed Portugal of its holdings and its trade, the little country was shorn of its old glory. In 1755 Lisbon was all but destroyed by one of the most severe of recorded earthquakes. (The shock of that disturbance, it has been said, was felt from Scotland to Asia Minor.) The disaster occurred during the hour of High Mass, and fire spread from the church candles to surrounding buildings. A tidal wave swept up the Tagus and broke over the lower town. It has been estimated that as many as forty thousand of the city's population perished. News of the disaster spread about the world. Members of the English clergy held that Lisbon had been destroyed because its inhabitants were Catholics; survivors of the catastrophe attributed it to the fact that they had misguidedly harbored a few Protestants in their midst. In any case, Lisbon was almost immediately rebuilt along "modern" lines that were revolutionary at the time, as the broad avenues and trim houses that may be seen today recall to mind.

The view above of Lisbon was engraved in 1619, about 150 years before the terrible earthquake that changed the face of the city; Saint George's Castle, left, was one of the few ancient structures that was spared the devastation.

155

Only its overview outdoes Pena Palace for spectacle (below); a grounded merman, above, glowers his displeasure from the castle.

A Spanish proverb observes that "to see the whole world and leave out Sintra is truly to travel blindfolded." Blessed by a cool climate and majestic, verdant surroundings, the small town was for centuries favored by the kings of Portugal as a summer residence. In the sixteenth century the poet Camões celebrated the beauty of this picturesque mountain landscape in his great work *The Lusiads,* Portugal's national epic. His contemporary, Gil Vicente, referred to the area as an earthly paradise — a sentiment echoed in the later writings of such distinguished English travelers and authors as Robert Southey, George Borrow, and Lord Byron. Late in the eighteenth century another Englishman, the wealthy, eccentric William Beckford, paused long enough in Sintra to build on its outskirts a palace of pure white stone in the Moorish style, now known as Montserrate, with a surrounding park. The park, which was systematically cultivated by subsequent British owners, contains rare plants, giant tree ferns, and other flora brought there from all corners of the earth. The high-lying lawns, as perfect as any in England, command a superb vista overlooking the Atlantic Ocean in the near distance far below. In the summer of 1808, within the town itself, was signed the Convention of Sintra, in accordance with which the British and Portuguese allowed Napoleon's troops, with their arms and baggage intact, to evacuate the kingdom unhindered aboard English ships — an agreement whose terms were not popular among the Portuguese. By May, 1811, the French were out of all the rest of Portugal for good.

As they are shown in the 17th-century view above, Sintra's many castles seem like a number of orogenic outthrusts; the Moorish royal palace, which has been rebuilt twice, dominates the foreground.

Writing of Sintra's mountains in his poem *Childe Harold's Pilgrimage*, Byron tells of "the horrid crags, by toppling convent crowned," using the word *horrid* in the romantic spirit to evoke a sense of awesome and exciting wonder. When he wrote, the dilapidated remains of the Convento de Pena (*pena* meaning "crag"), a small monastery built centuries earlier, stood in isolation on one of the highest of those peaks. Allegedly it had been built by King Manuel I, who used the aerie as a lookout post to spot the returning fleet of Vasco da Gama after its epic journey to India in 1499. Between 1840 and 1850 Ferdinand II, German consort of Queen Maria II, built over and about this "toppling convent" the huge palace of Pena that now so prominently dominates the crag and the surrounding countryside. For his architect, Ferdinand chose another German, Baron Eschwege, who provided him with an imaginative construction that combines a bewildering variety of styles. A statue of Eschwege in the guise of a medieval knight stands on a nearby rock. When Maria died, Ferdinand lived on in his lofty extravaganza, comforted by an opera singer who was his mistress.

RANCE abounds in more varied historic sites than any other country in Europe, or in the world. That enviable heritage can be traced in good measure to the nature of the land itself. For, taken as a whole, France displays a greater variety of natural features than can be found in virtually any other European country—lush river valleys and salty marshes, fertile plains and wooded hills, rugged mountains and inviting coasts. France has also enjoyed the rare advantage of direct outlets both to the ancient world of the Mediterranean, with all its storied treasure and wisdom, and to the newer worlds that opened about the Atlantic, with their untold resources and limitless horizons.

Those physical facts have played a significant part in shaping the history of France. The diverse and promising aspects of the land have, over millenniums of time, attracted settlers and plunderers, migrants and conquerors, merchants and adventurers from all quarters of the Continent and beyond. With the waning of the fourth and last Ice Age, as glaciers melted and as bleak steppes and tundras gave way to forests and other forms of vegetation, predatory humans followed the different breeds of animals that moved into that new habitat. In subsequent centuries other, civilized peoples—Greeks and Romans—moved up from the south along ancient trade routes to traffic in northern commodities; and from the north and east came nomadic hordes, peoples from outlandish places, hungry for the sun and the warmth, the glamour and the treasure of the more sophisticated southern world.

At one point, in the fifth century, Attila, aptly called the Scourge of God, led his band of ruthless, marauding Huns into the land; but he was turned back before he could devastate the country. Less than three centuries later the fanatical warriors of Islam, vanguard of a civilization far more advanced than anything known in France at the time, stormed up over the Pyrenees from Africa and Spain to proselytize this fair western world in the name of Mohammed—and they, too, were repulsed, with consequences of enormous importance to the destiny of Europe.

In the end, it was the Roman occupation of Gaul (as France was known to the ancients) and the gradual Christianization of the country that laid firm foundations for the development of French society. It was largely through these agencies that over long years of trial was forged an amalgam of the highly disparate traditions of the classical civilization of the southern world and the tribal cultures of the northern reaches. Overlaying that basic pattern, the passage of transients and the influx of immigrants have made the country a major crossroads of the world, a place where stimulating and civilizing influences from every direction mingled and matured and ultimately endowed France with a cultural importance out of all proportion to the limited size of the nation. As the pages that follow clearly indicate, every corner of France bears the imprint of events and circumstances that have over the ages contributed to the rich history of the country.

The "Marseillaise" calls Frenchmen to arms in this relief from the Arc de Triomphe, Paris.

Prehistory

The record of human accomplishment in France can be traced far back in time, virtually to the very emergence in Europe of *Homo sapiens*—the first known representatives of the human race—during the fourth and last Ice Age. Long before they had evolved a written language or learned to construct permanent shelters, these "sapient" men were creating convincing and suggestive images to relate their experiences and to express their hopes and fears in graphic form. Toward the end of the Old Stone Age, between about 15,000 and 10,000 B.C., this early art came to a remarkable peak in such life-like renderings of living creatures—of the game and the predators whose habits the artists knew so well—as are still preserved on the walls of caves at Lascaux in southwestern France, and at a number of comparable sites. Precisely what occult purposes these astonishing creations may have served can only be guessed, but they must have been the common purposes of some group or tribe. This was more than mere decoration, for some of the Lascaux drawings can be reached only by crawling on hands and knees into dark crevices. Most likely the artists who fashioned such images with earthy pigments were "professionals," men who may have been relieved of communal duties because of the importance put upon their special aptitude. As such they were among the earliest specialists in history. Their images are often superimposed one on another, as though their magical message—to insure a successful hunt by previsioning it, to ward off famine by reproducing a plenitude of slaughtered beasts, or whatever—needed repeated statement for the reassurance of the community. For endless centuries these historic treasures were sealed and hidden until, altogether by accident, in 1940 they were rediscovered by neighborhood boys whose dog had fallen into a hole that led to the underground caverns.

Images of beasts (below, and detail, above) in a Lascaux cave; the sunlit Dordogne valley, opposite, seen from a cave opening

Gateway for Greece

MUSÉE DE CHÂTILLON – GIRAUDON

PHOTOGRAPHS ALBANE, PARIS

PHOTOGRAPHS ALBANE, PARIS

Over five feet tall, the Vix krater is decorated with handles (detail, top) cast in the shape of a serpentine-legged grotesque and with a frieze that alternates the figure of a walking warrior with that of a chariot driver (detail, bottom).

FRENCH EMBASSY PRESS AND INFORMATION DIVISION

Marseilles is the oldest large city in France. More than twenty-five hundred years ago—about 600 B.C.—Greek mariners landed at what is now called the Old Port of the city and founded there a settlement known as Massalia (or, in Latin, Massilia). This was to be the mother of a cluster of Greek colonies in Gaul and Iberia, and a base for trading and exploring ships that may have ranged far beyond the Pillars of Hercules, from Senegal to Iceland. The settlement also became a principal gateway for Greek merchants who bartered with the inland tribes of Gaul. In 1953 a colossal sculptured bronze *krater*, or wine vessel, of Greek workmanship, dating from the sixth century B.C., was unearthed from the tomb of a Celtic princess in the heart of Burgundy at Vix, near Châtillon, far north of Marseilles. No bronze object at the same time so huge and so magnificent has been recovered in Greece itself or any of its colonies. Why such an extraordinary treasure was sent to that remote hinterland site has not been explained, but its presence there suggests the enterprise of such Greek traders as those who operated out of Marseilles and who might have taken it as tribute to barbarian tribesmen controlling trade routes to northern Europe. In later years Cicero observed that without the services of Massalia, Rome never would have been able to conquer Gaul. Even then, when Rome dominated the Mediterranean world, the city remained for a time a vital center of Hellenic culture in the West. Conservative Romans sent their sons to school at Massalia rather than to Athens, whose moral reputation was then dubious. Over the course of subsequent centuries, this vital contribution of ancient Greece was overlaid by the swirling currents of Western history. However, in spite of many turbulent periods, the city's eminence as a port was rarely challenged. In 1249 it supplied the vessels needed by Saint Louis for his Crusade, and out of such endeavors Marseilles established trading posts in Asia Minor and Africa. Trade with the East reached heights of splendor late in the Middle Ages. In 1524, to bolster the city's defenses, Francis I had built on a rocky island in the outer bay the Château d'If—a structure to be forever associated with the stories of Alexandre Dumas about the count of Monte Cristo.

The island on which the Château d'If (above) stands is one of several sheltering a harbor where Greeks from Phoenicia about 600 B.C. established Massalia; 15th-century Marseilles is shown as a walled city in the woodcut below.

BIBLIOTHÈQUE DE LA VILLE DE MARSEILLE

163

In 124 B.C. Roman troops marched into southern France, a region largely inhabited by the "Gauls beyond the Alps." They had been summoned by Massalia, then an ally of Rome, for protection against those barbarians who had drifted down from the north and who had proved to be troublesome neighbors. Veterans of the army were settled on the land; the rich hinterland of Marseilles became the Provincia Romana. The regions later known as Provence and Languedoc soon sprouted with typical Roman structures— triumphal arches, theaters, arenas, temples, baths, and stadiums—a fair number of which remain standing. The great bridge and aqueduct known as the Pont du Gard was built during the reign of Augustus. With its three tiers of arches made of blocks of uncemented golden-colored stone, it is one of the lasting marvels of that time and place. At the topmost level a five-foot-deep channel carried an abundant supply of clear water that passed through aeration and filtering stations to the nearby city of Nîmes from a source more than thirty miles away. In its architectural perfection, as it spans the valley of the Gard River, it seemed to one recent observer "more than anything else, the completion of a landscape that had been left unfinished by mistake." At Nîmes itself, the Maison Carrée remains the best preserved of all Roman temples. Thomas Jefferson described it as "the most beautiful and precious morsel of architecture left to us by the ancients." "Here I am, Madam," he wrote the comtesse de Tessé, "gazing whole hours at the Maison Carrée, like a lover at his mistress." And with this vision in his mind's eye he designed, or rather redesigned, the Virginia State Capitol at Richmond.

Roman Gaul

A Roman temple, the Maison Carrée at Nîmes, was depicted (below) by Hubert Robert in the 18th century and used as a model by Jefferson in his design for Virginia's capitol (above).

The arches of the Pont du Gard (opposite) supported an aqueduct and a Roman road.

About midway in the first century B.C. Julius Caesar undertook the campaign that swiftly brought all Gaul under Roman rule. The Pax Romana, the Roman Peace, superseded the anarchy and intertribal strife that had prevailed in much of the land for so long, and Gaul was soon Romanized. In the following centuries Gaul in fact became more Roman than Rome itself. Throughout present-day France there are innumerable reminders of this phase of the country's ancient past, nowhere more plentiful than in the south. For its gladiatorial games and other diversions, the amphitheater at Arles in Provence could accommodate about twenty-six thousand spectators, virtually the whole population of the city at the time the arena was built (a century earlier than the Colosseum at Rome). As in other Roman arenas, the sand was dyed red so that blood from the savage combats of men and beasts would not show. Today the structure is used for the genial Provencal variety of bullfights, in which nobody gets hurt—including the bull. Nearby, less than half the original structure of a huge theater still stands. It could seat an audience of ten thousand in its semicircular tiers, whose diameter was greater than the length of an American football field, and whose huge scenic wall rose higher than a ten-story modern building. About a dozen miles northeast of Arles, excavation of the ruins of the ancient city of Glanum, on what is known as the Plateau des Antiques, has revealed the only foundations of Greek houses yet discovered in France. At some point in the early history of that community the citizens developed a new city hard by the site of the original one. The town of Glanum was originally founded as a center for quarrying and cutting stones needed for the development of Arles. Its ruins in turn became a quarry for building nearby Saint Remy. On the outskirts of the present town of Saint Remy, two splendid monuments—a so-called mausoleum and a triumphal arch—stand as lonely witnesses to what was once a populous and animated Gallo-Roman city. Authorities claim that the arch was erected by Caesar's orders shortly after 49 B.C., to commemorate the capture of Massalia by his forces after that city had, with ill luck, taken the losing side of Pompey in the power struggle between the two men. The "mausoleum" appears to be rather the cenotaph of two personages of disputed identity, perhaps the grandsons of Augustus Caesar, represented by sculptured figures within its circular colonnade. Both monuments must have once dominated some major public place, now overgrown with stone pines shaped by the wind, and in the spring bright with poppies.

Relics of the prosperous Gallo-Roman city of Glanum: near St. Remy a "mausoleum" (above, left) and a triumphal arch (left). And at Arles, a spacious amphitheater and a theater (opposite)

Detail from a 15th-century altarpiece shows Avignon (above) with its famous bridge and in the distance Mont Ventoux; left is Petrarch's sketch of the nearby Fountain of Vaucluse.

The Artists' Provence

For centuries past artists and writers have been attracted by the historic interest and the dramatic nature of the Provence countryside. During the fifteenth century artists of this region created some of the most beautiful paintings of all times. In 1480 one of them included as a background detail of a celebrated altarpiece a landscape view of the medieval city of Avignon and its surroundings. The bridge of Saint Bénézet, famous throughout the world because of the popular song about it, spans the Rhone River and leads from the west bank to the Palace of the Popes in Avignon. This enormous and splendid fortified structure, covering about seventy thousand square feet, still rises majestically above the red-tiled roofs of the city's houses. Here, from 1309 to 1377, a succession of French popes challenged the authority of Rome. That period of time was so close to the seventy-year captivity of the Jews in Babylon that it has been called the Babylonian captivity of the papacy. Petrarch, a good Catholic who had occasion to witness the notoriously luxurious life at the papal court, referred to the Avignon papacy as the Whore of Babylon: "Nest of treachery . . . Handmaid of wine-bibbing, sloth, gluttony in whom lust does its utmost. . . ." Such scarifying epithets appear in the midst of Petrarch's idyll of his own "mad love" for the Laura of his poems. To escape the tormenting charms of that lady he retreated to the Fountain of Vaucluse, an enchanting spot a dozen miles from Avignon. In the spring of 1336, to elevate his flagging spirit, Petrarch climbed to the summit of Mont Ventoux, thirty miles northeast of Avignon, shown on the skyline in the altarpiece. His account of that ascent is one of the earliest known records of anyone climbing a mountain for the sheer pleasure of such an adventure.

Paul Cézanne, one of the greatest pioneers of modern art, was born in Aix-en-Provence and spent long periods of his life in that region, painting its people and its landscapes. During the latter part of his life, the peak of Mont Sainte Victoire was visible from his studio window. In the countryside near that mountain, in 102 B.C., the Roman general Gaius Marius had won momentous victories over the threatening barbarians — victories that, it is said, deferred for four centuries the sack of the Roman world. (It is also said that to this day more than a quarter of the male population of Provence are christened Marius.) Again and again Cézanne used Mont Sainte Victoire as a motif in the ultimate refinement of his unique talent. Vincent van Gogh spent the most tragic but artistically the most fruitful and rewarding part of his life in Provence, recording its scenes at Arles, Saint Remy, and elsewhere with his hallucinatory vision. (Cézanne thought it was the work of a madman.) His drawing of a cypress is one of innumerable studies of this tough and flexible tree, which stands everywhere in Provence as a practical defense for town and field against the howling winds of the mistral. The tree was, van Gogh wrote, as beautiful "in line and proportion as an Egyptian obelisk . . . a splash of black in a sunny landscape."

Two Provence views: above, a cypress by van Gogh; opposite, one of Cézanne's many depictions of Mont Ste. Victoire

Walls of Resistance

Romans once occupied the site of Carcassonne, the greatest and most picturesque of the medieval walled cities whose remains are still to be found throughout France. In the fifth century the Visigoths seized the escarpment, added a new ring of fortifications to the Roman entrenchments there, and used it as a base for their conquest of southern France. Three centuries later the Franks took control of the fortress town. With its triple ring of crenelated walls and its fifty-four towers, constructed at various times, its flying balconies, and other intricate defenses, Carcassonne long remained an impregnable frontier post of Languedoc, the region west of Provence. However, in 1209 a motley army of two hundred thousand crusaders from the north, under the Norman count Simon de Montfort, swarmed over that region and among other acts of violence and pillage laid siege to Carcassonne and forced its inhabitants to capitulate. Damage to the city was later repaired; the structure was reinforced, and it became again a mighty fortress. Subsequently, the role of the city changed, and its walls and towers deteriorated until, in the middle of the last century, during the romantic period, complete restoration was begun by Viollet-le-Duc.

When he set out to restore the walled city of Carcassonne, Viollet-le-Duc executed a design (above) for a gate, the Porte Narbonnaise, which was realized (below) in the renovated structure.

170

The avowed purpose of those crusading northerners—
Frenchmen, Germans, Flemings, and others—was to
wipe out the heresies that flourished in and about
Languedoc. The "heretics" were actually not Christians
but Albigenses—named after the city of Albi, which was
a center of their activity—who adhered to the ancient
Manichaean belief in the coexistence of good and evil.
Jesus, they attested, had lived only in semblance. When
the Christian clergy (including Saint Bernard of Clairvaux) could not dissuade the Albigenses from their
faith, the armed crusaders moved in to eradicate such
dissidence—with the lure of plunder to goad them on. By
such means and by a subsequent inquisition, Albigen-
sianism was ultimately eradicated. Bernard de Castanet,
"the most terrible of inquisitors," was rewarded for his
efforts with the episcopacy of Albi. There, by extortion
and other dubious fund-raising devices, he built as a
personal memorial the huge fortified cathedral that still
stands in Albi. It is one of the most remarkable religious
structures in France, made of brick and more like a
citadel than a church, with its tall, narrow windows set
between powerful vertical buttresses; it has only two
doors and no transept. In this spacious keep, large
enough to hold a great troop, conforming Christians
might well feel secure against the assaults of their
errant, vengeful brethren. Bernard was so hated by the
people of his diocese, who greeted him with cries of
"death," that he was removed to the city of Le Puy. But
the grim "lair of the helmeted inquisitor" that he planned
stands little changed on the exterior from its original
design, save for a Flamboyant Gothic porch added
centuries later.

*The Romanesque church of St. Cecilia
at Albi (above) rises near a Roman
aqueduct visible through a Renaissance
viaduct; a porch in the High Gothic
style (below) was subsequently added.*

During the darker days of the Middle Ages men lived in their small world, in constant fear of the strange world beyond. Towns survived if their sites were defensible—protected by rivers or marshy ground, or strategically situated on some commanding height, either behind walls as at Carcassonne or under the protection of fortified castles to which townspeople could flee in times of peril. Thus the town of Gordes in Provence clings to its hilltop, about the site of an early fortress with its surrounding ramparts. The ruins of Les Baux, also in Provence, remain on a stark chalk cliff, from which point of vantage one of the most powerful feudal dynasties of the south once launched its wars against neighboring rivals. The feudal seigneurs of Les Baux—the English author John Addington Symonds called them "a burning, raging, fiery-souled, swift-handed tribe"—claimed descent from King Balthasar, one of the Magi who came from the East to pay homage to the infant Jesus. The castle that once stood at Les Baux may have been as large as the Palace of the Popes at Avignon, and the life there as luxurious. On this grim crag, in the thirteenth century, Provençal troubadours sang the praises of the warlords of the place, and the cult of courtly love flourished in rooms furbished with storied tapestries, oriental carpets, and gold and silver plate in abundance. By the sixteenth century Les Baux had become a stronghold of Protestantism, and in 1632, weary of the arrogance of its troublesome barons, Louis XIII had the castle and its ramparts leveled. In time the other structures disintegrated or were demolished. The site stands as a ghostly apparition of its proud past—one of the most picturesque and the eeriest of France's historic places. (Bauxite, the principal ore of aluminum, was first found here in 1822 and takes its name from the town.)

The town of Gordes (above) remains perched on a lofty hilltop; but in its arrogance, Les Baux (opposite) was reduced to a ghost town.

173

The structures at Les Baux had been built of local stone, and when they crumbled, their ruins became hardly distinguishable from the rock-strewn, moonlike landscape. North of Languedoc, at Le Puy, in the mountainous Auvergne province of central France, the chapel of Saint Michel d'Aiguilhe ("Saint Michael on the Needle") has perched for nine centuries atop its rocky pinnacle, like some organic extension of that almost incredible natural formation. (The building may have replaced a much earlier temple dedicated to the Roman god Mercury). The town of Le Puy, one of the principal gathering points for French pilgrims headed toward Santiago de Compostela in Spain, was celebrated for its miraculous statue of the Virgin, which was venerated even by the Moors from Córdoba. Tradition claims that Saint Louis, returning from his Crusade in Egypt, gave the statue—or a statue—to the cathedral of Notre Dame du Puy, near Saint Michel. The fact is that the church was dedicated to the Virgin, and her cult that flourished there spread throughout France and to Spain. As early as the middle of the tenth century, Bishop Godescale of Le Puy conducted a tour of two hundred monks to Santiago, and in the cusped arches and zebra work of the portal of Saint Michel can be seen the influence of Moorish architecture—proof enough that returning pilgrims brought back more than cockleshells and tales of miracles from the world beyond the Pyrenees. Notre Dame du Puy, which rises on its own, somewhat less spectacular eminence, incorporates not only similar Moorish designs but also architectural elements that recall the great Spanish cathedral at Santiago. It was at Le Puy that about A.D. 990 the local bishop called a great outdoor meeting of his diocese to persuade the lay nobles "to observe the peace, not to plunder the property of the church or the poor, and to restore what they had already taken. . . ." When the barons refused to give such a pledge the bishop, who had armed some of his people, brought them into play. Under this pressure the nobles capitulated and signed a "Truce of God." The movement thus initiated was one of the most significant developments of the Middle Ages.

St. Michael on the Needle (opposite) sits atop one of Auvergne's peaks at Le Puy; local volcanic stone was used in its Moorish decoration (portal arch above). The cathedral of Le Puy attracted pilgrims (below) en route to Santiago, Spain.

Auvergne

Santiago pilgrims also paid homage to an image of Our Lady of the Market in the Romanesque church (opposite) at Clermont; from a field nearby, Urban II summoned recruits for the First Crusade—such Christian warriors as these (below) figured in capitals from the church's choir. In another field, Vercingetorix the Gaul (honored in the gold coin above) defeated Julius Caesar.

The countryside of Auvergne is studded with old volcanic peaks that, like the one at Le Puy, often rise in dramatic formations. (In French, the word *puy* means the summit of such a mountain.) Many of the churches of Auvergne make use of black and red volcanic rock in their structures, producing singular and attractive accents of color. With its use of such materials, with its elevated lantern towering above the transept, and with its cluster of rounded, radiating chapels, Notre Dame du Port at Clermont-Ferrand, the capital of Auvergne, is a paradigm for a number of churches within a radius of twenty miles or so of that city. The celebrated little Black Madonna of Notre Dame, modeled on a Byzantine icon, has for centuries remained the object of pilgrimages. The church was specifically designed to accommodate the swarms of the faithful who visited the site. It was at Clermont-Ferrand that in 1095 the French-born ex-Cluniac monk Pope Urban II delivered one of the most moving orations recorded in history. No building in that area at the time was large enough to contain the audience that gathered to hear his message. In the open air, therefore, he addressed the huge assembly, praising the valor of the Franks, calling upon his listeners to remember the heroic deeds of their ancestors, and urging them to forget their petty squabbles and civil strife at home and to take up arms against those infidels who were desecrating Christianity's most cherished shrines in the Holy Land—for which endeavor, he counseled them, they would be rewarded on earth as in heaven. Thus was launched the First Crusade. The pope himself was surprised and almost embarrassed by the response to his exhortation. Such was Urban's eloquence that even women, monks and priests, old men, and children had to be restrained from marching off with the able-bodied men. Long centuries before, another event of dramatic importance had taken place on the plateau of Gergovie, not far from Clermont-Ferrand. There, in 52 B.C., the heroic Gallic leader Vercingetorix beat back the Roman legions in a bloody encounter. It was a glorious victory, but it won only a temporary respite for the Gauls. In another battle that shortly followed, Vercingetorix was conquered by Caesar and taken prisoner. When that young barbarian chieftain, ceremoniously clad in gold-studded armor and handsomely mounted as if for parade, finally threw down his arms before his victor, all serious opposition on the part of the Gauls was ended.

LUC JOUBERT, PARIS

SCALA

Burgundian
Sites

At Vézelay, northeast of Auvergne in Burgundy, the saintly Bernard of Clairvaux, whose fame as a churchman rivaled that of the pope, preached the Second Crusade on March 31, 1146. To dramatize his message Bernard tore up his own garments to provide material for banners for the crusaders. Among the host of pilgrims who gathered at that Eastertime to hear this great and superbly eloquent man was the king of France, Louis VII, who was thus inspired personally to lead a Christian army to the Holy Land. His dauntless queen, Eleanor of Aquitaine, determined to go along with him and his following of nobles. "The villages and castles are deserted," Bernard exulted in a letter to the pope, describing the results of his preachments, "there is none to be seen save widows and orphans whose husbands and fathers are alive." This crusade was actually a total fiasco, although en route Eleanor made the best of things by carrying on a notorious affair with her youthful uncle, Raymond II, prince of Antioch. Some years later, in 1190, King Philip Augustus of France and Richard the Lion-Hearted of England met at Vézelay before undertaking still another crusade. Meanwhile, the basilica of Saint Mary Magdalene was rebuilding on its hill overlooking a wonderful panorama of opulent Burgundy countryside—the hill of inspiration, as it has been called—at Vézelay. This construction followed a disastrous fire at a time when a thousand pilgrims had gathered there to venerate the relics associated with the saint—what amounted to a tragic mass cremation. The appeal of those relics was so great that Vézelay became a very important stage along the pilgrimage route—so great that a larger structure had to be built to accommodate

the throngs who went there to benefit from the miracles that might be wrought in their presence. However, in order to defray the enormous cost of the new construction the abbot felt obliged to impose additional taxes on the local population, which believed that its burdens were already heavy enough. The controversy reached a sudden, violent climax when the townsmen took matters in their own hands and killed the abbot to put an end to his demands. Nevertheless, the construction was completed. Then, late in the thirteenth century other relics of Mary Magdalene were disclosed at a church in Provence, which occasioned some misgivings about those in Vézelay, although these had earlier been authenticated by the pope. The influence of Vézelay thereafter diminished; the pilgrimages dwindled, and the fairs and markets that had enlivened the community lost their earlier importance. In the sixteenth century, during the wars of religion, it was pillaged by fanatical Huguenots and then further destroyed during the French Revolution. When the novelist Prosper Mérimée, who was also Inspector of Historical Monuments, viewed the structure in the last century it was virtually a shambles. Then, for almost twenty years, the incomparable Viollet-le-Duc worked to restore the church to its early splendor. Its stands today as one of the most gracious religious monuments in Burgundy. Fortunately, the original central portal of the church survived the ravages of time and accident (and the incidents of restoration). It still displays one of the greatest masterpieces of medieval relief sculpture, showing the Savior in the act of transmitting his redeeming grace and the Evangel to all the world.

With its basilica of Mary Magdalene, the town of Vézelay (above) dominates a stretch of the Burgundian fields; when he studied the ruins of the basilica, Viollet-le-Duc found and sketched its remnants (opposite, left). Only one portal (opposite, right), with superb 12th-century reliefs, had been preserved virtually intact.

179

Little remains (opposite, top) between the main entrance and a distant belfry in the once-flourishing monastery of Cluny (below). Above, grape pressing in Burgundy, depicted in a French tapestry executed about 1500

During the Middle Ages the history of France—of most of Europe for that matter—remained intimately and inseparably linked with the history of the Church. For long years the Church was plagued by problems that stemmed from the barbarian invasions on the one hand and from the decadence of its own administration on the other. Then, in the course of the tenth century, by a series of internal reforms and reorganizations, the ecclesiastical structure gathered new spirit and fresh strength. The single fact that lends unity to the next three centuries was, indeed, the authority exercised by the Church, a binding force that was felt not only in spiritual matters, but in art and literature, science and law, politics and economics, and, recalling the Crusades, even in war. It was in the monasteries that the latent and powerful spirit of Christianity and the seed of learning that informed it had survived the violence of the invasions that stormed across Europe in the days following the disintegration of Charlemagne's empire in the ninth century; and it was in good measure through the agency of the monasteries that the Church carried out its reforms and made its influence felt. The most important of these monasteries was the one at Cluny, in French Burgundy (where some of the finest wines of Europe have been produced from time out of mind). By papal decree the abbot of Cluny was responsible only to Rome, and neither king nor bishop could interfere in the affairs of the order's management. Cluny became, in fact, the headquarters of a monastic empire that embraced virtually all Europe within its spiritual jurisdiction; its emissaries carried the cultural influence along with the discipline of the order in every direction. At the height of its power Cluny controlled more than a thousand associated establishments spread as far apart as Scotland and Jerusalem. (In the eleventh century William the Conqueror pleaded urgently for Cluniac monks to help him strengthen his work and position in England, offering to pay for them with their weight in gold; but his bid was refused on the grounds that there was greater need for such emissaries elsewhere.) For almost half a millennium the abbey church at Cluny, today a sad but vastly impressive ruin (it was almost entirely destroyed during the Napoleonic period), remained the largest and most sumptuous building in Christendom — that is, from about A.D. 1100, when it was built, until the great cathedral of Saint Peter was raised at Rome in the sixteenth century. So large and sumptuous was it, indeed, that Bernard of Clairvaux, who was head of the rival Cistercian order of monks and a man of ascetic disposition, felt obliged to remonstrate against the "immoderate" length, the "immense" height, and the "supervacuous" width of the edifice, as well as against the "monstrous" imagery of its sculptures, the "curious carvings and paintings which attract the worshiper's gaze and hinder his attention." It was to Cluny that Peter Abelard ultimately fled for refuge when, following his tragic romance with Héloïse, his critical theological arguments earned him the wrath of Bernard. (Bernard was also a misogynist who believed that Eve was the original cause of all evil.)

Francis I lured Renaissance artists to the fortified chateau of Amboise, his early residence; here Leonardo (self-portrait below) came and died, it is said, in the king's arms.

The chateau at Amboise that perches on its height above the Loire River is only a minor portion of the complex of buildings, at once a fortress and a palace, that occupied the site in the sixteenth century. Construction on a large scale was started in 1492 by Charles VIII, who had been exposed to the rich delights of Italy's Renaissance culture in the course of invading that country, and with his taste for luxury he turned to Italy for treasures to furbish the chateau and to Italian craftsmen, artists, gardeners, and tailors to equip his establishment and adorn his grounds and his person. However, in 1498 he died of an unusual accident, and the heyday of the chateau came only with the occupancy of Francis I. Then a succession of wild beast fights, masquerades, and divers other entertainments followed one another in rapid succession. Francis had also been beguiled by his experience in Italy as a would-be conqueror, and by the most lavish patronage he tempted to his court the greatest talents of the time. "I will choke you with gold," he promised Benvenuto Cellini to entice him to France, and he did indeed lure that braggart, liar, and exquisite Italian craftsman to his court. The aged Leonardo da Vinci also came north at Francis's urging. He was promised seven thousand pieces of gold and "a palace of his own choice in the most beautiful region of France." Leonardo acquiesced, only to die shortly after his arrival — as legend has it, in the arms of the king at Amboise.

Chateaux & Palaces

As a solemn reminder that the end of life is not pleasure, even for royalty, more than eight hundred years after it was first consecrated by Pope Calixtus II in 1119 the abbey church of Fontevrault still stands near the banks of the Loire River. The order of Fontevrault had been founded twenty years earlier as an unusual religious establishment in which monks, nuns, lepers, the sick, and women of high rank who had withdrawn from the world were housed in five separate buildings. More unusual, over the centuries monks and nuns alike were ruled by abbesses—women chosen from the nobility (between 1099 and 1792 five of the thirty-seven abbesses were from the house of Bourbon). When she died, Eleanor of Aquitaine was buried at Fontevrault in 1204, and, after various misadventures, her reclining tomb effigy remains there, along with those of her second husband, French-born Henry II of England, their son Richard the Lion-Hearted, and a daughter-in-law, Isabelle of Angoulême, third wife of King John of England, successor to Richard. Eleanor's vast holdings in France, combined with those of her second husband, even while he was king of England (he was also duke of Normandy and count of Anjou), remained for centuries a formidable obstacle to the unification of France under the indisputable rule of a French monarch. From this union of Henry of Anjou and Eleanor of Aquitaine dates the beginning of the long and bloody strife between England and France.

At Fontevrault Romanesque arches rise above the tombs of Eleanor of Aquitaine and Henry II, her husband, the French-born king of England.

It was not until the end of the fifteenth century that most of the land that is France today was finally incorporated in the royal domain. With the conclusion of the Hundred Years' War in 1453, the last English invaders—the Goddams, as they were called—had been driven back across the Channel, thanks in part to the inspired help of Joan of Arc. Then, by craft and guile, by patience and persistence, by luck and struggle—and with bloodshed—the French kings overcame the fractious and scheming lords who had long insisted upon their feudal privileges in defiance of royal authority. It was with the relative tranquillity thus established in the land during the following years of economic recovery and progress that royalty and nobility alike could afford to abandon their fortified keeps in favor of more gracious and livable habitations. In 1519 Francis built an additional extravagant residence, Chambord (above), in the valley of the Loire River. With its four hundred forty rooms, its fifteen large staircases and sixty smaller ones, and its veritable village of terraces atop the main structure, it is the largest of the many chateaux that were soon to sprout in this long and remarkably pleasant valley.

A miniature village (see aerial detail) tops Francis I's extravagant chateau at Chambord; here ladies watched hunters riding to hounds in the fields and forest below. Above is a hunt from a detail in a manuscript illumination.

(In planning this vast establishment Francis had hoped to rechannel the Loire to bring it to the foot of the chateau, but his engineers and architects were fazed by such a gigantic task, and a smaller river was diverted instead.) Such sumptuous buildings were in fact not so much permanent residences as way stops in the pursuit of courtly pleasures. Set amid thousands of acres of forest (enclosed by a wall twenty miles long), Chambord served ideally as a "hunting lodge"; and Francis and royal successors were passionate hunters. The finest dogs of Europe were brought to Chambord for breeding; the royal pack consisted of hundreds of such hounds. From the lofty terraces, winding among large clusters of spires, bell-turrets, gables, and chimneys, courtiers could relieve their tedium by watching the huntsmen pursue their game, as well as the tournaments and other festivals held on the grounds below. (Among those intricate passages they could also dally and intrigue.) In later years, when Louis XIV was in residence at Chambord, Molière's *Le Bourgeois Gentilhomme* had its first presentation there. When the king evinced his pleasure at the performance, his courtiers quickly followed suit.

Fontainebleau (above), set in the midst of a magnificent forest about forty miles from Paris, remains one of the most impressive of the many great establishments that were built in the Renaissance manner during the sixteenth and seventeenth centuries—palaces and chateaux that were formally planned and designed with deliberate attention to such amenities as were never imagined in the Middle Ages. Work was started on the new structure in 1527 by order of Francis I, and it was added to and refurbished by subsequent French kings. (In later years it was one of the favorite residences of Napoleon Bonaparte, who restored the entire palace and grounds.)

Francis added new luster to the kingly name. His court, wherever he held it, comprised the most brilliant gatherings of lords and, especially, ladies that Europe had yet seen; a court that in its splendor foretold the extravagant displays at Versailles under Louis XIV more than a century later. For the embellishment of Fontainebleau, Francis imported some of the most prominent artists of Italy, notably including Francesco Primaticcio, Il Rosso, and that "faultless painter" Andrea del Sarto. With the presence of such foreign talent, a French school of painting matured at Fontainebleau. The art of this school was derived from the mannerist style that had developed in northern Italy, a style that is characterized by refined elegance and that often incorporated learned allegorical conceits and esoteric (and erotic) symbolism in its decorations. Four centuries later, another, totally different school of painting evolved in and about the neighboring village of Barbizon, an informal school whose artists—such men as Jean Baptiste Camille Corot, Jean François Millet, Theodore Rousseau, and Narcisse Diaz—found inspiration in the forested landscape near Fontainebleau, one of the most beautiful wooded tracts in France.

186

In mid-career Francis I broke ground for Fontainebleau and recruited artists to embellish the vast structure. The Fontainebleau School, which developed at the chateau, is represented by the 1595 painting (right) of Diane de Poitiers congratulating Gabrielle d'Estrées in their bath with a pinch: a pleased Gabrielle was pregnant by the king, Henry IV. Starting in the 1830's the forest of Fontainebleau became a favored subject often depicted by artists of the Barbizon school, as in the painting by Narcisse V. Diaz shown below.

OVERLEAF: *At Versailles Louis XIV, the Sun King, built the greatest of palaces.*

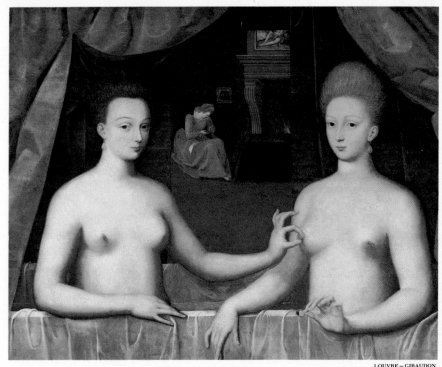

PHOTO BULLOZ

Queen at nineteen, Marie Antoinette liked to escape the public formalism of such places as Versailles' Hall of Mirrors (right) and play at the simple life in her village, Le Hameau; she peopled it with men to grind corn in the water mill (above, top) and girls to wash clothes in its pond. Her pleasures ended when a Revolutionary mob of women (see painting, above) seized her and the king and returned them to Paris.

With Louis XIV—the Grand Monarch, the Sun King of "terrifying majesty," in his own view the divinely appointed instrument of God's will—the French monarchy reached the apex of its power and its glory. To reflect the splendor of his role as supreme ruler of the most important and powerful state in Europe (as France then was), Louis commissioned the finest artists and artisans of the land to plan, build, and decorate for him and his court, without regard for cost, a complex of buildings and gardens at Versailles, outside Paris, that would astonish the whole world with its grandeur. (Louis was himself occasionally disconcerted as the price of his extravagance mounted, and at one point he burned his architects' accounts.) When it was all completed in 1688, Versailles did indeed impress the world. Here was an inimitable declaration of the Sun King's eminence, such eminence as no European monarch had attained since the days of Rome's greatness. Envious rulers and princes of other lands were tempted to emulate this magnificent display of pomp and circumstance, but their numerous "little Versailles'" were pale reductions of the scale and opulence of Louis' great creation, whose grandeur

190

ARCHIVES PHOTOGRAPHIQUES

to this day is indescribable and almost unbelievable. Even Mark Twain, who liked to scoff at European conceits and pretensions, was overwhelmed by the spectacle of Versailles: "You gaze, and stare, and try to understand that it is real," he wrote, "that it is on the earth, that it is not the Garden of Eden. . . ." Five thousand courtiers were accommodated in the vast reaches of this palace, five thousand more clustered about it in the adjacent village—all subservient to the king's pleasure and his bounty. In later years, Marie Antoinette would with extravagant simplicity play the role of an innocent shepherdess in her monumental and precious little *hameau* on the fringes of the palace grounds—until in 1789 the hard-bitten market women of Paris, seven thousand strong with cannon in tow, "invited" her and Louis XVI back to the city where they both were to lose their heads as the Revolution reached its climax. It was in the great Hall of Mirrors at Versailles in 1871, at the conclusion of the Franco-Prussian War, that William of Prussia was proclaimed the German emperor. Forty-eight years later in that same hall the treaty that ended World War I was signed.

191

Alsace

By the terms of the treaty of 1871 that resulted from the absurdly quick victory of Prussia and her allies over the French, most of Alsace and Lorraine was ceded by France to the new Germanic empire. Louis XIV had taken over that territory in northeast France from the Hapsburg emperor in the seventeenth century, and it was to be returned to France in 1918. During World War II Germany again took over the area, then was forced to relinquish it once more at the end of that conflict. As an intellectual and commercial center of Alsace, the city of Strasbourg has long played an important part, forming a bridge between the two great cultures with which it has alternately been allied. At its strategic site on the Rhine, Strasbourg was a major crossroads of northern Europe. It was here in A.D. 842 that two grandsons of Charlemagne made a pledge of mutual support (in opposition to a third grandson), taking an oath that was issued in the vernacular commonly used by their troops—the first written examples of those dialects that would later develop into the separate French and German languages. With its single spire, which has been called the most Gothic of all spires, the cathedral of Notre Dame at Strasbourg stands as a monument to the city's dual heritage and a repository of its history. When he took possession of the city in 1681, Louis XIV was greeted at the threshold of the cathedral with religious fervor. The foreign fiancées of both Louis XV and Louis XVI were ceremoniously met at Strasbourg as they entered France to be wed. (It was here in 1792 that Claude Joseph Rouget de Lisle, a young officer of the French Revolutionary army, composed a song that the troops from Marseilles sang as they marched into Paris and that became the national anthem of the borning republic.) At one point during the Revolution when antireligious sentiment was at a peak, plans were made to pull down the cathedral's spire. However, one inspired citizen managed to coif the tower with a Phrygian bonnet, the liberty cap favored by the Revolutionaries, made of tin, painted bright red, and thus saved the monument from destruction. In the picturesque city of Colmar, a quintessentially Alsatian community called the little Venice, is displayed the world-famous Isenheim altarpiece, painted by Matthias Grünewald, one of the most unusual masterpieces of fifteenth-century art.

In the quiet Alsatian town of Colmar (below) hang Matthias Grünewald's masterful Isenheim altar panels; a detail from The Crucifixion *is reproduced above.*

Strasbourg cathedral's single spire dominates the city.

193

Reims & Chartres

In the nineteenth century Goethe thought the Strasbourg cathedral was the truest possible expression of emerging German nationalism. However, its debt to earlier French Gothic structures is substantial. The famous sculptures that adorn its portal, piers, and arcades are related to those in the great cathedral at Reims. That latter structure, so sacred to the French, in itself resembles an immense sculpture, at once huge and solid and as delicate as lacework. Reims is to France what Canterbury is to England. In 496, long before the present cathedral was built, Clovis, the first Merovingian king, was baptized at Reims, and in later centuries the successive kings of France were traditionally anointed and crowned there. It was to Reims that Joan of Arc brought Charles VII, whose pedigree and hence his claim to the throne had been questioned, for his coronation. With this rite in this place, Charles became the indisputable monarch of his country. Pounded by a furious artillery barrage in World War I, the great structure remained standing, to be restored to its former glory after the war. When an earlier church at Chartres burned in 1194 it was decided to rebuild the structure, with the confident expectation that its principal relic, the Virgin's tunic salvaged from the fire, would attract enough pilgrims bearing gifts to cover the expense. And so it happened. The "new" Chartres that rose majestically from the ashes to tower above the surrounding plains became the most celebrated of all Gothic structures. To Henry Adams in later years, it expressed "an emotion, the deepest man ever felt—the struggle of his own littleness to grasp the infinite."

The coronation procession for Louis XV passes (right) near the great arched portals of the cathedral at Reims, where French kings were traditionally crowned. Opposite is Chartres, the most celebrated of French cathedrals, which with its 8,000 images in stained glass and sculpture is a visual encyclopedia of medieval faith.

Brittany

The first known architectural constructions in France were raised several millenniums before Christ on the Brittany peninsula. Here, at Carnac and other sites, may still be seen those mysterious, impressive arrangements of giant stone slabs known as dolmens, cromlechs, and menhirs — rude and distant ancestors of the great Gothic cathedrals that were built scores of centuries later. It is hard to imagine how such huge, enormously heavy stones could have been quarried, transported, and put in place. Some weighed hundreds of tons, and one, now fallen, stood seventy feet high. Well-organized group effort was obviously required, and that the resulting structures served some religious purposes seems most likely. They are only rough shapes, but they appear to be everlasting. Brittany is the most westerly province of France, its jagged coast reaching far out into the sea between the Bay of Biscay and the English Channel. The swift tides can reach heights of more than forty feet, and the sea behind them can be savage. At one point on the Penmarch peninsula, the shock of storm waves pounding against the rocks can be felt nineteen miles inland at Quimper. The ruggedness and heroism of Breton sailors is proverbial. In 1534 one of them, Jacques Cartier, sailed to look for gold in Newfoundland and Labrador, and instead discovered the Saint Lawrence River in Canada, which he mistook for Asia. For centuries Bretons fought against Franks, the dukes of Normandy and the counts of Anjou, and the kings of England and France to preserve their independence. Standing at Brittany's old frontier with France, the city of Fougères is a memorial to such struggles. Its impressive feudal castle, whose walls and large towers are among the most massive in Europe, stands on a rocky height almost encircled by the Nançon River. However, in spite of that stronghold and of the might of the Breton barons, Fougères was often invested by enemy forces. Francis I incorporated the duchy of Brittany with France in 1532, but Bretons have never lost their deep-grained spirit of independence.

Monuments Historiques de la France

At the western tip of France, Brittany
juts into a sea (right) that has claimed
the lives of so many Breton sailors. At
Carnac, long files of monolithic menhirs,
shown in a 19th-century print (opposite), stand like sentinels. Proudly
independent in spirit throughout its
history, Brittany long protected its
frontiers with such fortifications as the
towers at the city of Fougères, above.

ROGER — VIOLLET

197

Brittany received its modern name from the fact that about A.D. 500 the area was settled by Britons who had been driven from their homeland by the Anglo-Saxons. It is a land of many legends. According to some of these, it was the land where King Arthur and his knights sought the Holy Grail, the cup that Christ used at the Last Supper, and that, it was said, Joseph of Arimathea brought to Brittany from Palestine. When Christianity was introduced into Brittany, many of the ancient menhirs that were still venerated were converted to the purposes of the new religion by being carved with Christian symbols or crowned with crosses. These in turn became remote forebears of the carved granite calvaries representing Christ crucified and episodes of his Passion that were erected everywhere in Brittany in the late Middle Ages, and that remain a characteristic feature of the Breton countryside. The example at Guimiliau, fashioned late in the sixteenth century, represents two hundred figures. A composition at the corner of one of the platforms depicts the story of Catell-Gollet (Catherine the Lost), a young servant girl who went astray, fell into the clutches of the Devil, and was condemned to hell's eternal fire — a grim lesson to which the parish priest could call the attention of flirtatious young ladies. For the rest, these ubiquitous folk sculptures are graphic lessons in sacred history, ever visible before the local congregations. The postimpressionist artist Paul Gauguin often turned to the local traditions and monuments of Brittany, including the calvaries, for models and inspiration. In several of his compositions he sought to express the "great rustic and superstitious simplicity" that he found among the Breton peasants and that deeply moved him. Thus, his painting *The Calvary—Green Christ*, dated 1889, is obviously modeled on the moss-covered stone pietà from the calvary at Brasparts in Brittany.

A calvary from Guimiliau (opposite) in Brittany; above is Paul Gauguin's The Calvary—Green Christ, *shown with its source.*

No other historic place in Europe presents a more spectacular appearance than Mont Saint Michel, on its island off the Normandy coast just beyond the northeastern border of Brittany. Perched on a rocky eminence, which rises with dramatic boldness from surrounding tidelands, Mont Saint Michel has rightly been called the wonder of the Western world. (Because of the huge and menacing tides that swiftly ebb and flow about the foot of this cone-shaped rock, and the quicksands that threatened the unwary pilgrim, the great mound has also been called Saint Michael in Peril from the Sea.) The first building constructed on this site was raised, according to tradition, in A.D. 708 by the direction of the Archangel Michael, who appeared in a vision before Aubert, bishop of nearby Avranches. In the course of subsequent centuries a gigantic cluster of other structures developed about the precipitous slopes and at the peak of the rock —shops, inns, residences, dungeons, crypts, cloisters, garrison quarters, redoubts, and so on—all culminating in the superb Gothic abbey church whose sharp spire surmounted by a statue of Saint Michael reaches high toward the heavens. In the course of those centuries, also, the flow of pilgrims to this shrine has been constant, even during the Hundred Years' War, when the English held the neighboring regions but upon payment of a toll granted safe conduct to faithful wayfarers. As a matter of course the early church was fortified, in spite of its almost unassailable situation, and its ramparts were never breached. (It survived the Second World War undamaged.) In the eleventh century, while Mont Saint Michel was building, the duke of Normandy was richer and more powerful than the king of France—strong enough, indeed, in the person of William the Bastard, better remembered by history as "the Conqueror," to cross the Channel and conquer England to become monarch of that island kingdom, as well as ruler of his own considerable fief in Normandy. In years to come the royal heirs and successors of William, with their allies, would challenge the kings of France for sovereignty over their hereditary dominions and the kingdom itself in long and sanguinary encounters.

MUSÉE CONDÉ — GIRAUDON

Normandy

St. Michael aloft along Normandy's coast: at upper right, suspended before the abbey of Mont St. Michel in a 15th-century illumination from the Duc de Berry's Book of Hours *and opposite, in statue form atop the spire of the remodeled abbey. At Dives sur Mer, Duke William of Normandy (on horseback, in a detail from the Bayeux tapestry, right) prepares to embark for England.*

It was only with the end of the Hundred Years' War in 1453 that the Anglo-Norman pretenders (Englishmen now) lost their serious claim to the French throne. During the Hundred Years' War between the two countries, as if in response to a widely whispered prophecy that an armed virgin would drive the English from French soil, Joan of Arc had appeared, raised the siege of Orléans, and persuaded the hesitant King Charles VII to be anointed and crowned at Reims. But before the war ended, the heroic Maid fell into the hands of the enemy. In 1431 she was convicted of witchcraft and heresy and burned at the stake in the old marketplace of Rouen, then held by the English. The French king made no gesture to aid or comfort her. It was another eighteen years before he could ride triumphantly into that city. Situated on a curve of the Seine River downstream from Paris (it serves as the port of Paris), Rouen was the ancient capital of Normandy. Some years ago an eminent art historian wrote that the city was "like a rich book of Hours in which the center of the page is filled with figures of God, the Virgin, and the saints, while fancy runs riot in the margins." He was referring to the city's splendid sculptured cathedral, whose shimmering façade the impressionist Claude Monet painted so often and so lovingly; its other notable churches, Saint Ouen and Saint Maclou, and still other structures that give the city a profile that never ceases to astonish; and its old quarter of picturesque stone and half-timbered houses. Richard the Lion-Hearted was born at Rouen and bequeathed his heart to the cathedral chapter after church treasures had been sold to help ransom him when he was captured during the Third Crusade.

Church spires rise above Rouen (opposite), where Joan of Arc was burned by resentful Englishmen, her unburned heart thrown into the Seine; here, too, died William the Conqueror. These churches and parts of the old city, with half-timbered houses (left) and other reminders of a rich past, survived the bombings of World War II.

East of Deauville beach lies Villerville, painted (above) by Boudin; Étretat (below), by Monet.

Aside from its strategic situation facing the nearby shores of southern England across the Channel, the Normandy coast presents a variety of physical features that have long attracted vacationers, tourists, and artists. A short section of that coast stretching about fifteen or twenty miles west of the mouth of the Seine estuary, known as the Côte Fleurie (the "flowery coast"), is celebrated for its beauty and the quality of its light —and in such villages as Deauville (in season, during July and August), for the brilliance of the social scene and the variety of entertainment that is offered. Over the past century or so no town in France has played host to such a dazzling succession of international celebrities as Deauville—Princess Eugénie and King Farouk, Alphonse XIII and the duke of Morny, Maurice Chevalier and Mistinguette, the French champion prizefighter Georges Carpentier and his attentive manager, Baron de Rothschild and the great London dandy Berry Wall, among a long file of others more or less prominent and wealthy who enjoyed being seen there. The colorful scenes along the beach have been favorite subjects for such well-known artists as Eugène Boudin, a native of Normandy, the Dutchman Johan Jongkind, Raoul Dufy, and many others. The famous impressionist painter Claude Monet repeatedly pictured the spectacular arch cut by the sea through the rocky cliffs at Étretat, another popular resort on the coast just east of his home city of Le Havre. The combination of sea, rock, and sky was ideally suited to Monet's brilliant palette.

Over the years before they settled down and became converted into Frenchmen and Christians, the Norse pirates found this coast attractive for other reasons. By way of the inviting estuary of the Seine, passing the site of what is now the great port of Le Havre, they found their way up that long river, deep into the interior of France. Early in the tenth century the king of France was obliged to cede to these marauders a large area on either side of the river west of Paris. It was barely a century and a half later that the Norman duke William the Conqueror, blessed by the pope, embarked from a port near Deauville with his following of some twelve thousand knights and foot soldiers, crowded into thousands of vessels, to seize the crown of England. Eight hundred seventy-eight years later, on D-day in the late spring of 1944, that coastal stretch was the scene of such violence and slaughter as can be remembered only with sickening anguish. There it was, however, at Utah and Omaha beaches and adjacent spots not far from Deauville, that the Allied forces, in a mighty gamble against the weather, the tides, and the entrenched German forces, established and quickly secured the vital beachheads that opened the road to Paris, and on to Berlin. The half-sunken ruins of landing ships and other wreckage have been left at some points as memorials to the heroic actions that took place there. It took two years to clear the destruction at Le Havre. In the years that followed that picturesque old port was reconstructed as a modern city, and more important than ever as a "gateway to the Atlantic."

War debris (below) marks Utah Beach, while crosses (above) stand at American graves near Omaha beach.

Paris

In France all roads ultimately lead to Paris, the epicenter of national life. According to a venerable myth perpetuated in the first book printed in the French language, the city was founded by Paris, son of King Priam, following the Trojan War. Romances based on that epic war enjoyed wide popularity in the Middle Ages. (As told in such historical fiction Rome and London were also founded by Trojan heroes.) Another equally unlikely and agreeable legend tells that Hercules on his way to the Garden of the Hesperides brought settlers from the heights of Arcadia and left them on the slopes of what is now known as Montmartre (Mount of the Martyrs). The butte of Montmartre, the highest point in Paris, is today crowned by the huge, glistening basilica of Sacré Coeur (consecrated in 1919), which vies with the Eiffel Tower (and very recently with some tall skyscrapers) as a commanding feature of the Paris skyline. It was a favorite haunt of such outstanding artists as Maurice Utrillo, Maurice de Vlaminck, Henri de Toulouse-Lautrec, and others who have left colorful records of the streets and structures of the butte—and of the gay night life for which this section of the city has long been celebrated. Some two thousand years ago the Gallo-Roman god Mercury was worshiped on these heights, which for a time were called the Mont de Mercure. An enduring tradition relates that in the third century A.D., because his proselytizing zeal offended those who worshiped other gods, a Christian missionary to Gaul named Denis was beheaded as he was being

led to the pagan temple on the hilltop. Then, we are told, the saintly man performed a miracle by picking up his severed head, washing the blood from it at a convenient fountain, and carrying it in his arms until he found his eternal resting place. Within a few centuries a Christian basilica was raised over the site he selected, seven miles north of the center of Paris, to glorify his martyrdom. Denis became the patron saint of France, and the monastery of Saint Denis, dedicated to his memory, became for a time the richest and most important in the country. As rebuilt in the twelfth century under the abbot Suger, the church became the pioneer example of Gothic religious architecture and the burial place for the kings and queens, princes, and nobles of the realm in years to come. It was here that Joan of Arc hung up her arms in 1429. Here also, to conclude the long and bitter religious wars of the following century, Henry IV renounced his Protestantism to appease his Catholic subjects and to gain entry into Paris, otherwise denied him by its hostile citizens because of his faith. "Paris is well worth a mass," he conceded, and once ensconced in the capital he went on to heal the wounds of his sadly lacerated kingdom. During the French Revolution the abbey was sacked, the mortal remains in its royal tombs dug up and thrown into a common ditch, and many of the tomb effigies destroyed. Under the ever-watchful and studious eye of Viollet-le-Duc the structure was restored during the reign of Napoleon III.

The god Mercury (opposite), worshiped on Montmartre; St. Denis (above) carrying his head to his final resting place (below); Montmartre street with Sacré Coeur today (opposite, left), and as painted by Utrillo

Gargoyles (above) from Notre Dame (below), the cathedral of Paris. St. Germain des Prés (opposite), oldest church in Paris

The heart of Paris is the Île de la Cité, a boat-shaped island that cleaves the Seine River as it flows toward the sea. This insular area, long known as Lutèce (or Lutetia), was once the center of the Parisii, an insignificant tribe of Celtic fishermen and boatmen who trafficked along the lower course of the river. For centuries following the Roman occupation of Gaul there was little to indicate the important part the community, renamed Paris in the fourth century A.D., would one day play in the history of France, Europe, and the world at large. It was not until the time of the Capetian kings, a line that reigned from 987 to 1328, that the city became the fixed and permanent capital of the kingdom and the cultural and intellectual center of the Western world. Under Philip Augustus (1180–1223), the seventh of those fourteen rulers, the principal thoroughfares of Paris were paved for the first time. Near the western border of the city Philip built an impressive fortress known as the Louvre, remnants of which may still be seen amid the masonry of the enormous structure that was to develop from it. Also during Philip's reign the great Gothic cathedral of Notre Dame, begun in 1163, rose in all its majesty on the Île de la Cité. Across the river in the Latin Quarter stands Saint Germain des Prés (Saint Germain in the Fields), built more than a century before Notre Dame and the oldest surviving church in Paris.

Looking northward at the Place de la Concorde, from left: Hôtel Crillon, Luxor obelisk, Madeleine (behind obelisk), Ministry of

Excavated Roman baths in Paris

Following Caesar's conquest of Gaul, Paris soon became a Roman town. Provincial and relatively unimportant as it was, Paris had its arena, which although smaller than the one at Arles, for example, yet could seat ten thousand spectators. Its remains can still be seen on a hill on the Left Bank of the Seine. Adjoining what is now the Cluny Museum stand the ruins of the great Roman baths that measured more than one hundred yards across. Nearby, the present Rue Saint Jacques and the Rue Saint Martin follow the route of early Roman highways that led to the south and west, elements in the network of solidly paved roads that spread out across the breadth of Roman Gaul, and that quickened the way to and from Rome itself. With the gradual collapse of the Western Roman Empire, Paris, like the rest of Gaul, felt the repeated shocks of barbarian invasions. Even the great new empire forged by Charlemagne was not immune to such incursions. In his later years, it is said, that aging emperor wept at the prospect of the menacing advances of the Vikings, whose dreaded long boats with their high dragon prows were ever more boldly slipping up the Seine to plunder the river valley. Paris was sacked in 845, and for forty years to come was subject to repeated assaults. However, in the slow, often agonizing reformation of Roman Gaul into the kingdom of France, Paris was to play an increasingly important role. From the twelfth century on, the history of France is the story of the progressive centralization of the country about this capital city. Throughout the central area of the city there are many reminders of the successive stages through which Paris passed in reaching its present appearance over the centuries of change and growth. In

210

the Marine (this building and its twin — the Crillon — were planned by Jacques Ange Gabriel). Sacré Coeur rises in the background.

the eighteenth century Paris was the most populous city in the most populous nation of Europe, and it kept spilling over its old boundaries of forts and walls into the adjoining countryside. Midway in that century plans were made to lay out a large square on waste space at the western limits of the city as a regal setting for a statue of King Louis XV; beyond that area a wooded path led through the Champs Élysées into open fields. First known as the Place Louis XV, the area was later renamed Place de la Révolution. With its statuary, fountains, and esplanade covering almost a hundred thousand square yards, it is today possibly the most celebrated urban space in the world. At the north side two magnificent identical structures, divided by the Rue Royale, were raised to house members of the nobility and to serve as state offices; today one serves as headquarters for the Ministry of the Marine and the other has become the luxurious Hôtel Crillon. On January 21, 1793, Louis XVI lost his head to the guillotine in this elegant setting, as some months later did Marie Antoinette, Madame Du Barry, Charlotte Corday, and more than a thousand others — after which gruesome spectacles the area was again and ultimately renamed Place de la Concorde. Forty-odd years later, during the reign of Louis Philippe, an Egyptian obelisk from Luxor was raised at the center of the square, a gift from the viceroy of Egypt and a monument devoid of political connotations except, perhaps, as a reminder of Napoleon's campaigns in Egypt. The installation of this great monolith in 1836 attracted a crowd of two hundred thousand spectators. It is the oldest monument to be seen in Paris, more than three thousand years older than the surrounding structures.

Oldest house in Paris, 3 Rue Volta

211

In 1806 Napoleon Bonaparte ordered a huge arch honoring the armies of France to be erected at the western limit of the Champs Élysées—a triumphal arch in the Roman style to be more than twice the size of the great Arch of Constantine in Rome. The emperor did not live to see the monument completed; the work was finally done, in fact, barely in time for the chariot bearing his remains to pass beneath it in 1840 on the way from Saint Helena to their final resting place in the chapel of the Invalides. With its elaborate sculptures, its observation platform, and its impressive site, the Arc de Triomphe is one of the celebrated attractions of Paris. In 1854 Baron Georges Haussmann, then in the process of "rebuilding" the city at the command of Napoleon III, added seven new boulevards to five earlier thoroughfares that radiated from the area surrounding the arch and lined them with buildings of uniform design. With its starlike pattern this surrounding area was almost inevitably known as the Place de l'Étoile, until in recent years it was renamed Place Charles de Gaulle. Across the Seine, on the Left Bank, the Eiffel Tower surveys all Paris. It was built to ornament the Universal Exposition of 1889, celebrating the centenary of the French Revolution. When it was built it was the world's tallest (984 feet) and most daring structure, a prodigy of engineering skill and inventiveness. Two and a half million rivets were used to secure its weblike steel elements. Starting in 1887, hundreds of acrobatic workmen labored to raise the monument to its commanding height in time for the opening of the exhibition. The extreme boldness and novelty of its design brought cries of protest from many authors and artists who felt it violated the serene skyline of Paris. (From the highest of its three observation platforms, it was said, one got the best view of the city, for from such a vantage one did not have to look at the ugly tower itself.) However, over the years since then the gigantic construction has won the affection of the world. It has become the very symbol of Paris.

L'Étoile (right), so named for the five roads radiating from here in 1806 when Napoleon ordered the raising of a triumphal arch to honor all the armies of France; the Arc de Triomphe stands now at the center of the star. At left, commemorating the French Revolution, is the Eiffel Tower, itself a revolutionary architectural monument.

The Pont Neuf, most venerable and massive of the bridges that connect the left and right banks of Paris, as depicted in a 17th-century painting. An equestrian statue of Henry IV, the vert gallant, *stands near the tip of the Île de la Cité; buildings of the Louvre are on the Right Bank of the Seine.*

Paris has long been a favored school for artists of all nations, and a source of their inspiration. As one consequence, few cities in the world can boast such complete and colorful graphic records of the daily life and the changing scenes that have illuminated their histories over the centuries. In a number of important aspects time has treated historic sites and monuments of the city very kindly. The Pont Neuf, oldest and most celebrated of Paris bridges, spans the Seine at the western tip of the Île de la Cité. Completed during the reign of Henry IV, first of the kingdom's Bourbon rulers, it was the first bridge across the river to be built without houses on it. Before any street in the city had such an innovation, it had sidewalks for the convenience of pedestrians. Today, more than three and a half centuries after its completion, its ample roadway accommodates heavy motor traffic with less strain than many more modern thoroughfares. Henry IV continues to be one of the most popular kings in French history. He was, as a popular rhyme put it, the *vert gallant*—a king who not only could drink and fight, but could make love along with the best of them—accomplishments that did not diminish his reputation among his countrymen. Four years after his death at the hands of an assassin in 1610, a bronze equestrian statue was raised in his memory, the first such effigy to be displayed on a public route. A copy of it now stands by the roadside, from which one views across the river on the Right Bank the great architectural pile of the Louvre.

Time has barely dimmed the elegance of the Place Vendôme, planned with the authority of Louis XIV and executed more than two hundred fifty years ago under the direction of Jules Mansart, the illustrious architect who had supervised the construction of the Palace of Versailles among other remarkable monuments that glorified the reign of the Sun King. The colossal statue of Louis that once adorned the central spot of the place was torn down during the Revolution and later replaced by a tall column with a spiral sheath of bronze made from the hundreds of cannon Napoleon captured at the battle of Austerlitz. A statue of Napoleon in the role of Caesar originally capped the column, but when Napoleon fled to Elba it was replaced by one of Henry IV, which was in turn pulled down when the emperor returned to Paris. After other changes the whole column was destroyed during the riots of 1871. (The painter Gustave Courbet was imprisoned for his alleged part in this destruction.) It was then restored by the Third Republic with Napoleon as Caesar again on top, as it now stands. At the end of the last century the famous house of Paquin, whose dresses adorned the most elegant ladies of the period, opened its doors on the Rue de la Paix, leading into the Place Vendôme. At closing time the thousands of girls and women who worked at Paquin's flooded the street, a daily event celebrated by artists and songwriters of the *belle époque*. The gigantic transformation of Paris into the "capital of capitals" was one of the first undertakings of Louis Napoleon as emperor. Under Haussmann's direction eighty-five miles of new streets, notably the *grands boulevards*, were slashed through old sections of the city; thirty-two thousand gas lamps were installed to brighten the scene. As a finishing touch the vast Opéra, the largest theater in the world, was designed by Charles Garnier. Its Grand Staircase and Grand Foyer, embellished with colored marble from all over the nation, became a stage for France's most brilliant society.

Above: Up and down the staircase of the Opéra; French society in Detaille's painting parade as if on stage. Below: At closing time chic midinettes file out of the fashionable house of Paquin, the couturier, near the Place Vendôme.

OVERLEAF: *Paris, in all its variety*

he Low Countries—Belgium, the Netherlands, and Luxembourg—occupy a relatively small area in the western corner of Europe bordering the North Sea where it narrows into the English Channel. As their general designation suggests, these countries are made up of low-lying territory for the most part. Their boundaries are political and historic rather than natural, except for the seacoast, much of it made over by man, which through many centuries has opened up wide vistas to the world at large. On the land side only manmade signs give any indication that the traveler is passing from one of these countries into a neighboring state—into northwestern Germany from the Netherlands (popularly known as Holland), into northwestern France from Belgium, or into either Germany or France from tiny Luxembourg. That easy accessibility from all directions has over the centuries made the Low Countries chronically a theater of war. The additional fact that throughout medieval and modern times this area has been one of the wealthiest in Europe has increased its lure to aggressors from other lands, as well as to traders and settlers. Although the unity of the region, so neatly termed the Low Countries, seems clearly apparent to foreigners, the natives of the three countries have ever been aware of their own differences. And although they have had old experience of being minor parts of much larger political entities, such as the Frankish kingdom and the Hapsburg empire, they have also separately known international importance out of all proportion to their size. Until relatively modern times both Holland and Belgium controlled far-flung empires, which greatly contributed to the prosperity and the cosmopolitanism of the homelands. In the seventeenth century Holland commanded a large colonial empire, holdings that for about a half century included a trading post, New Amsterdam at the tip of Manhattan Island, on what was to become the wealthiest small area on earth. But at the time, Dutch gains in silk, tea, and spices from trade in the Orient were of far greater importance than trading for furs in the New World. This was Holland's golden age—an era spanned by the life of Rembrandt, one of the world's most renowned artists—recalled not only in his paintings and those of his illustrious contemporaries, but in substantial parts of the urban and rural Dutch landscape as it has survived to our day. (It was also the age of the "tulip mania," when traders and thieves made and lost millions trafficking in the exotic bulbs brought into the country from Asia Minor.) Early in the fifteenth century, two hundred years before Rembrandt, members of another school of Netherlandish painting from Flanders (what is now western Belgium and the adjoining area of northern France) re-created the world about them with an intimate realism and extreme precision that effected a revolution in the history of art—a new conquest of the visible world and one of the finest achievements of the age. That world is happily still visible in those parts of Belgium where good fortune and care have preserved the evidence of an abundant, distinctive history.

A highly characteristic Netherlandish landscape view, including windmills and a canal

*Ghent's medieval Castle of the Counts,
below, protected this river crossing.*

Belgium

In the wake of the Norman invasions there emerged in the Low Countries late in the ninth and early in the tenth centuries a hardy new breed of rulers, the local counts, who despite their nominal allegiance to the kings of France or England, or the emperor of Germany, wielded absolute power over their petty principalities. These feudal princes encouraged the growth of new settlements by granting charters to places on natural harbors and well-placed waterways that were potential trading outlets. Count Baldwin, the "Iron Arm," founder of the dynasty of the counts of Flanders, established a castle in 870 at the confluence of the Scheldt and Lys rivers around which the town of Ghent developed. Commerce soon stimulated the nascent textile industry, and with it mushroom expansion, so that by 1100 Ghent was the largest town of the Low Countries and well on its way to becoming the leading clothmaking center of Europe. As a guard against Ghent's volatile burghers, Count Philip of Alsace in 1180 reconstructed the ancient castle, one of the many seats occupied by the Flemish counts, providing a circular curtain wall in front of a massive square keep and other refinements. During the century following the acquisition of Flanders in 1385 by the dukes of Burgundy, the Castle of the Counts was converted into a chapter house for knights of the Order of the Golden Fleece. In their quest for the appropriate trappings of power, the French dukes tapped the talents of Flemish painters, sculptors, musicians, and architects and brought about the golden age of art in the Flemish provinces. In 1432 Jan van Eyck completed in his Ghent studio the colossal polyptych known variously as the Ghent altarpiece or the *Adoration of the Lamb*, the most famous painting in present-day Belgium and one of the outstanding examples of Christian art. Depicting a universe in miniature, with some two hundred fifty figures and fifty species of plants and flowers, this mystical work was donated by Josse Vyd, a wealthy merchant, to Ghent's cathedral, then under construction. Over the course of the centuries this masterpiece has weathered a number of vicissitudes. It was nearly destroyed by Calvinist iconoclasts during the religious uprisings of 1566; the Hapsburg emperor Joseph II attempted to remove the wing panels portraying Adam and Eve in a "shocking" state of nudity; French revolutionaries carried the altarpiece to Paris, where it remained until 1815; several panels were amputated during World War I and sent to Berlin; and in World War II the Gestapo added the altarpiece to Göring's collection in Austria, whence it was finally returned to its rightful home in Ghent's cathedral of Saint Bavon.

A detail from Jan van Eyck's Ghent altarpiece is shown above. The masterpiece is in the Flamboyant Gothic cathedral of St. Bavon (below), begun in the twelfth and then completed in the sixteenth century.

PHOTO RESEARCHERS – PIERRE BERGER

As the medieval Flemish towns expanded into bustling metropolises bristling with belfries, lofty churches, and ornate guildhalls paid for by proceeds from the export of linen, fine wool, cotton, and silk, life became increasingly fraught with confusion and upheaval. Competition between cities for supplies of raw wool—native sources were inadequate and the precious commodity had to be imported from England—conflicts over foreign entanglements, and fierce internecine struggles between patricians and burghers, burghers and artisans, and the craftsmen of one guild and those of another kindled discontent. Ghent, particularly, was wracked by constant civil strife from the fourteenth through the sixteenth centuries. Its proud, energetic, quick-tempered citizens were by tradition resistant to authority. Merchants and weavers alike found themselves in frequent opposition to the counts of Flanders, who arrogantly referred to themselves as "first after God" and took little interest in the lives of their subjects. When England's King Edward III threatened to cut off his country's vital wool supply upon the outbreak of hostilities with France, the people of Ghent rose against the count of Flanders, who honored his feudal ties to France, and chose as their councilor general in 1336 Jacob van Artevelde, a brewer, who made an alliance with Edward III, recognized his claim to the French throne, and rallied all of Flanders behind him. One snowy January day in 1340 Edward was proclaimed king of France in Ghent's Friday Market, thus inciting the Hundred Years' War. Public favor was short-lived, however, and when Edward left Ghent without repaying a loan, an angry mob slew Van Artevelde.

BELGIAN CONSULATE GENERAL, NEW YORK

222

The guildhouses below, constructed between the twelfth and sixteenth centuries, line the Graslei Quay at Ghent's inland port. A statue honoring the Flemish patriot Van Artevelde (opposite, below) stands in the Friday Market. The placid canal opposite is one of the many manmade waterways crossing West Flanders.

Quays, Castles, and Canals

BELGIAN CONSULATE GENERAL, NEW YORK

As evidence of its long history of strife, the Belgian countryside is strewn with fortified castles that are scarcely more distant one from another than the chateaux of the Loire Valley in France. Although the Belgian strongholds are less impressive in scale and polished in plan than their French counterparts, these sturdy structures, with all their roughness and lack of refinements, reflect a greater diversity of style and vigor than their neighbors to the south. Many of these edifices have suffered the worse for being captured, recaptured, battered, and burned over the years and are now in ruins. Only a precious few have survived the vicissitudes of the centuries relatively unscathed or have benefited from intelligent restoration, and they now serve to enhance our understanding of the civil and military architecture of the Middle Ages. The early rulers of Belgium's principalities erected their feudal fortresses to use as bases for waging continual wars against their neighbors. In the thirteenth century Godefroid de Hallebeke, seneschal of Brabant, chose the bucolic village of Beersel (Flemish for "lair of bears") as the site on which to raise a castle whose prime function was to defend the nearby town of Brussels. Ironically, the stronghold suffered its first assault from the very people whom it had been designed to protect.

PHOTO RESEARCHERS—PIERRE BERGER

224

AERIAL PHOTOGRAPHY, BELGIUM

In 1306 Beersel was besieged, pillaged, and extensively damaged by troops from Brussels under the command of Louis de Maele. The buildings were repaired in 1357, and in 1375 Beersel became a possession of the noble De Witthem family, who retained the property until 1591. The castle's most illustrious occupant was the powerful lord Henri III de Witthem, a knight of the Golden Fleece who served as chamberlain to Emperor Charles V. At the time of his death in 1575, Henri owned enough property to be considered one of the most important landowners in the Low Countries. Beersel subsequently passed by marriage to the dukes of Arenberg and later belonged to the princes of Mérode and a certain Captain Villemons. In 1818 the fortress was transformed into a cotton mill, which was abandoned shortly thereafter. Restored today, this mysterious dwelling, with its moats, drawbridge, machicolations through which molten lead was poured, dank dungeons, and three round towers pierced by a curtain wall, constitutes an invaluable witness to bygone days. Other well-preserved castles in Belgium include Vèves, a tiny fifteenth-century stronghold near Celles in the foothills of the Meuse Valley, which, with its slate-capped towers, is perhaps the most romantic, and the moat-encircled castle of Jehay, situated in the fertile Hesbaye region. Rising in tiers of ruddy brick, this sprightly structure was raised during the Renaissance and reveals a new emphasis on decorative form that stands in marked contrast to the severe military aspect of its medieval predecessors.

The indomitable old fortress of Beersel (left) stands in the lush Brabant countryside outside Brussels. The feudal castle of Vèves (opposite, above), in the picturesque Meuse Valley, was completed in the fifteenth century. Encircled by its moat, the Renaissance castle of Jehay (above, left) is in a fertile market region close to the town of Liège.

225

Cityscapes

PHOTO RESEARCHERS—FRITZ HENLE

Scenes of Brussels' flamboyant seventeenth-century Grand' Place include the guildhalls illuminated at night, below, and views of the town hall, opposite.

226

Lined with rich baroque guildhalls and dominated by the tall graceful spire of the town hall, the great medieval market square, or Grand' Place, in the heart of modern Brussels bears mute witness to the vicissitudes of the city's past. When Philip the Good, duke of Burgundy, acquired Brabant in 1430, he made Brussels the seat of his court and government. Such monuments as the Flamboyant Gothic town hall, begun by Philip's son Charles the Bold, recall the Burgundian presence. During the sixteenth century under the Hapsburgs and their regents, Brussels became the administrative capital of the entire Netherlands. Emperor Charles V introduced the horrors of the Inquisition to the Grand' Place in 1523, when the first martyrs of the Reformation were burned alive there. The tide of popular resentment against the Hapsburgs culminated during the religious risings of the 1560's. Charles's son, Philip II, dispatched the duke of Alva and ten thousand troops to Brussels to restore order. Proclaiming that "everyone must be made to live in constant fear," the duke inaugurated a reign of terror and arrested all suspected insurgents, including the Flemish patriots Counts Egmont and Horn, who were beheaded in the Grand' Place on June 5, 1568. Although the scene of much bloodshed, the market square survived intact until 1695, when Marshal Villeroi, at the behest of France's King Louis XIV, bombarded Brussels. The red-hot cannonballs that fell on the Grand' Place destroyed most of its wooden guildhalls. Reconstruction of the buildings began almost immediately under the direction of the city architect, Guillaume de Bruyn, whose harmonious ensemble represents one of the finest examples of early town planning. As much a symbol of Brussels as the Grand' Place is the nearby Manneken Pis, a fountain created in 1619 surmounted with a bronze statue of a young boy unself-consciously performing a natural function.

The Manneken Pis (below), Brussels' dear mascot, unabashedly waters his quarter.

Rubens's Assumption of the Virgin *over the high altar of Antwerp's cathedral (above)*

Shortly after the Hapsburgs superseded the dukes of Burgundy as rulers of the Low Countries late in the 1400's, the city of Antwerp came into the ascendant. Foreign traders residing at Bruges left that city when the Zwyn estuary began silting up and transferred their business to Antwerp on the navigable Scheldt. Under the patronage of Emperor Charles V, who early in his reign realized that this port city, with its bankers and merchants, was a potentially greater source of wealth than his gold mines in Mexico or Peru, Antwerp developed into the economic capital of Europe. Its Bourse, or exchange, dedicated in 1531 "for the use of merchants of every race or language," came to wield exclusive control over the money market of the known world. Even Queen Elizabeth I of England was not too proud to borrow from the Bourse. Virtually every important town of Europe established its commercial headquarters at Antwerp. By the mid-sixteenth century this cosmopolitan center boasted more than one hundred thousand inhabitants, with a hundred ships entering and leaving its harbor daily and more than a thousand mercantile concerns. In the wake of the merchants came architects, sculptors, and painters, and Antwerp became known as La Metropole des Arts. As one Venetian envoy remarked, "I was astonished and wondered much when I beheld Antwerp, for I saw Venice outdone." During these boom years numerous religious and civic buildings, including breweries, guildhalls, and markets, arose. The town hall was completed in 1565 by Corneille de Vriendt in an Italianate style, unusual for that epoch, and reflects, perhaps, the fact that this seaport was open to foreign influence earlier than the rest of the country.

Antwerp's great prosperity began to decline in the second half of the century under Charles V's son, Philip II, an intolerant Catholic and promoter of the Inquisition, whose repressive rule fanned the religious strife that accompanied the Reformation in the Low Countries. Protestant iconoclasts sacked and desecrated the city's Gothic cathedral of Notre Dame in 1566. A decade later, Spanish troops rampaged through Antwerp to obtain booty in lieu of the wages owed them by Philip II, massacred seven thousand citizens, and forced thousands of Protestants to flee. And in 1585 Antwerp, after a yearlong struggle to free itself from the Spanish yoke, capitulated under siege. Although Antwerp stagnated in the 1600's and trade came to a halt after 1648, when Holland gained the right to the mouth of the Scheldt, the city retained its powerful cultural tradition. There was a renewed demand for religious art to fill the churches cleaned out by the Calvinists, which reached its apotheosis in the paintings of Peter Paul Rubens, born in 1577, who spent most of his prolific career at Antwerp and influenced contemporary architecture and the craft of tapestry weaving as well. In Rubens's baroque masterpieces in Antwerp's cathedral we witness an exuberant affirmation of the Counter Reformation.

A woodcut of 1515, opposite, top, depicts Antwerp's bustling port. The Italianate town hall below, left, reflects the city's mid-century opulence. Begun in 1352, the cathedral of Notre Dame, below, is the largest Gothic structure in the Low Countries.

RAPHO-GUILLUMETTE PICTURES—JEAN ROUBIER

PHOTO RESEARCHERS—PIERRE BERGER

229

Many of the towns of Flanders and Brabant reached the pinnacle of their fortunes during the Middle Ages and then, almost immediately, began the long and painful process of decline. Often the very factors that contributed to their success contained the seeds of their decay. Damme today is a pale shadow of the rich commercial port on the Zwyn arm of the North Sea that served as the golden artery of Bruges' greatest days. Passing through this congested center was Bruges' extensive Flemish trade with the coasts of Europe and Scandinavia. The Zwyn estuary began silting up in the fourteenth century and eventually rendered Damme's harbor unusable. By the time Charles the Bold, duke of Burgundy, married Margaret of York at Damme in 1468, an event commemorated by statues of the couple in a niche of the picturesque town hall, completed the same year, the city had collapsed commercially. Louvain, the capital of the dukes of Brabant, experienced boom growth as the center of the clothmaking industry, and by the fourteenth century boasted more than one hundred thousand inhabitants, most of whom were involved in textile manufacture. The weavers, however, were a turbulent lot, and throughout the 1300's they waged a continual communal struggle against the ruling patrician class, culminating in the insurrection of 1378, in which angry workers tossed thirteen city magistrates from the windows of the town hall onto the pikes of the populace below. Reprisals for the defenestration came in 1382, when Duke Wenceslaus took Louvain and severely punished its citizens, many of whom fled to England or Holland, whither went their craft skills. The last duke of Brabant, John IV, attempted to make amends for the repression that had resulted in the town's economic ruin by founding the University of Louvain in 1426. Under the dukes of Burgundy, who inherited John IV's domains when he died without issue in 1430, the university flourished, developing into one of the most celebrated institutions of Europe, and Louvain recovered somewhat. Wealth generated by the university helped raise the new Flamboyant Gothic town hall, which was completed in 1459 and reflects a resurgence of civic pride.

Louvain's rich Flamboyant Gothic town hall (opposite), with its turrets, pinnacles, open tracery, and wealth of ornament, is the finest edifice of its kind in Belgium. The Gothic town hall above was constructed in the fifteenth-century foreport of Damme.

231

Bruges

Basking in unworldly seclusion amid quiet canals, Gothic bridges, venerable spires, fortified gates, and street after cobbled street of quaintly gabled houses, Bruges in its physical aspect has scarcely changed since the Middle Ages, when it was the most important commercial city of northern Europe. In 1134 a tidal wave transformed the Zwyn estuary into a gulf of the North Sea that came within four miles of this walled city and was linked to it by canals and a river. Bruges consequently developed into a thriving port where merchants from all over Europe, induced by tax exemptions and other trading privileges, came to traffic in English wool, coal, and cheese, Russian furs, French and Rhenish wines, Spanish fruit, and Mediterranean spices in exchange for Flemish cloth, tiles, linen, and red dye, and such products as *dinanderie,* the celebrated copperware from the town of Dinant. By 1300 Bruges had become the western emporium of the Hanseatic League, a cartel of German free cities, with hundreds of resident merchants and its own houses, warehouses, and courts; the favorite continental port of the English, who at the time occupied large sections of France; and the successor to Champagne as the organizer of trade fairs. The burghers of Bruges and their wives did not hesitate to exhibit newly acquired wealth in their homes or on their persons.

As France's Queen Jeanne of Navarre remarked on her visit in 1301, "I thought I was the only Queen, but I see hundreds of them." Although popular revolts periodically marred the peace during the 1300's, Bruges suffered little damage, and in that epoch it seemed to present a never-ending panorama of sumptuous pageants, mystery plays, chivalric tournaments, and festivals. Under the dukes of Burgundy, who took the city along with the rest of Flanders in 1384 and made it their northern capital, Bruges blossomed into a center of the arts, rivaling Florence and Venice in Renaissance splendor. Yet, even during its cultural heyday Bruges was headed for economic disaster. The relentless accumulation of silt in the Zwyn channels caused ship arrivals to decrease steadily during the fifteenth century; by 1513 no vessel entered the estuary. In addition, England ceased furnishing Flanders with vital supplies of raw wool and began manufacturing its own high-grade cloth, thus competing with Bruges for its most important finished product. And in 1477 Mary of Burgundy, daughter of the last duke, married Maximilian of Austria, the future Holy Roman Emperor. Not only did the Hapsburg prince antagonize the citizens of Bruges, but he founded the dynasty that was to rule the Low Countries for the next three hundred years and involve them willy-nilly in the continuous Hapsburg struggles with France. As Louis XV later put it while standing over Mary of Burgundy's tomb at Bruges, "There lies the cradle of our wars."

The tomb of Mary of Burgundy rests in Bruges Cathedral (top, right). A party of boaters passes under one of the city's numerous bridges in the sixteenth-century miniature at top, left. Modern Bruges seems untouched by time, opposite and above.

OVERLEAF: *The town of Dinant, in Namur, nestles beneath a steep cliff alongside the Meuse River.*

233

Gateways to Holland

Above is the town of Zierikzee, and opposite, above, is its 14th-century gateway, with two towers to guard roads along the canal. Opposite, below, is the Hoofd-toren, or harbor tower, at Hoorn.

Between the end of the Roman occupation and the thirteenth century, Dutch history is a litany of quarrels among competing patches of sovereignty and shaky dynasties. Union was neither possible nor desired. Trade developed only slowly, and towns remained few and for the most part of only local significance. The creative efforts of this period were devoted to building dikes and draining the land. Every able-bodied man was bound by self-interest and community law to contribute his share of labor. A typical local ordinance of the time commanded: "You shall keep the law of peace against family and neighbors. Clean the sluices . . . heighten the sea dikes and dams . . . repair the roads and make drainings under the roads." Even so, the land remained vulnerable to threatening seas. In the thirteenth century a series of major storms flooded the marshlands of North Holland and Friesland, permanently destroying the natural barriers along the coast and converting the vast freshwater lake, the Zuider Zee, into an arm of the sea. Though it wreaked havoc with thousands of acres of manmade farmland and took many lives, this remaking of the map was a blessing in disguise for dozens of communities. Towns that had never had access to the sea became seaports—just when international trade was expanding rapidly. Some joined the Hanseatic League, an association of about seventy cities. Others, such as Hoorn and Amsterdam, chose to compete in the open market. Within a hundred years these newcomers had not only made the Hanse's mercantile skills their own but had become master shipbuilders and sailors, well on their way to driving the old monopoly out of business.

The Dutch had caught herring off their coast for centuries, not for the purpose of trade but for home consumption. Only in the latter half of the fourteenth century was a means of preserving the highly perishable fish at sea devised, and from that time forth the Dutch, as one observer put it, fished more gold from the sea than other nations mined from the earth. The new development made it possible for Dutch vessels to range farther for their catch than competing English or Hanseatic ships. The chronicler of Hoorn proudly described what followed: "Our shipping increased steadily, as did the number of our sailors. . . . Thus we sailed them out of the water and appropriated the trade for ourselves." In witness to the new prosperity, towns embarked on great building projects: defensive walls were raised, town halls built, canals extended. Zierikzee in Zeeland, one of Holland's best-preserved towns, is fair witness to the character of such old communities. The catch was tightly supervised by the College of Great Fishery. This quasi-governmental organization controlled all activities relating to the herring, from the grading of fish to the commissioning of ships and the pay of their crews. The college even practiced an early form of conservation in limiting the fishing season. To simplify regulations only five towns — Brielle, Delft, Enkhuizen, Rotterdam, and Schiedam — were licensed as ports. The fishermen of other water towns had no choice but to trade at one of the appointed places. Thus protected, the herring industry not only managed to survive the coming political upheavals, but also helped prepare the Netherlands for leadership in the age of exploration.

237

Holland's Liberation

Above is an equestrian monument to William of Orange in The Hague. Below is a 16th-century sculpture of Philip II of Spain. The stripped and whitewashed Buurkerk in Utrecht is opposite.

In 1555 Philip II, successor to his father, Charles V, as Holy Roman Emperor, inherited the Low Countries as part of his vast domain. His Dutch subjects, accustomed to making their own decisions in religion, in politics, and in the conduct of their economic affairs, did not take kindly to his attempts to impose a unified order on such concerns of their daily lives. Beyond that, Philip was a Spaniard by birth and temperament and was passionately Roman Catholic; he was bound to antagonize Protestant Dutchmen. When they objected to his edicts, issued in 1559, designed to quash the Reformation in their country, he sent in his troops. Despite the military superiority of those occupation forces, in quick and violent reaction the Dutch rebelled. Crowds attacked Catholic churches, smashing icons and burning paintings. Philip's response was devastating: in 1567 ten thousand soldiers under the duke of Alva entered Holland and began the years of the "Spanish Fury." Thousands of "heretics" were put to death and their property confiscated. Prominent among the young noblemen who began to organize opposition to this tyranny was William of Orange, one of Philip's stadholders, or viceroys, who was charged with ruling several important Lowland provinces. For a time William tried to direct his protests against the king's agents rather than against Philip himself. But as the brutalization of the Dutch people continued, the issue was drawn. Though nothing was solved by it, the lifting of the Spanish siege of Leiden in 1574 was in retrospect a turning point in the war. Dutch marine guerrillas—the daring and romantic Sea Beggars—sailed up to the walls of Leiden over thousands of acres flooded by resisting farmers to bring relief to the beleaguered city. The Dutch, traditionally fragmented, were now cooperating under William's brilliant leadership. This new spirit led to the Union of Utrecht in 1579, sealing the alliance of the eight northern United Provinces and leading ultimately to independence.

The Dutch Scene

Compared with other Dutch towns, Amsterdam was a late starter. According to legend it was founded by a Frisian, a Viking, and a dog who were shipwrecked at the mouth of the River Amstel. In fact, it was settlers from Frisia who about 1200 erected the first dam and other earthworks in this area—a sea dike along the Ij (a broad inlet) and two other dikes on either side of the Amstel. This created a crescent-shaped area above the marshes that lent itself to commercial exploitation. In order to ship goods past the dam the cargo had to be unloaded from sea-going vessels to shallow-draft lighters and vice versa. Amsterdam's fortunate location in Europe's middle latitude, its protected harbor (later deepened by dredging), and its easy access to the Zuider Zee, the Baltic, the Rhine, and almost every commercial town in the inner Lowlands, made growth beyond its early bounds inevitable. But expansion in this "golden swamp" entailed enormous community expense and was resisted by clergy and politicians until its population had grown to the bursting point. Then in 1585 the first of a series of plans was put into action. A new wide strip of land was created along the city's north perimeter by driving a double row of mammoth wooden pilings into the harbor's bottom, then pumping out the water and replacing it with land fill. Following the visionary thinking of Henrikje Staets, a spider-web system of concentric and radial canals was effected, and there gradually emerged that rarest of creations, a well-planned city.

Daniel Defoe described the citizens of Amsterdam as "the Middle Persons in Trade, the Factors and Brokers of Europe. They buy to sell again, take in to send out, and the greatest Part of their vast Commerce consists in being supply'd from All Parts of the World, that they may supply All the World again." Prudent policies had carried Amsterdam to this secure position. Slow to join the Orangist cause, the city escaped becoming a victim of fire and sword. Yet it had a reputation for tolerance, and when Antwerp's Protestant and Jewish merchants were driven out of Belgium, many of them chose to settle here. Thus Amsterdam was almost overnight the heir to centuries of mercantile experience and the economic capital of the recently established Dutch republic. To keep pace with the city's new possibilities, a chamber of assurances was created in 1602, a new bourse in 1608, an exchange bank in 1610, and a lending bank in 1614. Traders and kings came here to finance their enterprises at the most favorable bank rates in Europe. Always Amsterdam remained scrupulously, pragmatically neutral. Everyone called it friend; no one could afford to call it traitor. Also chartered in Amsterdam at this time was one of six chambers of the United East India Company. Despite efforts by the States-General to spread the power and profits, Amsterdam once again gained control, and with it a strong voice in foreign policy: as the company's most powerful policymaker warned, "We cannot carry on trade without war nor war without trade." Amsterdam would lose some of its bluster at the end of the eighteenth century as England and France proved stronger militarily than the Dutch, but it would remain the power center of the Netherlands for the long years to come.

An aerial view of Amsterdam (top) shows its complex pattern of canals. Ships from the Indies were unloaded at the 16th-century Montelbaans Tower (left), at the junction of four canals. Opposite is the fortresslike American Hotel, a 19th-century Amsterdam landmark.

241

Above are the syndics, or governors, of Amsterdam's Cloth Drapers' Guild at an annual meeting, painted by Rembrandt in 1661–62 — the artist's largest commission during his late years and his greatest group portrait.

Without the craft guilds, seventeenth-century Amsterdam would never have prospered and expanded as it did. The expulsion of the repressive Spanish Crown had left a power vacuum in Holland, and unlike other areas of Europe, there were no strong religious or political groups around which the country could build. The craft guilds filled this function most effectively. As they grew, the guilds generated the capital that made possible the growth of Amsterdam and other Dutch cities. In their general purposes the guilds were roughly comparable to present-day labor unions, but the breadth and depth of their significance to the community were far greater: they exercised control over the lives of their many members almost from cradle to grave. At about the age of twelve a boy was apprenticed into the home of a master craftsman; several years of successful performance would earn him the title of journeyman; with skill and luck, in time, he would have a "masterpiece" approved by the local guild and would himself become a master. Thereafter every aspect of his work — its quality, quantity, price, the conditions under which it was done, even his right to advertise it — was regulated by the guild. In return, members enjoyed protection of their local market monopoly and of prices, as well as protection from competition with "outsider" craftsmen from other towns. And they would regularly celebrate their prosperity with lavish feasts in the town's best tavern or their own handsome hall. For a Dutch guild master, life was most abundantly beautiful.

242

John Evelyn, inveterate English traveler, was astonished at the ubiquitousness of paintings in Dutch households. "The reason of this store of pictures and their cheapness, proceeds from their want of land to employ their stock, so that it is an ordinary thing to find a common Farmer lay out two or £3000 in this commodity." The most important supplier of paintings was Amsterdam, and its most important artist was Rembrandt Harmensz van Rijn. Rembrandt was born in 1606, just three years before the Dutch and Spanish signed their truce. He grew up in a time of expanding prosperity, and when he went to Amsterdam in 1631, he achieved a quick success as a portraitist, a landscape painter, and an engraver of international repute. By the late 1630's he had many pupils who not only paid for the privilege of studying under the master but worked on portions of his canvases. With the leading men of the community as his patrons, Rembrandt was tempted to live the life of the merchants around him. However, as Dutch tastes shifted to the more elegant, superficial styles of van Dyck and the French school, Rembrandt's work, grown solemn and profound, was less sought after, and the artist slipped ever more deeply into debt. At this time also, his wife, Saskia, died. Unable to put his affairs in order, Rembrandt declared bankruptcy in 1656. Yet he continued to produce such major works as the group portrait illustrated here.

Below is the house in Amsterdam where Rembrandt lived for 25 years, now a museum housing examples of the great artist's work. Below, right, is an etched Rembrandt self-portrait.

Once the palace of the counts of Holland, the Binnenhof (below) now houses Parliament. The Dutch coat of arms, above, reads "I will prevail."

William II, count of Holland, gave The Hague its start in the thirteenth century. Choosing a forested site a few miles from the North Sea but behind the natural defenses of high sandy hills, he built a hunting lodge—'s Gravenhage, or "the Counts' Enclosure." This same William soon after became Holy Roman Emperor, and in 1248 he upgraded his original modest structure to the status of a royal residence and built the Binnenhof. William's son Floris V, not an emperor but a count of Holland, added the Ridderzaal, or Knights' Hall, in 1230 when he outgrew the palace, and successive counts continued the building of the complex, which by then had become the residence also of a good many of the Dutch aristocracy and a small but prosperous community of linen merchants. From the very outset The Hague was unique in that it had no ramparts. Property, which in the older cities was given inflated value to pay for the maintenance of municipal security, was here relatively cheap, and the houses were built with generous spaces around them. When he visited here early in the 1500's, the Florentine Francesco Guicciardini described The Hague as "the prettiest, richest, and largest open village on the continent. There are now more than a thousand dwellings, many of them grand, and a magnificent royal palace." Unfortunately, this "village" would soon suffer mightily for its openness.

When war with Spain broke out, The Hague found itself all but defenseless. The court moved to safer precincts, followed by the nobility, leaving behind only the poor and the middle class. Occupied alternately by the troops of Philip II and of William of Orange, the gracious royal seat fell into disrepair. Weeds grew in the streets, and the impressive Groote Kerk was used as a stable. As long as William of Orange was alive, the real center of Dutch power would be wherever he was; but in 1586, just two years after his death, the States-General were formally installed in The Hague, and when the powerful Republic of the United Provinces was ultimately created, the ancient palace buildings of the counts of Holland became its headquarters. With peace came city expansion. Canals were added, new residences were built in the baroque and French classical styles to replace many of the medieval structures, and cultural life bloomed. So too did internal divisions: in 1618 William's grandson, Stadholder Maurice, ordered Jan van Olden Barneveldt, chief political officer of the realm, beheaded in the Binnenhof courtyard. All the while the capital's citizenry remained impotent, for rival cities had refused them a voice in government. It was Louis Bonaparte who finally gave The Hague power to match its prestige: he transferred the capital to Amsterdam, making The Hague just another city with municipal privileges like all the rest. After Napoleon's collapse The Hague resumed its role as political capital of the Netherlands. Since 1899 it has served as one of the chief world centers for negotiations covering international peace.

The Huis ten Bosch, below, was built about 1650. In 1899 it played host to the first world peace congress.

When William of Orange moved his royal seat to Delft in 1583, the old town was still known chiefly for its breweries and linen manufactures. William settled into the abandoned convent of Saint Agatha, renamed it the Prinsenhof, and continued the war of independence. He had less than a year more to give to the effort, for Philip II of Spain had put a very tempting price on his head. A patent of nobility and twenty-five thousand gold coins would go to anyone who would murder the "chief disturber of Christendom." All over Catholic Europe, would-be assassins plotted. One of them, a twenty-seven-year-old zealot named Balthasar Gerard, succeeded. Gerard disguised himself as a Calvinist, gained entrance to the palace, and on July 10, 1584, mortally wounded the stadholder. He escaped from the palace, but he was captured and tortured to death with a degree of cruelty unusual even in those imaginative years. The peace of Delft was again disturbed in 1654, when early on an October morning a tremendous explosion occurred. "The arch of heaven seemed to crash and burst," wrote one of the survivors, who added that the sound could be heard by ships at sea. It was, in fact, the city's arsenal—eighty thousand pounds of gunpowder left over from the Eighty Years' War had been accidentally set off. More than two hundred houses were leveled, more severely damaged, and untold numbers of citizens killed.

The Oostport, or East Gate (opposite, top) is a rare vestige of Delft's old city walls. Its southern gate, shown above in a painting by Vermeer, faces the Schie River. The Pilgrims passed this way en route to America, and the church in Delfshaven where they held their last service is shown opposite, bottom. An 18th-century Delftware plate is shown below.

Among the survivors of Delft's gunpowder explosion was the young Jan Vermeer. Twenty-two and a newly named master painter in the local guild of Saint Luke, in the next twenty years he went on to become the supreme painter of Dutch light and space, the artist who would make seventeenth-century Delft interiors seem almost as familiar to us as our own. For all his evident genius, Vermeer lived a difficult and finally disappointing life. Though apparently well liked and admired locally, he never enjoyed a sufficient income. In 1672 Vermeer was forced to sell his own beloved ancestral house on the main square, opposite the Prinsenhof, and move to smaller quarters. There, three years later at the age of forty-three he died, leaving his wife and eight children destitute. His paintings were dispersed at auction, not to be seriously noticed by critics for two hundred years. Meanwhile Delft was gathering an international reputation for another kind of artistry—that of painted earthenware. In 1604 a Portuguese ship, laden with one hundred thousand pieces of blue and white Ming porcelain, was captured by Dutch privateers, and the cargo sold with great fanfare in Amsterdam. Enterprising Delft potters, seizing a new opportunity, found ways of imitating the precious Oriental ware in glazed and decorated earthenware. Vigorously promoted, this local industry helped to fill the city's warehouses, left all but empty by the declining trade of the brewers. By the time of Vermeer's death, such rough but charming copies of Chinese porcelain were replaced by forms decorated with flowers, landscapes, and scenes of daily life. By the 1800's this Delftware, as it was called, found a market even in the Orient.

247

Hoorn's main square (above) is lined by tall, narrow houses and municipal buildings, including the impressive 1609 Weigh House, unusual in its blue stone construction. The Haarlem Butchery (top, right) was designed by Lieven de Kay about 1602 and is a fine example of northern Renaissance building. Veere's Gothic Stadhuis, opposite, dates from 1474, with a Renaissance bell tower from 1599.

When they speak of Dutch monuments, architectural historians rarely mean castles or chateaux. The Dutch nobility who might have built them never gained the measure of power enjoyed by the French, German, or Italian princes, nor with few exceptions, such as the counts of Holland, were they able to maintain their ducal claims long enough in any one place to make the grand architectural gesture. Neither has Dutch ecclesiastical architecture left us a great legacy. Due in part to the desecrations of the Protestant iconoclasts of the sixteenth century and also to the depredations of centuries of warfare that tended to take their highest toll among soaring church edifices, much of the grandeur of the northern Gothic originals has been lost. It is rather in civic architecture—in the guildhalls, markets, city gates, town halls, and burghers' residences—that Dutch creativity is to be seen at its fullest. Most of these date from the sixteenth and seventeenth centuries, when architects began to build in a distinctive native manner. Working in a predominantly Calvinist society for hard-driving merchant-burghers, they might have been expected to produce an ascetic, gloomy style, but the cheerful, sensible Dutch could not suppress their natural enthusiasm for home, for material comfort, or for public display. With red brick for their walls, white sandstone for their trim, large casements for their windows, and steeply gabled tile roofs as a characteristic profile, architects created the traditional Dutch townscape. Occasionally, as in "water towns," where men engaged in Oriental trade lived, flights of fancy added a certain exotic flavor. There onion domes, Moorish tracery, oddly misplaced classical scrolls, and miniature obelisks ornament public halls and houses as reminders of far-off splendors.

248

During the late 1500's the Protestant Dutch provinces, under the leadership of William the Silent, prince of Orange, waged stubborn resistance against King Philip II of Spain and in so doing began to build up the fleet that assumed hegemony over the seas in the seventeenth century. Dutch Sea Beggars, as they were called, equipped and manned vessels that attacked Spanish shipping and gradually liberated the coastal towns of the Netherlands from the Catholic yoke. At this time the lonely coastal regions also saw the rise of such fortified communities as Willemstad, which, with its heptagonal plan, was founded on the desolate Hollandschdiep estuary by its namesake, William the Silent, in 1583, the year before he was assassinated by a Catholic fanatic in Delft. Early in the seventeenth century the directors of the Dutch West India Company specified such a multipointed bastion for the infant community of New Amsterdam at the tip of what is now Manhattan Island. By the time that Czar Peter the Great of Russia visited the Netherlands in 1697, the Dutch fleet was world renowned. Tradition has it that the young ruler saw a Dutch ship anchored at Saint Petersburg and immediately determined to create a Russian navy. He not only sent his countrymen to Western Europe to study seamanship, shipbuilding, and navigation, but decided to go abroad himself and learn these skills firsthand. The czar traveled incognito under the pseudonym Peter Mikhailov in order to avoid the tedious protocol of state visits.

Peter the Great is portrayed as a shipwright above. The czar briefly resided at Zaandam, below. Willemstad's star-shaped fortifications are shown opposite.

After crossing Prussia, he made straight for the inland town of Zaandam, in North Holland, whose famous shipyards produced nearly three hundred boats annually. Wood was floated down the Zaan River, Zaandam's major artery, to the town's shipyards, where it was sawed by windmills, which at one time numbered in the hundreds. Here Peter was hired as a workman at the Lynsz Teeuwisz shipyard, and he found lodgings in the humble hut of one Gerrit Kist. During his stay Peter quickly mastered the shipwrights' tools, and at night, when he was not studying mathematics, physics, or chemistry, he joined his fellow carpenters in convivial bouts of smoking and drinking. The sovereign remained at Zaandam for only eight days. After having his disguise penetrated unexpectedly by the duke of Marlborough, the czar was so pestered by curious townspeople that he was forced to move to Amsterdam. Peter the Great subsequently returned to Zaandam many times to visit his former abode, and in 1717 he brought along his wife and a large retinue so that they might be moved by the rusticity of the cabin and its crude appointments. "Nothing is too small for a great man," Peter would remind his friends when they exclaimed at its austerity and poverty. Following Peter's death, the dwelling became the property of the imperial Crown of Russia. Among the many monarchs who came to Zaandam over the years to pay their respects to and contemplate this edifying relic was the emperor Napoleon. Late in the nineteenth century Czar Nicholas II, to protect this touching family heirloom from flood or fire, enclosed the hut in a stone building in an elevated spot where it could defy the years and bequeathed to Zaandam a statue of his celebrated ancestor holding carpenters' tools in his hands.

Gouda's town hall, seen through a casement window, is opposite. Above, left, is a seventeenth-century bas-relief of cheese weighing. Above, a nineteenth-century caricature shows a Dutchman enjoying his churchwarden's pipe.

When Desiderius Erasmus, the great Renaissance philosopher, arrived as a student in Gouda just before 1475, this old Dutch market town was a prosperous, long-established member of the mercantile community. An important center of the medieval cloth trade, it sent fabrics via the network of interconnecting canals not only to all parts of the Low Countries but also to destinations in England and on the Baltic. Young Erasmus, hurrying on his way through the town's spacious marketplace, would most likely have been attracted by the brightly painted farm wagons heaped high with what looked like pale yellow cannonballs (in whose stead, as legend has it, they were once actually used). In fact the wagons carried Gouda cheeses, brought to town for the official weighing before being dipped in crimson wax for export. Gouda, along with Texel, Leiden, Alkmaar, and Edam, produced one of the Netherlands' most profitable trade goods, and great care and ceremony were taken to insure that the town's reputation for the cheeses would always be upheld. Gouda also took pride in its pipe making, a specialty that developed in the seventeenth century along with the Dutchman's love affair with tobacco. Gouda craftsmen first saw pipes in the hands of Prince Maurice's British mercenaries, stationed here in the 1580's. The English stay was short-lived, but their smoking gear left a permanent impress. Gouda, the cheese maker, was soon made doubly prosperous by its pipes, as poets wrote odes in praise of tobacco, and doctors told of its medicinal value. A hundred years later fifteen thousand people were working in clay-pipe factories, and Gouda's long-stemmed "churchwardens" were the most prized in the Netherlands.

Luxembourg

Isolated by the rugged range of forested hills known as the Ardennes, the diminutive duchy of Luxembourg, with its storybook castles and meandering rivers, has pursued its own course of development quite independently of the other Low Countries. In 963 a nobleman named Siegfried from the Moselle region erected a castle on the ruins of an ancient Roman citadel on a steep escarpment above the Alzette River. From this fortress a town and feudal province that were called Luxembourg grew up. Siegfried's heirs referred to themselves as the counts of Luxembourg and extended and strengthened their domains by waging successful warfare. At the time of the Crusades these lords protectors sallied forth from such strongholds as Esch-sur-Sûre to the Holy Land, and after a long absence they returned debt-ridden to Luxembourg, where they sold, gambled, and generally mismanaged their estates into bankruptcy. In the twelfth century a new dynasty restored Luxembourg's prosperity and prestige. One of that line, Countess Ermesinde, between 1225 and 1247 created a centralized government, established courts of justice, granted individual freedoms, founded institutions of education and culture, and tripled her country's territory. Luxembourg entered its greatest period in the fourteenth century, when its ruling house made a bid to dominate all Europe. Several counts were elected to the post of Holy Roman Emperor and held sway over dominions that extended from the North Sea to Moscow and from the Baltic to the Alps.

Another count, John the Blind, became Luxembourg's national hero when, early in the Hundred Years' War, he joined the French ranks at the Battle of Crécy in 1346 and was slain. England's victorious King Edward III was so impressed with the sightless warrior's valor that he declared, "The battle was not worth the death of this man," and adopted the three ostrich feathers that had adorned John's helmet for his own coat of arms, as well as John's motto "*Ich dien*" (I serve). Luxembourg's epoch of imperial glory had long since passed when the country became a province under Duke Philip the Good of Burgundy in 1443. For the next four centuries Luxembourg was dominated by Burgundy, Spain, France, and Austria. After the fall of Napoleon in 1815, the men who met at the Congress of Vienna determined not to liberate Luxembourg. They feared that its fortified capital at the pivot point of Europe would be used as a pawn in the struggles between major powers. By the treaties of 1815 Luxembourg became a grand duchy attached to the Confederation of German States, which garrisoned Prussian troops there for the next fifty-two years, and was simultaneously made the personal possession of King William I of the Netherlands, who in 1839 ceded half the country's territory to Belgium. It was not until the 1867 Conference of London that the European powers certified Luxembourg's autonomy, independence, and neutrality.

In a scene of the capital city of Luxembourg (opposite), the Promenade de la Corniche may be seen following the ancient ramparts. The town of Esch, in its fairy-tale setting along the banks of the Sûre River (below), contains the ruins of a medieval castle.

The British Isles

"British Isles" is a term referring to the group of islands off the northwestern coast of Europe, comprising Great Britain — that is, England, Scotland, and Wales — and Ireland. Although they lie in approximately the same latitude as Labrador, thanks to the surrounding ocean the islands enjoy a generally favorable climate. Estuaries along the eastern coasts provide inviting entrances to the inlands from the nearby Continent. The winds and the tides of the intervening straits and channels, on the other hand, have long given the islands a measure of security from unwanted intrusions. This combination of accessibility and defensibility has been a major factor in the historical development of the British Isles. Thus, in ancient times relations between their Celtic inhabitants and the Gallic tribes across the English Channel were so close, and ominous, that in 55 B.C. Julius Caesar undertook the conquest of Britain to secure the Romans' position in that remote borderland of their empire. The Roman occupation was never complete by any means (it did not include Ireland and scarcely penetrated Scotland) and was often disturbed by resisting native tribesmen and offshore raiders. Nevertheless, by the time Roman officialdom quit Britain in the fifth century, Roman culture, customs and manners, had been absorbed into British life over a large area. In succeeding centuries Britain suffered invasions from Germanic peoples — the Anglo-Saxons and Jutes, who added their own cultural influence to the land's heritage. Then came the Danes in large numbers. That troubled period came to an end with the conquest of England by William of Normandy. This was the last successful invasion of the island. Within a century and a half the crucial contest for authority between royalty and nobility resulted in the signing of the Magna Charta, the greatest of English constitutional documents, which led to the development and steadily growing power of parliamentary rule that has distinguished British government ever since. In the fourteenth and fifteenth centuries the assertion of English claims to French territory resulted in the Hundred Years' War, in which, after notable victories on the Continent, England was ultimately defeated. The beginning of modern history in Britain starts in the following century with the reigns of Henry VIII and Queen Elizabeth, one of the most glorious periods of English history. At that time was seeded the British Empire, which at its height late in the nineteenth and early in the twentieth centuries became the greatest empire the world has ever known. From the prehistoric constructions at Stonehenge and the remains of Hadrian's Wall to the magnificence of Saint Paul's Cathedral and the stately pile of the houses of Parliament, from the white cliffs of Dover to the forbidding castles of Scotland and Ireland, and from the small Saxon churches to such great cathedrals as Salisbury and Canterbury, the long experience of the British islanders remains to be read on the face of the land.

The white chalk cliffs of Dover are a natural symbol of Britain's ancient insularity.

Early England

The remains of Hadrian's Wall, below, still extend across the English countryside. A 4th-century Roman mosaic floor, opposite, above, was laid at Lullingstone Villa, in Kent. A handsomely designed Celtic shield from the Iron Age is opposite, below.

OVERLEAF: *The massive stone constructions at Stonehenge on the Wessex plain*

PAUL CAPONIGRO, SANTA FE

Scattered about the world are groups of mysterious structures built of huge stones in various arrangements. Many of them, such as those near the coast of Brittany in France (see page 196), may be two thousand years older than the pyramids of early Egypt. In medieval times it was believed that the extraordinary cluster of such "buildings" at Stonehenge in England (see pages 260–61) must have been erected by a race of giants in the remote past. It is safer to assume that these megalithic constructions were raised by Wessex tribesmen about four thousand years ago. Man is the only creature on earth concerned with the passage of time. Time has been basic to all religions, associated as it is with such ideas as reincarnation, foretelling the future, resurrection, and the worshiping of heavenly bodies. And that concern with time is inseparable from almost all scientific development. When they began to connect the changing seasons with the sun's progress across the sky, our distant British ancestors built such great calculators as Stonehenge, where the rays of sunrise and sunset fall along a line between the huge, carefully dressed monoliths at the summer and winter solstice. It has been claimed that Stonehenge was built as a druid temple. No doubt it was a holy place, a sepulchral site, but it dates more than a millennium and a half before the druids arrived in England. As in the case of other such piles, it remains a matter for wonder that prehistoric men, guided by occult purposes, could have quarried, transported, shaped, and raised such monumental rocks and arranged them with such nicety.

MINISTRY OF PUBLIC BUILDING AND WORKS, LONDON

In 55 B.C., under the all-conquering Caesar, Roman forces were landed in Britain. However, for almost a century thereafter Rome's foothold in the distant island remained tenuous. In A.D. 43, responding to an appeal from a Kentish chieftain who had long lived in Rome, the emperor Claudius dispatched four legions—about forty thousand men—to put down the local British rulers and to organize their territories into a major province. Claudius himself led the final victorious assault by his troops against the native warriors. Even then the Britons fought back. Some twenty years later they all but annihilated a Roman legion, burned Roman communities, and massacred more than seventy thousand Romans and Britons friendly to Rome. With their wild flowing hair, their hideous war cries, and their scythed chariots they could be terrifying opponents. To further secure the province, in A.D. 122 the emperor Hadrian crossed to Britain, personally surveyed the long line from the Tyne to the Solway Firth, and had built the seventy-three-mile wall that bears his name as a defense against the wild tribes of northern England. The people of the British Isles who so often disputed the possession of their land by the Romans were Celts, people who until the Roman conquest had been for five centuries the most important body of people in Europe and who had found in Britain an island of resistance. They were skilled artisans who lavished loving care on their worldly luxuries, as some unknown maker did in the disciplined design and ornamentation of the ceremonial shield here illustrated. Celtic influence long outlasted the Roman occupation of Britain. To this day Scotland, Wales, and Ireland are regarded by their own inhabitants, and by the rest of the world, as the last stronghold of the Celts.

259

During the Roman occupation life in a good part of Britain became progressively more civilized, orderly, and prosperous—more Romanized. In the towns even the workmen spoke Latin. Christianity had found its way to the islands, where it flourished. In the fifth century, when the Roman legions were withdrawn to face threats closer to the heart of the empire, all this was undone. Barbarian hordes swarmed across the ruins of Hadrian's Wall; others stormed the coasts of England. Out of this turmoil, toward the end of the fifth century, emerged the heroic figure of King Arthur, who a millennium and a half later remains in our minds the great Christian leader, the paragon of chivalry, the formidable warrior who fought to save his people from heathen invaders. Century after century the legend of this fabulous character has spread about the world, growing with time to dreamlike proportions. Skeptics have long ago argued that the Arthurian story was a myth generated by the needs of a desperate people and perpetuated by romancers. But recently historians and archaeologists have probed deeply into the evidence and have concluded that Arthur did exist, not as a king in shining armor, but as a rough, gallant general who in fact fought the marauding invaders of his country to the death.

Arthur epitomizes regality in a 15th-century tapestry (opposite, top). At bottom, opposite, are the ruins of Tintagel Castle, his legendary birthplace. A miniature (above) depicts the Battle of Hastings; below is Battle Abbey, built by William after his victory.

Five centuries or more after the death of King Arthur, early in the autumn of 1066, England suffered the most portentous invasion in its history. Leading an armada of some seven hundred ships laden with men, horses, and equipment, William the Bastard of Normandy crossed the Channel to assert his claims to the British throne. He was taking a chance on having a fair following wind (he had no oarsmen) and not too much of it to raise high seas, but his landing was safely engineered at Pevensey, on the southeast coast of England. It was a remarkable feat of navigation, accompanied by the best of luck. On October 14 William engaged the hastily assembled forces of his adversary, Harold, the reigning king of England, several miles from Hastings and defeated them in a fierce battle, during which Harold was killed. On the spot where Harold died William decreed that the altar of a great commemorative church should stand, where its remains still do. The Battle of Hastings marked one of the decisive days in all history. Had Harold prevailed, the entire course of England's destiny — and its culture, art, and literature — would have been different. William would have been only dimly remembered, not as "the Conqueror," but simply as "the Bastard."

The same day that Thomas à Becket was dispatched to the angels (delicately pictured in the ivory below), stories of miraculous happenings in Canterbury Cathedral (opposite) began to circulate, and within a short time pilgrimages to the church began. The pilgrims above are from a miniature illustrating Chaucer's tales.

Church and School

The medieval cathedral at Canterbury has been called the mother church of all England. On September 5, 1174, that early structure caught fire and in the words of a contemporary quickly became "a despicable heap of ashes, reduced to a dreary wilderness, and laid open to all the injuries of weather." Reconstruction of the hallowed building was almost immediately undertaken by a French architect, one William of Sens, "a man active and ready and as a workman most skilful both in wood and stone," who was hired for the purpose by the canons of Canterbury after a stiff competition with other master builders. Early in the job William fell fifty feet from the perch where he was supervising the upper arches of the vault; disabled, he returned to France. However, his plans were faithfully carried out by his English successor, and the new cathedral became the first demonstration of the Gothic style in Britain (as the cathedral at Sens had been the first in that style in France, where Gothic architecture was born). A few years earlier Thomas à Becket, archbishop of Canterbury, who had fled England for fear of persecution because his views on church policy contradicted the aims of King Henry II, had been received at Sens with particular hospitality. When Becket returned to England in 1170 his differences with the king were immediately heightened. On December 29 four armed knights hacked the archbishop to pieces in the cathedral. The bloody slaughter was one of the most dramatic events in English history, marking in tragic tones the struggle for supremacy between Church and state. To what degree the king was responsible for that high crime remains uncertain, but the event shocked the whole Christian world. In his horrid death Becket won eternal glory. Only three years later he was canonized as a Christian martyr, and his tomb at Canterbury became a shrine that attracted pilgrims from all over Europe. Two centuries after Becket's grotesque murder, Geoffrey Chaucer wrote his immortal tales of pilgrims journeying to the Canterbury tomb. Six centuries after that T. S. Eliot related the story of the saint's martyrdom in his *Murder in the Cathedral.*

The American novelist Henry James called Salisbury Cathedral "a blond beauty among churches." It is without doubt one of the most impressive examples of the Gothic style in England, a style that increasingly became the peculiar and eloquent national idiom of the country, distinctively different from the Gothic language of France. When he saw Salisbury for the first time, the famous nineteenth-century architectural critic Augustus Pugin exclaimed: "I have traveled all over Europe in search of architecture, but I have seen nothing like this." The great structure was raised in open country between 1220 and 1258, a remarkably short time, and it was the first purely Gothic building in the land. With its towering spire (at 404 feet the highest in England), added in the fourteenth century, it became a celebrated landmark of the Wiltshire countryside, visible for miles about. Early in the last century the landscapist John Constable spent several weeks with the bishop of Salisbury. The gray stone cathedral, in its typically English setting of arching trees and bucolic delights, captured the artist's imagination. In the years to come the noble structure, as it could be seen from the bishop's grounds and from the surrounding meadows in all weather and from every point of view, provided the subject of a number of his finest paintings. Unlike the cathedrals in France and Germany, those in England were typically not closely hemmed about by the older houses of a city. Rather they were more frequently placed in a parklike setting apart from a city's clatter and clutter, together with their bishops' residences, cloisters, and related buildings of ecclesiastical function. Shortly after the basic structure of Salisbury cathedral was completed, work was begun on its adjoining cloisters, which are the oldest and largest of any English cathedral. (The library of the cloisters preserves one of the four original copies of the Magna Charta.) A town immediately began to spring up around the cathedral area, and in 1227 under a charter of Henry III it was declared a free city, to be "forever" part of the bishop's demesne.

When it was consecrated in 1258 Salisbury Cathedral boasted neither the cloisters (opposite), begun a few years later, nor the spire and flying buttresses; the church has changed little since John Constable painted it (below), and its surroundings are still almost as bucolic.

In Cambridge and Oxford, England is endowed with two of the world's most ancient and distinguished universities. Both have undergone continuous development since their modest beginnings almost nine centuries ago. The town of Cambridge was originally a Roman fort and subsequently a Saxon and then a Norman community. William the Conqueror built a castle here late in the eleventh century as part of his design to establish order in the land he had recently invaded and conquered. That structure has long since disappeared. Early in the following century the town assumed new importance with the advent of Benedictine monks from nearby Ely. These holy men gave Cambridge a scholastic and ecclesiastical reputation, and, in effect, they formed the nucleus about which the university would develop. By the end of the next century Cambridge was organized into residential colleges, which increased in number and importance throughout the Middle Ages—and down to our own day. (Two of these, founded in the nineteenth century, were pioneers in providing university education for women.) King's College was founded in 1441 by King Henry VI. Its famous chapel, which towers above the surrounding town and university, was inspired by Sainte Chapelle in Paris, the exquisite structure built by Saint Louis to house the sacred crown of thorns. The first stone of King's Chapel was laid in 1446 and the building was completed in 1515, a magnificent example of the Perpendicular Gothic style. With its lofty and intricate fan vaulting, its tall stained-glass windows, and its numerous heraldic carvings, among other features, it is the pride and glory of King's College. Adjoining its chapel, as an interesting contrast, a screen wall with a heavily pinnacled gateway was raised in the mock Perpendicular style of the nineteenth century, during the Gothic revival in England.

THE SCIENCE MUSEUM, LONDON

Sir Isaac Newton, shown in the contemporary portrait above, attended Cambridge and served on its faculty from 1669 to 1701. Below is the Gothic Revival wall that connects with King's College Chapel, opposite.

RAPHO-GUILLUMETTE PICTURES—J. ALLAN CASH

The beginning of Oxford, one very old story recounts, was a nunnery founded in 727 on the present site of Christ Church by Saint Frideswide in gratitude for her deliverance from an over-ardent suitor and thus for the preservation of her treasured virginity. (She remains the patron saint of both the city and the university of Oxford.) Be that as it may, by the time the Domesday Book was compiled, in 1085–86, by order of William the Conqueror, Oxford was a flourishing town, among the largest in the kingdom with its four thousand inhabitants. Within a generation or so, young scholars were gathering there to learn from the wise monks and teachers of the place. In 1167, during a quarrel with Becket, Henry II ordered English students who were in Paris to return to England to ensure that "there may never be wanting a succession of persons duly qualified for the service of God in Church and State." Presumably some good proportion of these repatriated scholars found their way to Oxford. The university was a-borning. Throughout the Middle Ages Oxford remained a principal center of learning. In the thirteenth century the great English scholastic philosopher and scientist Roger Bacon (called the Admirable Doctor) became one of the university's most celebrated graduates and teachers. Bacon's contemporary John Duns Scotus (called the Subtle Doctor) also taught there, expounding among other things his theory that the state arose from the common consent of the people in the social contract. As at Cambridge, over the course of centuries separate colleges were established, and they multiplied. Between the accession of Queen Elizabeth in 1558 and the civil wars of the following century the university was greatly enlarged. Old buildings made way for new ones. By the time the print here illustrated was engraved in 1675, nineteen colleges had already been established. Unlike Cambridge, the town at Oxford had grown large and important before the founding of the university. During the civil wars of the seventeenth century Oxford was the Royalist capital. Although it was besieged by the Parliamentarians, no damage was done to its buildings. Enough of those early buildings have survived to make an overall view of Oxford one of the most engaging prospects in all England. Almost every period and style of British architecture is represented in a fine example by an outstanding master builder or architect—more of them than can be mentioned, much less described, in these pages. The great Gothic spire of Saint Mary's Church contrasts with the Italian dome of Radcliffe Camera, built by James Gibbs in the eighteenth century. Standing above the city wall as it has for five hundred years, the low but graceful tower of the Merton College Chapel rises nearby that of Magdalen, described by King James I as "the most absolute building in Oxford"; the Ashmolean Museum, built in the Greek Revival style of the 1840's, stands a few streets away around the corner from the roughly contemporary University Museum, built in the Gothic Revival style—all varied and history-laden structures that enchant the eye and excite the imagination.

Domus híc Regia, Sedes Episcopalis, Cathedralis Ecclesia, & Collegium in Universitate Oxoniensi, Musis & pietati addicebatur sub S. Frideswide auspicijs; post varias denique utriusq; fortunæ clades et magnifica, sed in irritum cedentia molimina. An. 1546 in Ecclesiam Christi, ex fundatione R.

The engraving of Oxford University below depicts the already impressive complex in 1675. Three centuries of continuous building since have turned modern Oxford (overview at right) into a living architectural museum.

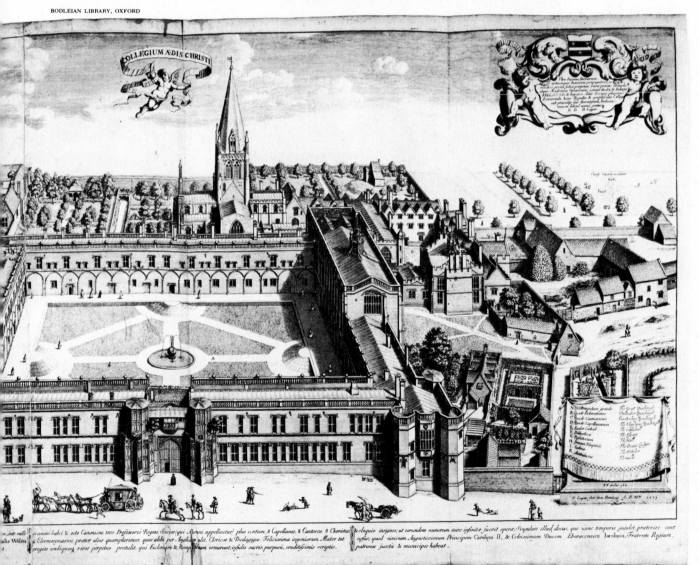

House and Castle

Merrymaking takes place around a yule log blazing in the chimney-less great hall of Penshurst, a 14th-century manor (top). Little Moreton Hall, opposite, in north-west England, is an impressive example of Tudor half-timbered architecture. Shakespeare's birth-place (above) represents the more modest dwellings of the time.

Almost four centuries ago, in one of his most memorable legal pronouncements, the great English jurist Edward Coke reminded his countrymen that as a matter of common law "the house of every one is to him his castle and fortress." He wrote at a time when, following the long, peaceful, and prosperous years of Elizabeth's reign, the manor house was actually no longer conceived of as a castle and fortress but rather primarily as a dwelling place. The need had passed for massive impregnable walls, for drawbridge and moat, for windows that were mere protective slits from which to aim arrows and other projectiles instead of ample outlooks on a verdant world. A new need was felt for more private and specialized conveniences than were provided, for example, by the great manorial halls of medieval times: those lofty rooms of all purposes where everyone—"knight, page, and household squire" —lived, ate, and slept, where the estate business was administered, and where in inclement weather the tenderer livestock was given shelter. Such a hall, without a chimney but with an open hearth at the center of the room and an outlet for smoke in its high, timbered roof, survives at Penshurst Place in Kent. The new manor house of Elizabeth's time was built of lighter and more graceful materials, with accommodations to the queen's taste, should she pay a visit on her royal progress from place to place. Black and white half-timbered structures were ubiquitous features of the Elizabethan landscape, and none was so conspicuously handsome as Little Moreton Hall, built in 1559, with its elaborate tracery of decorative structural timbers outlined against the white plaster of the outer wall. Anne Hathaway and Will Shakespeare were born and lived in half-timbered houses, modest in scale but of thoroughly pleasant appearance, with their inevitable flower borders, such as lined the streets and byways of Tudor villages. England at this time, it seemed to Shakespeare, was "this other Eden, demi-paradise,/This fortress built by Nature for herself/. . . This blessed plot, this earth, this realm, this England." One less rhapsodic observer, a traveler, noted that Englishmen think "there are no other men than themselves, and no other world but England; and whenever they see a handsome foreigner, they say that 'he looks like an Englishman.'"

When Henry VIII of the house of Tudor succeeded to the throne of England in 1509, he found in Thomas Wolsey an aide of rare genius. Wolsey, once a student at Oxford, had been chaplain to Henry VII. In the new king's service the young prelate rapidly rose to power and prestige. By 1515 he was not only a cardinal of the Church but lord chancellor of the realm, a man who more than any other ably supported the absolutism aspired to by his monarch. The emoluments of Wolsey's offices were enormous, wealth that he spent with princely ostentation. His household was composed of five hundred persons of noble birth, including knights and barons of the realm. In 1515 he built as his main residence, some fifteen miles southwest of London, Hampton Court, one of the finest and most interesting surviving examples of Tudor architecture and a palace of regal pretention. It was during Wolsey's ministry in 1520 that Henry met with Francis I, king of France, in an unexampled exhibition of pageantry at a spot near Calais that was called the Field of the Cloth of Gold, in a vain effort to resolve their conflicting imperialistic ambitions. That splendid and pompous performance (a depiction of which is displayed in the palace) was, however, a diplomatic fiasco. The magnificence of Hampton Court, meanwhile, excited the envy of Henry, and in 1526 Wolsey thought it prudent to give it over to the king, who made it his favorite residence, as it would be that of other English sovereigns until the time of George IV. Long before, in the reign of William the Conqueror, Windsor Castle (twenty-three miles west of London) had been established as the chief residence of England's royalty, and thus it remains. It was designed by William to serve as one link in a chain of castles surrounding London. Added to, rebuilt, restored, and refurbished by successive monarchs over the following centuries, it has become a vast and rich conglomeration of historic structures.

The famous painting of Henry VIII arriving at the Field of the Cloth of Gold (below) hangs in Hampton Court. Opposite is a view of the gatehouse at the palace through the archway named for Anne Boleyn.

OVERLEAF: *Windsor Castle*

Blenheim sprawls symmetrically over seven acres; the grand court as shown in the 18th-century engraving above covers three of them. Opposite, top, is the garden façade of the mansion. The first duke's memorial (opposite), one of the finest English baroque sculptures, is in the palace's chapel.

Sarah Jennings and John Churchill, both children of gentry, talented, intelligent, and driven by ambition for wealth and rank, married in the court of Charles II. John, who by virtue of having crushed a domestic rebellion was made a major general by James II, managed to jump nimbly to the side of William and Mary when they overthrew James. Eventually they made him earl of Marlborough. Sarah had been an attendant and intimate friend of Mary's easily influenced sister Anne since girlhood, and when Anne ascended the throne in 1702 the Churchills became the real power in England. At precisely that time England went to war against France and Spain, and however inevitable the choice of Marlborough to lead the English forces, it was also the right one. He was one of the greatest strategists, tacticians, and formulators of wartime diplomacy ever. Many important victories during the next few years resulted in bulging coffers and the title of "duke" for Marlborough. In 1704 he smashed the French at Blenheim, stunning them for decades to come. Queen Anne was hard-pressed to think of a splendid enough reward, but Sarah as usual had an idea: John might like a place in the country as a retreat between triumphs. In 1705 the queen signed a bill that gave a royal estate near Oxford to Marlborough and directed that an elegant mansion be raised at royal expense. The palace itself was Marlborough's idea. As one of his descendants wrote: "He set himself to see that his exploits were worthily commemorated, and took it as a matter of course that no memorial could be too magnificent." In choosing a designer for his monument Marlborough ignored the logical choice—old Christopher Wren, who had built Saint Paul's—and named a younger man, John Vanbrugh, who was both architect and dramatist. Delighted with the commission, Vanbrugh got to work immediately, and within three months the cornerstone was laid.

That auspicious beginning notwithstanding, there was little but trouble getting the massive edifice—to be the largest mansion in England—off the ground. Though this was the nation's gift to its conquering hero, no one seemed to be responsible for paying the thousand workmen and countless suppliers, even before Queen Anne tired of the Churchills' manipulations and dismissed them. Because of the trickle of funds and because the architect proved so whimsical as to pull down a good deal of what was already in place, the building pace slowed considerably after the first burst, but construction did continue throughout Anne's reign. Another of Vanbrugh's fancies was to raise a thirty-three-room bridge over a river on the estate, much to the disgust of the duchess. For years she unavailingly argued with the man to dispense with his extravagance, and in 1716 she forced him to resign and took over as contractor herself. Three years later, ailing but by then in favor with King George I, the duke was finally able to take up residence in the baroque mansion. The tightfisted Churchills, however, had to pay a great deal of its enormous cost. As his memorial it was the duke's favorite resting place, and he was able to spend two more summers there before his death in June, 1722. The duchess, who never liked it, added finishing touches after his death and rarely went there again. When he visited the fourth duke of Marlborough at Blenheim Palace, George III exclaimed: "We have nothing to equal this."

Longleat

Stratford Saye

Castle Howard

The medieval tradition of building was strong in England. It stemmed from generations of craftsmanship whose principles and practices were intuitively understood by master builders and their workmen. And it endured long after fresh concepts of architecture had been introduced in the Italian Renaissance, concepts that were attended by new and more formal patterns of living. It was not until late in the sixteenth century that the very words "architect" and "architecture," derived from their Italian equivalents, first appeared in the English language, along with many other expressions that were soon to become part of a necessary vocabulary for those who designed and built structures of any consequence. Most of the great houses that sprang up about the English countryside late in the Tudor period and during the seventeenth century bore witness to the wave of interest in the new style that superseded the Gothic. In the symmetry (another one of those new words) of their plans and their use of classical motifs they gradually changed the appearance of the architectural landscape, as a comparison between Little Moreton Hall (pages 272–73) and the buildings illustrated on these two pages clearly indicates. The new architecture was a commanding fashion among English gentlemen of taste and means.

Stratfield

Mereworth Castle

Hatfield House

Holkham Hall

Those gentlemen who had inherited ancestral mansions in the Gothic or Elizabethan style made haste to modernize them—or to tear them down and rebuild them in the new fashion if they had the wherewithal. It was in this spirit that Henry VIII made changes in the royal apartments at Hampton Court, deemed "so very old built, and so irregular" (for the new style was a matter of interior convenience as well as external show). Thus the fashion spread. "If a man should wear the old bonnet, tunic, and vest of King Henry the VIII's days now," observed one seventeenth-century reporter, "or build a palace after the Gothic style as it was then, he would be pointed at as a madman." Not everyone approved of such changes. There were those who resented the new refinements and proprieties that were dictating the course of daily life—who pined for the "good old days" when manners and fashions were more traditional, native, and "natural."

By the eighteenth century the craze for building in the classical mode
had become what one contemporary called the "epidemical madness"
of the age. A knowledge of architecture was considered a necessary
part of any gentleman's intellectual equipment, and a grand tour
of Europe to study Continental models of excellence was *de rigueur*
for young men of rank. In England the great mansions were opened
to a gaping public on certain days of the week. On the Continent the
fame of England's great estates led Catherine the Great to commission the celebrated potter Josiah Wedgwood to produce for her an
imperial table service decorated with views of English countryseats.
The first big surge of interest in the new style sent architects scurrying
to the published designs of Andrea Palladio (see pages 100–101) for
guidance. Lord Burlington's Chiswick House, built in 1729, was the
most famous of many English copies of Palladio's Villa Capra at
Vicenza. Later in the eighteenth century another classical revival
was fired by the light and graceful adaptations of Roman forms and
ornaments designed by the brothers Robert and James Adam. In
1762 Sir Hugh Smithson, a man of munificent habits and "correct
taste," commissioned the Adamses to modernize his wife's home,
Syon House. It became one of the Adamses' most memorable artistic
accomplishments and the finest advertisement of their firm.

*William Kent modeled Chiswick
House, above, after Palladio's Villa
Capra. Robert Adam employed many
bold color schemes in Syon House,
opposite; the entrance hall is white
with black floor tiles and furnishings.*

282

The geometric perfection and enormous scale of Bath's architecture are evident in the aerial view at top. Opposite is the exterior of George IV's Royal Pavilion at Brighton; the aquatint of its music room above is from a book of views of the place produced by the architect Nash for George IV to give to his visitors.

The town of Bath in Somersetshire in southwest England was famed in Roman times for the restorative quality of its bubbling hot springs and for the luxurious blandishments that inevitably become a part of life at such spas. (Tacitus thought the use of these waters and all that went with it was part of a subtle plan to enervate the "rude and primitive" Britons, thus to ease them into more willing submission to Roman rule.) Early in the eighteenth century the elegant Beau Nash, as master of ceremonies and accepted leader of society, brought Bath back into high fashion. By the second half of the century the city had become one of the most beautiful in Europe. Under the architects John Wood, father and son, an ambitious scheme of town planning was undertaken. The senior Wood thought in terms of architectural masses in which the individual dwelling-house became a component of a larger structure with a continuous façade, all designed with a classical regard for symmetry. To a substantial degree his project was successfully carried out, although there were those who rebelled against the idea of living in a home that was but a fraction of a building instead of the traditional detached unit. However, the thousand-foot sweep of the Royal Crescent was one of the most completely satisfying architectural creations in England.

When in 1750 Dr. Richard Russell discovered the beneficial qualities of sea water in treating certain disorders, Brighton was quickly transformed from a small fishing village into a popular resort. As one contemporary wit observed, fashionable people rushed there to be cured, like tongues, by dipping into brine. As Prince of Wales and spendthrift leader of a dissolute society, the future George IV was attracted to Brighton in his youth. In 1784 the press reported that he was seeking a house in Brighton, having been "advised by his physician to sea-bathing as necessary to perfect the re-establishment of his health." There he met, fell madly in love with, and clandestinely married the young, twice-widowed Catholic Mrs. Fitzherbert. As a summer residence, the young prince took over a house that had been remodeled into a pavilion to suit the extravagant royal taste and to accommodate the round of royal pleasures. This was not enough. In 1815 the Prince Regent commissioned the prominent architect John Nash to transform the Royal Pavilion into an exuberant Oriental fantasy; with its bulbous domes and minarets it seemed a free poetic paraphrase of some theme from *The Arabian Nights*. Inside and out this extraordinary fabrication was the extreme architectural expression of a romantic age—an architectural "folly" of princely proportions.

London

HURLIMANN

HERSCHEL LEVIT

Although the Romans had invested the site and enclosed it with walls in the first century A.D., not until the ninth century under the rule of Alfred the Great did London emerge as an important town. Alfred refortified the area, and almost two centuries later William the Conqueror considered London so formidable that he treated with it separately in the course of his conquest. To add to the city's defenses he built there the White Tower, a fort that became the core of the Tower of London, which has witnessed some of the most dramatic and grisly episodes in British history. The most poignant of these concerns Edward V, who became king at the age of twelve. While awaiting his coronation, the terrified child and his younger brother were murdered by order of their uncle in their Tower apartment as they clutched one another, crying for their mother. The uncle then ascended the throne as Richard III. Over the centuries the Tower served as a royal residence as well as the jail of illustrious prisoners, and often enough the scene of their torture and beheading. In the thirteenth century Henry III remodeled the ancient fort into a true Gothic fortress and added a zoo. Today the Tower houses a superb collection of arms and armor, and when they are not in use, the crown jewels, carefully watched over by the "Beefeaters." It was also Henry III who had the old Norman abbey at Westminster (then a separate town) razed to make way for the magnificent Gothic structure, two hundred years in the building, which still stands today. Since William I every English sovereign, save two, has been crowned in the abbey; and it has long served as the burial place of England's illustrious sons and daughters.

William I's White Tower, much restored, is depicted above. Opposite is Henry VII's chapel in Westminster Abbey. It is filled with the tombs of many kings and queens and such memorials to the great as those in the Poet's Corner, left. Longfellow is the only American honored among the writers.

SHOSTAL

287

Until late in the seventeenth century London was still essentially a medieval city. In 1661 the indefatigable diarist John Evelyn, who had surveyed the up-to-date structures in the Renaissance style in Rome, Paris, and elsewhere on the Continent, complained bitterly of London's "Congestion of mishapen . . . Houses," of its "narrow and incommodious" streets, of their "uneasie" form of paving, and of the "troublesome and malicious" disposure of the spouts and gutters overhead, among other annoyances. Just five years later virtually all this was wiped out by a gigantic conflagration that left the old city a charred ruin. Within a week of that catastrophe Evelyn had presented to the king a plan for rebuilding the area in a modern manner, with wide, straight streets, crossing one another at right angles for the most part, and a series of conspicuous open spaces lined with trim structures. His vision was shared by the prominent architect Christopher Wren. However, questions of property rights and the general misery occasioned by the disaster prevented the realization of any such grandiose schemes. Nevertheless, as one contemporary observed, "the dwelling houses raised since the fire are generally very fair, and built much more convenient and uniform than heretofore." In the rebuilding of the city Wren played a notable part. Among his many structures, the fifty-two London churches he designed, with their tall, graceful spires rising high above low-pitched roofs, set a general pattern for Georgian churches. (They also set a model for the churches and meetinghouses that would become such a prominent and engaging feature of the American landscape in the following century and a half.) Wren's enduring masterpiece is the great Saint Paul's Cathedral, which replaced the old medieval church wiped out by the fire. With its superb dome, one of the finest in Europe, the huge edifice was completed in thirty-five years, during the episcopate of one bishop. The last stone in the lantern was laid by Wren's son in 1708. Among those who worked under Wren were England's finest craftsmen—carefully selected masons, carvers, carpenters, joiners, and others who constituted virtually a national school of building and decoration.

Some Englishmen and their dogs relish their vantage across the river from the holocaust ravaging London in a 1666 engraving, above. Below, Christopher Wren poses before a vision of his masterpiece, St. Paul's Cathedral (its façade is opposite). To save money attempts were made to rebuild from charred remains until a column buckled; Wren was told to design a new church. He wrote the dean: "I . . . comfort you as I would a friend for the loss of his grandfather by saying in the course of nature you could not longer enjoy him."

289

Buckingham Palace has often been harshly judged as an undistinguished architectural pile, but it has a secure place in the history of London and of England's royal family. It remains the official London residence of the sovereign since its establishment as such by Queen Victoria in 1837 (albeit she termed its exterior "a disgrace to the country"). The land on which the palace now stands was once planted with thirty thousand mulberry trees in an ill-informed and ill-fated experiment, sponsored by James I, to produce raw silk in Britain. The area then became a popular but disreputable loitering place known as the Mulberry Garden. Early in the eighteenth century, after a series of mansions that had been built beside the garden went up in flames, John Sheffield, duke of Buckingham and Normanby, there raised what was considered the finest private palace near London. Later in that century George III bought the building to serve him and his bride as a royal retreat, adding to the structure to improve its usefulness. Upon his accession to the throne in 1820, George IV decided to turn the place into a palace worthy of the name, and worthy of his own notorious reputation for heedless extravagance. When the king died in his turn, Queen Victoria moved in, and following her marriage to Prince Albert, she soon enlarged and modified the castle better to accommodate her fast-growing family. The erratic history of the construction was finally ended in 1913, when still further alterations were made.

SHOSTAL

To accomplish the major alterations at Buckingham Palace George IV hired the talented architect John Nash, who had also transformed the Royal Pavilion for the king. The total cost came to a staggering £ 719,000, to the great dismay of Parliament. Earlier Nash had also been called in to devise Trafalgar Square as one element of the most ambitious effort at urban planning London has ever known. The square was to serve as an anchor to a large throughway linking Saint James's and Whitehall with the British Museum and Bloomsbury, and as the junction of several famous roads—Fleet Street, Whitehall, Pall Mall, and Charing Cross Road. The square itself, as completed by other architects largely during the 1830's, remains a hub of London life and a national forum for mass meetings. At the center of this spacious composition rises the tall column commemorating Lord Nelson's great victory at Trafalgar over the combined French and Spanish fleets in 1805—a decisive English triumph that ended Napoleon's power on the high seas. It was in this grim battle that Nelson, after signaling his fleet, "England expects that every man will do his duty," fell dead from enemy fire. On the north side of the square the National Gallery houses one of the world's outstanding collections of art treasures; and at one corner of the square rises the steeple of James Gibbs's exquisite church, Saint Martin-in-the-Fields, whose design was closely followed for Saint Paul's Chapel, built in 1766 on lower Manhattan Island in New York City and still standing there.

Buckingham Palace (opposite), begun in 1703, has a twentieth-century façade. The National Gallery is at left in the background of the view above of Trafalgar Square, which is dominated by the Nelson Memorial. St. Martin-in-the-Fields, perhaps the finest Georgian church in England, may be seen in the center.

291

Queen Victoria, shown with Albert in the 1855 engraving at left, greatly loved her consort; but his Germanic ways antagonized her subjects. Later his sponsorship of the exhibition in the Crystal Palace (opposite) won him some popularity. After his death, Victoria raised the cast-iron Albert Memorial (below).

The Crystal Palace is no longer a landmark of London. Nevertheless, there are many still living who recall this phenomenal structure, and many more who delight in the history of those brief months in 1851 when the palace was a focus of interest for a wide world of visiting spectators. It was constructed with the active support of Queen Victoria's German consort, Prince Albert, to house a vast international industrial exhibition, which would provide, in Albert's words, "a living picture of the point of development at which mankind has arrived, and a new starting point from which all nations will be able to exert their future exertions." Millions of people came from all over to enrich their minds and kindle their spirits by viewing its displays—from schoolchildren to exalted foreign dignitaries and one eighty-four-year-old woman who walked all the way from Cornwall. In the end the building itself was the main spectacle. It was 1,848 feet long and 456 feet wide at its widest dimensions, and it covered nearly 18 acres of ground. It was four times the size of Saint Paul's Cathedral. Quite aside from those impressive statistics, it represented the most imaginative and daring architectural adventure of the nineteenth century. It was primarily the creation of Joseph Paxton, head gardener of the duke of Devonshire, who found his inspiration in the greenhouses he had earlier devised at the duke's Chatsworth estate. Made of a film of plate glass set in a network of iron frames and supports, audaciously flung in soaring domes and light, glittering arcades far over the stalls beneath, the building was a symbol of the new control man was assuming over the materials that nature provided. The whole complex was prefabricated—the first modular building constructed of uniform, interchangeable, mass-produced parts. It was completed barely seventeen weeks after the first column was raised. When the fair was over, the great structure was easily dismantled and re-erected at Sydenham. It was totally destroyed by fire in 1936.

The British Parliament, made up of the House of Lords and the House of Commons, has met at Westminster since the days of Henry VIII. Only once in the year do the two bodies meet in joint session, on that annual autumn occasion when the reigning monarch ascends the throne in the House of Lords and declares Parliament open. The solemn and brilliant pageantry of that occasion is a formality rooted in ages of accumulated tradition. In ceremonial procession the royal presence is preceded into the great chamber by Rouge Dragon Pursuivant and Portcullis Pursuivant, Lancaster Herald and Richmond Herald and Arundel Herald Extraordinary, Black Rod, Norroy and Ulster and Clarenceux Kings of Arms, the Cap of Maintenance, and the Sword of State—each the symbol of an ancient observance that contributed to the evolution of parliamentary government in England. Here, in the fourteenth century, Richard II, last of the Plantagenets, was deposed; here Charles I was sentenced to death; and here were held the historic trials of Sir Thomas More and of Warren Hastings. On October 16, 1834, the old palace of Westminster, where Parliament so long had met, was irrecoverably damaged by fire. In spite of the continuing vogue for the classical style, especially for large secular public buildings, it was decided that the new houses of Parliament, the most important public buildings in the nation, would be designed and constructed in the Gothic manner. This was considered appropriate because that whole area of London had long been closely associated with buildings of medieval origin.

Ninety-seven architects competed for the commission to design the new parliamentary buildings. After long and bitter wrangling, the assignment was finally given to Sir Charles Barry, curiously enough, a man well known for his work in the classical style. His gigantic production was in fact conceived in terms of classical symmetry, clothed in Gothic detail. Thirty-two years after the project was commissioned the buildings were completed. They covered eighty acres of ground with a three-hundred-yard frontage on the Thames. As Sir Kenneth Clark has observed, today they remain more admired than they ever have been; in his words, they seem "to embody all that is most characteristic and most moving in London." At night, a light in the clock tower indicates that Parliament is sitting. Later in the century the Tower Bridge, so named because of its proximity to the Tower of London, was also built in the Gothic Revival style to span the Thames. (London Bridge, which according to the old popular song had so long been "falling down," has now been dismantled and packed off to be re-erected as a showpiece in Arizona.)

A strong undercurrent of feeling which held that Gothic was essentially an English style was responsible for the fabric of the Tower Bridge (top), begun in 1886, and the stately houses of Parliament, designed some 50 years earlier. The term "Big Ben" refers not to the conspicuous clock, but to its hour bell. The medal above showing Commons in session is inscribed: "Restored 1651 in the third year of freedom by God's blessing." It was struck to commemorate the trial of Charles I.

Scotland

Visitors to Holyroodhouse pass through the gate at left. The castle itself (opposite) is still a royal residence though little used; Holyrood Abbey, adjoining it on the right, was partially destroyed by Protestant reformers. Edinburgh Castle is almost lost in the haze (Auld Reekie) in the view of the city below. The needle-spired structure behind and left of the Greek Revival monument is Sir Walter Scott's memorial.

Edinburgh is one of the most picturesque cities in the British Isles. Although it had more remote origins, its true history began early in the seventh century when Edwin, king of Northumbria, built a stronghold on the high rock where Edinburgh Castle now stands at the center of the modern city. About the castle that was built on that site in the eleventh century grew the old town that would become the capital city of Scotland in 1437. Today, after centuries of vicissitudes that record dramatic episodes in Scottish history, the castle actually consists of a cluster of buildings of various ages, a group that impressively dominates the surrounding city from its rocky heights. In 1128, soon after his accession to the Scottish throne, David I founded the abbey of Holyrood, outside the fortress, which from an early date received the court, whose members preferred it to the bleak quarters of the castle a mile away. About 1500 James IV began to build, adjoining the abbey, Holyroodhouse, which was to be the principal royal palace of Scotland. It was to Holyrood that in 1561 Mary queen of Scots returned from France as the teen-age widow of Francis II, king of France, and dowager queen of that country. She spent but six years at Holyrood, years of tragic romance that eventually led to her bloody execution in 1587. After long centuries of contention over questions of sovereignty and religion, in 1707 the parliaments of Scotland and England were finally united, and thereafter the history of Scotland joined that of Great Britain. Later in the eighteenth century and in the nineteenth Edinburgh developed a brilliant reputation as a center of learning and literature. Colonial American students came to its celebrated university to take courses in medicine and law. The economist Adam Smith and the novelist Sir Walter Scott were among prominent personages associated with the city. Guided by good advice, in 1826 John James Audubon, the self-styled "American woodsman," came to Edinburgh, and here he found the first engraver for the plates of *Birds of America* and the first subscribers to this audacious publication.

In the grandeur of its architectural mass and the richness of its historical associations, Glamis Castle makes an undeniable appeal to the romantic imagination. Although portions of this picturesque structure are much earlier (with fifteen-foot-thick walls), the castle owes its general appearance to the first earl of Strathmore, who had it built late in the seventeenth century. Long before, in the eleventh century, the historical Macbeth was thane of Glamis. Basing his tragedy on early chronicles, Shakespeare quite naturally but inaccurately sets the first two acts of *Macbeth* at the later feudal castle that was built at Glamis. However, the castle has associations as dramatic and fearful as anything told in the play. According to oft-told accounts, Macbeth did indeed murder his king, Duncan, near here in 1040; and only a generation earlier than the poet's, a Lady Glamis was accused of witchcraft and of plotting to poison King James V and was burned at the stake. When her innocence was belatedly proved, her son built the present castle. Posed before a wild, mountainous landscape, Inveraray Castle also replaces a much earlier stronghold. The present "massive and uniform mansion," as Sir Walter Scott described it, was raised for the third duke of Argyll in 1746. With its round corner towers, its pointed arch windows, and its great battlemented tower rising from its heart, it was a very early manifestation of the renewed interest in the Gothic style that led to a widespread architectural fashion throughout Britain. No one was more influential in the revival of interest in the medieval scene than Scott himself, largely through his Waverley novels, with their wealth of archaeological detail. In the first two decades of the nineteenth century a flood of pamphlets on Gothic archaeology also fed the public interest.

Sir Walter Scott was enamoured of both Glamis Castle, opposite, and Inveraray Castle, below, because of their aura of Gothic romance. He claimed that Glamis had a secret chamber that only the earl, his heir, and one confidant might know about at a given time.

In 1811 Scott bought a farm on the banks of the River Tweed and on that property, to realize his dreams of baronial splendor and hospitality on a scale commensurate with his literary revenues, he built Abbotsford, an ambitious mansion in the Gothic style with a profusion of gables and turrets. Scott's medieval romances and his other tales were a raging fashion in America as in England, and the author was the subject of almost universal adulation. Among the many pilgrims who visited the Abbotsford shrine was Audubon, who went there in 1827 with a portfolio of his drawings, hoping for the great man's endorsement, if not his patronage. Scott, however, was not impressed by Audubon's work. Washington Irving, on the other hand, spent four days with Scott at Abbotsford, rambling about the countryside and talking with him from breakfast until bedtime and earning Scott's encouragement to resume writing, which the American had forsaken because of his family's business troubles. When he returned to America Irving remodeled a farmhouse at Sunnyside, near Tarrytown, New York, in the Hudson River Valley—his "little nookery," as he called it—into a small-scale reminder of Abbotsford, and of a past that could never be recovered.

Abbotsford (shown at bottom) is still in the Scott family, thanks to the generous interest of the author's friends and creditors. The structure is recalled in Washington Irving's remodeled Sunnyside (below), located near Tarrytown, New York. Scott is buried in Dryburgh Abbey (opposite page).

When he died in 1832 Scott was buried amid the ruins of the ancient Dryburgh Abbey church, a spot on a graceful bend of the Tweed historic and romantic enough to satisfy the novelist's own colorful imagination. Here the ancient druids had once practiced their rites, and here, in the twelfth century, the original church was built, a large structure with a cloister to accommodate a community of monks, canons, and working brethren. It enjoyed a prosperous growth until 1322, when Edward I, in his attempt to subjugate Scotland, ravaged the borderlands and burned the abbey. Once restored, it was burned again in 1385 at the hands of Richard II, then rebuilt and again pillaged and burned for the third time by English invaders in 1544. It was never again restored; only remnants from the various constructions remain—a Romanesque doorway, two pointed arches surmounted by a triforium gallery (as seen in the accompanying illustration), and other fragments that recall what was once a large, flourishing, and persistent center of religious activity. (Almost every stage of the old monastic buildings is represented by some surviving element.) It is a peaceful ruin, surrounded by many venerable trees, one of them —a yew—being at least coeval with the abbey. About 1700 the grounds belonged to Scott's great-grandfather, and but for an extravagant granduncle who became bankrupt and had to part with the property, it would have been inherited by the novelist. About this turn of events Scott remarked, "We have nothing left of Dryburgh but the right of stretching our bones there." He is buried amid the graves of his wife, his son, his son-in-law, and his ancestors. His tomb is a plain block of polished granite, inscribed with his name and the dates of his birth and death.

Glasgow as seen from its hilltop necropolis appears opposite, bottom. Though often vandalized, Melrose Abbey (above) still decorates "Scott country." Opposite, top, is the interior of Glasgow Cathedral. A Scott character says of it: "It's a brave kirk—nane o' yere whigmaleeries and curliewurlies . . . about it."

Near the south bank of the Tweed, in the heart of the "Scott country," stand the ruins of Melrose Abbey, once an elaborate and profusely ornamented church, and one with a violent history. (Scott used the abbey as a prototype for the building on which centers the story in his novel *The Monastery*.) David I founded the original abbey, which was dedicated in the summer of 1136. Lying as it did directly in the path of invading forces from England, the building was several times wrecked, and little of that early structure remains. In 1326, in a period between such raids, Robert Bruce, king of Scotland and in his later years bitter adversary of the English (although he had been brought up at the English court), repaired and rebuilt the abbey. Mindful of an unfulfilled vow he had made to visit the Holy Sepulcher, Robert requested that upon his death his heart be carried there. However, the faithful follower to whom he had entrusted this mission was killed while fighting the Moors in Spain, and Robert's heart, it is said, found its last resting place at Melrose Abbey under the high altar. The present ruins are largely from a later rebuilding of the church, which was undertaken late in the fourteenth and in the fifteenth centuries. This building in turn was plundered in 1545 during another English raid and was still later bombarded by the forces of Oliver Cromwell. After that the ruins were freely used as a quarry for neighboring constructions. What remains of this edifice, however, clearly indicates that it was a large and splendid Gothic pile influenced by French architectural styles. (After Bruce secured the independence of his country, Scotland turned largely to France for architectural inspiration, and the master mason of Melrose may well have been a Frenchman.) Scott immortalized the east window, with its "slender shafts of shapely stone," in *The Lay of the Last Minstrel*, his first important original work. In 1566 Mary queen of Scots made her husband commendator of the abbey, but the next year that unfortunate was proscribed and fled to Norway. (He died insane, a prisoner of the Danish king.) In 1918 the ruins of the abbey were presented to the nation by the duke of Buccleuch.

Ruins though they are, the remains of Melrose Abbey are well preserved as such. The best preserved (and restored) complete Gothic structure in Scotland is Glasgow Cathedral, "a brave kirk," as it was termed in Scott's *Rob Roy*, "that will stand as long as the warld." Mainly built in the thirteenth century, the church grew about the venerated tomb of Saint Kentigern (also known as Saint Mungo), an early missionary in Scotland. During the Reformation the structure was purged of all "monuments of idolatry," but the church itself was spared destruction through the efforts of the city's trade guilds. Here Oliver Cromwell once endured a two-hour-long sermon in which he was denounced by the minister as a "sectary and blasphemer"; whereupon he invited the preacher to dinner and concluded the entertainment with a three-hour-long prayer. The smoke-blackened exterior of the church rises before a hill overlooking Glasgow, the largest city in Scotland, its most important seaport, and the center of a great industrial belt. On that height a nineteenth-century necropolis filled with curious architectural monuments to the dead remains one place in the city where the voice of its teeming activity is hushed.

Wales

Each August people gather at Llangollen in Wales for the colorful eisteddfod, a competition of musicians and poets that is followed with avid interest by the Welsh. The strong emphasis on native culture, so characteristic of a country that has produced many fine poets, singers, writers, and actors, seems almost to have been an outgrowth of the land itself. Wales is dominated by a massive mountain range whose soaring peaks, lonely valleys, and high moors made penetration by foreigners so difficult that the ancient language and old customs stoutly resisted the influence of new ways from the outside. The geographical isolation of little communities within the country made lasting political unity nearly impossible; it also kept the Welsh independent between the second and thirteenth centuries despite invasions by Romans, Irish, Vikings, Anglo-Saxons, and Normans. The members of each group made inroads and left some of their own culture behind, but they were unable to subdue permanently the fiercely proud Celtic tribesmen, who carried on continuous guerrilla warfare from their hidden fastnesses. Not until late in the thirteenth century, when Edward I of England built a series of six fortresses, was Wales overcome. Knowing the Welsh would not stand for a foreign prince, Edward sent his pregnant wife in 1284 to Caernarvon Castle, where she bore a son; Edward introduced the infant to the chieftains as a true Prince of Wales, who "spoke no English and had been born on Welsh soil." The heir to the British throne has been so called ever since. Edward also imposed on Wales the English language and law (though even today some one hundred thousand citizens speak only Welsh). The only serious challenge to English rule thereafter was Owen Glendower's brilliant rebellion against Henry IV, which ended unsuccessfully in 1408. A major social upheaval occurred in the nineteenth century with the discovery of huge coal and metal deposits in the south of Wales, which turned such little towns as Cardiff and Newport into factory cities with vast slums. As a consequence, the Welsh voted in many members of the developing British Liberal party, which eventually took control of Parliament from landowners; in 1900 Wales sent the first Labour Member of Parliament to London.

The church of St. Cadox, above, is the oldest center of Christianity in Wales. Opposite are the ruins of the church of Cymmer Abbey, a Cistercian monastery founded late in the 12th century; the structure was never completed.

OVERLEAF: *Caernarvon Castle in Wales was begun in the 13th century to help Edward I of England subjugate Wales.*

Wild O'Tooles and O'Brynes in the neighboring hills caused the first builders of Protestant St. Patrick's Cathedral in Dublin (below) to fortify it heavily. At top is the courtyard of Dublin's Trinity College.

Among the countries of Western Europe Ireland has the rare distinction of never having been occupied by the Romans. Whereas in Britain and on most of the Continent the overlay of classical civilization tended to efface or at least significantly modify earlier cultures, in Ireland the Gaelic language and other indigenous characteristics maintained unbroken traditions over long centuries. The history of the land only gradually and uncertainly emerges from age-old legends. Even the introduction of Christianity in the fifth century under the persuasion of Saint Patrick and others did not discourage Gaelic poetry, mythology, and laws. As a matter of fact, in the centuries immediately following the conversion of Ireland, the land enjoyed a brilliant age of Celtic Christian culture. Irish monks and monasteries were celebrated throughout Europe. It was about the year 806 that Irish monks produced that supreme illuminated manuscript known as the *Book of Kells*, now treasured in the University of Dublin, or Trinity College. (The university, founded by Queen Elizabeth in 1591, was established on the site of a twelfth-century Augustinian monastery. Its immense collection of books and manuscripts, now numbering almost a million entries, was started a few years later.) A plausible tradition recalls that Saint Patrick baptized converted Celts in a well at the site of the cathedral that bears the name of Patrick, the Apostle of Ireland. The church, originally consecrated in 1192, was replaced in the following century, and additions to the later structure were made in subsequent years. In the course of time the structure suffered from several fires and other vicissitudes, as well as from simple neglect. By the middle of the last century the cathedral was in a state of dilapidation, whereupon it was completely restored.

Ireland

Both Trinity College and Saint Patrick's are associated with the brilliant Dublin-born satirist Jonathan Swift. In spite of his rebellious behavior Swift was granted a degree by Trinity, and from 1713 to 1745 he served as dean of the cathedral. The year after he undertook that service the port of Dublin was commenced, and the city's commercial importance grew rapidly. In the following years Dublin began to assume its present appearance; architecturally it is essentially a Georgian city, and it was one of the most gracious of that period. One can recapture the charm of that aspect of the city's history from a view of Harcourt Street, which was once one of Dublin's most fashionable residential streets, although it is now given over largely to hotels and commercial offices. By virtue of the scale of its buildings lining a pleasant curve it is still one of Dublin's outstanding Georgian streets. In one of these houses was born Edward Carson, baron of Duncairn, Trinity graduate and organizer of Orange resistance to Home Rule; in another once lived Cardinal Newman; and in still another, converted into a school, W. B. Yeats was once a student.

Gracefully curved Harcourt Street is still lined with Georgian houses; one of them served as the bank for the Sinn Fein movement.

Starting in the eighth century Norse raiders interrupted a long period of Ireland's isolation. In one such raid, late in the ninth century, the freebooters occupied the ancient monastery at Monasterboice, and in retaliation Domnall, king of Tara (high king of all Ireland), slew hundreds of the Viking invaders. At this site three Celtic Christian figured crosses remain standing, the finest of which, named Muiredach's Cross after the abbot of that name who had earlier ruled the monastery, is more than seventeen feet high. Such standards, with their rude but expressive "illustrations," did in effect serve as edifying stone picture books for the unlettered. Cashel in Tipperary, another celebrated historic shrine, was the capital of the kings of Munster, one of Ireland's ancient kingdoms; it has been called the City of the Kings. (Kingship, disappearing in Gaul by the first century B.C., survived in Ireland. Besides being a ruler, the king had been from the beginning in a sense a sacred person.) On the massive limestone Rock of Cashel, rising one hundred feet from the center of the town, stands a tenth-century cathedral, an ancient cross, and a twelfth-century chapel. The last, called Cormac's Chapel after that king of Munster who had it raised, is a richly ornamented miniature Romanesque cathedral that marks a culminating point in Hibernian art. Probably no other monument in Ireland is more celebrated about the world than Blarney Castle, built in the fifteenth century on a rock overlooking the River Martin. Its international fame is due to an almost inaccessible stone that, when kissed, endows the performer with marvelous powers of eloquence and persuasion. To reach the spot for this purpose, the candidate must be hung head downward from the battlement above, firmly held by husky attendants, a feat that gives color if not truth to the hallowed legend.

Blarney Castle, opposite, basks in its emerald setting. Cormac's Chapel, at bottom, is part of the cluster of monuments at Cashel. Sculptures like Muiredach's Cross, below, were brightly painted after they were carved.

BOTH: SHOSTAL

The strange basalt formations in the Giant's Causeway (above) fascinate visitors. The Spanish Armada fired at some of the tall lava columns, mistaking them in the fog for the chimneys of an enemy's castle. Opposite, top, is Queen's University in Belfast. St. Patrick's Cathedral at Armagh (bottom) is the seat of the archbishops.

Belfast, in the north of Ireland, is a phenomenal city. In 1177 one John de Courcy built a castle at the site to command the river ford there—a strategic position over whose control frequent violent battles were waged by rival factions. The castle was destroyed and rebuilt over and over again. It was not until the seventeenth century that a small village, forming around the castle that was then standing, gave initial promise of the city that was to be—a promise brightened by the arrival of industrious French Huguenots following the revocation of the Edict of Nantes. Even so, less than two hundred years ago Belfast was still but an obscure village at the junction of a tidal estuary and a sand-blocked river. Then, in the course of the nineteenth century, the community developed at an extraordinary rate. Between 1800 and 1880 its population increased more than tenfold. (Queen's University was founded there in 1845.) Today it is the largest city and the principal seaport and industrial center of Ireland. Southwest of Belfast, the town of Armagh had at an early date become the leading city of Christian Ireland. Here in the fifth century Saint Patrick founded a church and a monastery. Today Armagh is the seat of the metropolitan archbishops, both Protestant and Catholic. The present Roman Catholic Saint Patrick's Cathedral, a nineteenth-century structure, stands on a hill where the saint, while walking with the local king, released a doe and a fawn he had saved from the royal archers. In the eighteenth century the Reverend Gilbert Tennent, a native of Armagh, emigrated to America, where he helped found the "Log College," which was to become Princeton University in New Jersey. At the northern tip of Ireland, eons ago, volcanic disturbances ejected great quantities of molten basalt, which, as it cooled, formed spectacular clusters of polygonal columns. As the surface lava eroded it exposed a red bank of iron ore. This so-called Giant's Causeway is one of the natural wonders of the world.

Scandinavia

*S*candinavia comprises those irregularly shaped peninsulas that reach up and out from the extreme northwest of Europe into the surrounding seas. The term "Scandinavia" has no political significance, but it connotes the linguistic and cultural affinities that, along with geographical proximity, for centuries have bound the history of what are today Denmark, Norway, and Sweden. Although the people of these three countries have shared many common experiences, their long interrelationships have by no means always been amicable. For a brief while, nearly six hundred years ago, all three were brought together in an uneasy union. However, both before and after that, problems of dynastic succession, commercial rivalries, and conflicting foreign entanglements often enough led to wars among them on land and sea. Today, as for long years past, they remain peaceable neighbors, each with a strong sense of its national identity. In the history of all three countries the sea has always been an important formative influence. More than a thousand years ago Norsemen, or Vikings, as Scandinavians of the past are termed, swept the seas in their formidable long ships and, among other bold adventures, reached the shores of the New World. As already told, in the tenth century these seaborne marauders took over a fair part of France, to be known as Normandy, from which territory a later generation, known as Normans, sailed off to conquer England. Other Normans became rulers in southern Italy and Sicily, and still others established themselves in the Greek islands and threatened Byzantium. Through that expansionist drive, Vikings and their descendants played a vital part in the history of Europe at large. At home, as the age of the Vikings drew to a close, the three distinct if unsettled kingdoms began to take shape, not without confusion and bloodshed. Christianity had been introduced into Sweden early in the ninth century, but the old pagan gods died hard. However, missionaries who gradually spread the Gospel were followed by monastic communities, through which scholastic and cultural influences were brought to the northern lands from the south. In spite of the wearisome record of contention and warfare that disturbed the peace throughout the Middle Ages and after, more positive accomplishments laid the groundwork for the emergence of the three modern nations. The great university of Uppsala in Sweden, for example, now a seat of learning renowned around the world, opened its doors to students in 1477. A century later King Christian IV of Denmark and Norway sponsored an architectural boom to which Copenhagen owes much of its present beauty and Oslo its very existence. To his enterprise we also owe such picturesque castles as Rosenborg, Frederiksborg, and others. In many other impressive ways the past of Scandinavia lives on into the present. Out of their total experience the three countries have developed standards of living that, with little evidence of extreme wealth or poverty, are the envy of most of their European neighbors.

The decorative instincts of Viking craftsmen ran to fanciful monsters such as this one.   315

A *twelfth-century English manuscript illustration (left) represents the beginning of a landing operation in that country by Danish raiders. The restored ninth-century Viking ship below is typical of the handsome craft employed in carrying out such invasions.*

Age of the Vikings

In the minds of many, the Viking era represents both the beginning and virtually the end of the history of the Scandinavian countries. In fact, it was neither. But the period in question, beginning about A.D. 800 and spanning two and a half centuries, is the earliest from which there are comprehensive physical remains. It is also the most widely known, if still not the most widely understood, period in Scandinavian history — one that in its wealth of color and its wide-ranging impact on the rest of Europe seems to dwarf everything that came afterward. To the west, England, Ireland, and the islands off Scotland were primary targets of invasion by these marauding mariners; England was part of the empire of two Danish kings, Canute II and Canute III, during much of the first half of the eleventh century. A party from western Norway is credited with founding the first permanent settlement in Iceland in 874; from there Vikings went on to Greenland and to attempts to colonize North America. To the south, they drove into what is now northern Germany (Schleswig-Holstein), France (where Paris came under attack from 845 to 887), and even Spain. And to the east, not only did Swedes establish settlements in the area of Estonia, Latvia, and Lithuania; they pushed on to Kiev and Novgorod — and inadvertently gave Russia its name (from the word *ruotsi*, meaning "rowing men" in Old Finnish). To navigation the Vikings gave a handsome and highly effective fighting craft, the long ship — high in prow and stern, narrow in beam, and very maneuverable. The Ladby ship, which was excavated in Fyn, Denmark, in 1935, is a noteworthy example of this seafaring legacy.

ROYAL DANISH MINISTRY FOR FOREIGN AFFAIRS

NATIONAL MUSEUM OF ANTIQUITIES, SCOTLAND

The excavation at Ladby (left) in Denmark reveals the contours of a long ship. Above is a Viking chessman unearthed in western Scotland.

The burial ground (above) near Norre Sundby, Jutland, is Denmark's largest from the Viking period. The runic stones (below) at Jelling, Jutland, stand near the oldest royal tombs.

Though the Vikings never succeeded in hewing out a lasting empire, they left their mark in many ways, both within and beyond the borders of Scandinavia. The rune stones that they carved, and the mounds containing their relics, are among the chief sources of our knowledge of these adventurers, whose preoccupation with seafaring and combat is mirrored in their remains as in their recorded deeds. A characteristic mark of Viking burial sites is a barrow with stones arranged in the form of an elongated oval to represent the outline of a ship. This pattern can be clearly discerned at the graveyard near Norre Sundby, in Danish Jutland, and it is recurrent in much of Scandinavia. Farther south in Jutland, at Jelling, are mounds believed to mark the oldest of Denmark's royal tombs: the resting places of Gorm the Old, who died about 940 as the first king of a united Denmark, and his queen, Thyre (or Thyra). At Jelling also are two of the most famous examples of runic stones. The larger, erected about 980 by Gorm's son and successor, Harold Bluetooth, is both a memorial to his parents and—as the inscription makes clear—a testament to Harold himself: "Who won . . . all Denmark and Norway and made the Danes Christians." Another thing made clear by this portion of the inscription is the gradual change within the Scandinavians themselves during the Viking era, which, contrary to popular belief, was not all pagan ritual and warfare. Recent excavation in Denmark and Norway has provided new exhibits for museums and fresh insight into the Viking way of life and death. The ship found at Ladby and another on view in Oslo were the tombs of a Danish warrior and a Norwegian queen, intended to convey them to Valhalla in the style appropriate to their station. The warrior was outfitted with full arms, a warhorse and other steeds, and hunting dogs; within the queen's ship were found the remains of a servant together with richly ornamented household furnishings and utensils. Excavation has turned up other craft built for actual travel and combat, and at the Danish sites of Fyrkat, in Jutland, and Trelleborg, in Zealand, it has uncovered the remains of Viking fortresses dating from about 1000 and notable for the mathematical exactitude of their design.

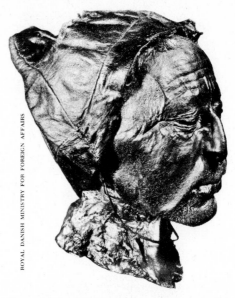

Above, the head of an Iron Age corpse found in a Danish bog. Below, a rune stone of the Viking age

Denmark

Hammershus (above), built on Bornholm's rocky coast in the thirteenth century, has been permanently Danish since 1660. Opposite are the interior of a restored Danish medieval church (top) and the massive church in Kalundborg, Zealand, designed by Esbern Snare and dating from about 1170.

Denmark's late medieval period was marked by the rise of a number of great fortified castles, whose fortunes reflected the changing pattern of the country's fortunes on both a national and international scale. Of the structures that have survived in some form, probably none is more familiar to travelers than Hammershus; surely none is more picturesque. The castle was built about the middle of the thirteenth century on the granite cliffs that form the northern coast of Bornholm, the Danish island in the Baltic Sea off the southern tip of Sweden. It was erected by Jacob Erlandsen, archbishop of Lund, for at that time Bornholm was under Swedish control, and Danish fortunes were at a low point. The end of the Viking era had seen the ambitions of Danish kings to establish strong central authority pitted against the forces of a growing aristocracy and of the Church. Waldemar I and Waldemar II emerged as strong rulers; under the latter Denmark gained dominion of the Baltic, including the important city of Lübeck and other territory in northern Germany and in Estonia. After his death in 1241, a century of national reverses followed. When Waldemar IV, last of the Estrith dynasty, assumed the crown in 1340, most of the country was under the rule of foreign princes, whom he systematically expelled. Hammershus became Danish late in the thirteenth century; in 1525 it was captured by the forces of Lübeck, then head of the powerful Hanseatic League; reverting to Denmark later in the sixteenth century, it was once more occupied briefly by the Swedes before becoming a permanent Danish possession, together with all Bornholm, in 1660. Long out of active service, the castle remains one of the stateliest ruins in northern Europe.

Christianity came to Denmark in 826 through the efforts of the Frankish missionary Anschar. But it was through the example of King Harold Bluetooth, as we have seen, that the new doctrine gained a national footing. A Saxon chronicle relates that Harold became a convert about 960 upon seeing a monk carry red-hot iron without burning his hands. Harold's son and successor, Sweyn I, reverted to paganism, but Sweyn II had founded six bishoprics and several hundred churches within Denmark and parts of present-day Sweden at the time of his death in 1075. His reign, moreover, developed a close association with the Roman Church. By the middle of the next century, monastic orders from abroad had begun to take root. Gradually the Church became secularized as its high offices and its lands passed to political noblemen. Demands for Church reform led to the introduction of the Lutheran Reformation in 1536. Meanwhile, medieval artists and architects found in churches a ready outlet for their talents. One of the most original of these was Esbern Snare, whose early-Gothic brick church stands in Kalundborg, in northwest Zealand. This fortresslike structure, built about 1170, employs a Greek cross as its ground plan.

321

Egeskov is both a Danish national monument and a private home.

Among Danish Renaissance castles, Egeskov has a rather special place: It is a manor house that is still a home rather than a museum or a picturesque ruin — a palatial home in strong contrast to the first farm dwelling that from 1405 stood on this site near the village of Kvaerndrup, in central Fyn. In 1545 Frands Brockenhuus, who built the present redbrick structure, acquired the site through marriage. A prominent military man, he secured the services of an architect, Martin Bussert, with a like background. The castle arose in the 1550's on an artificial island of piles in a small lake. Originally its access was gained through a system of drawbridges; today, long after the time when defensive measures were needed, Egeskov is still reached by way of a suspension bridge on the east and a causeway on the west. The castle has no background of historic events, but its handsome interiors reflect four centuries of very good living by a succession of wealthy owners, the most recent of whom has been Count Gregers Ahlefeldt-Bille. Though the interiors represent many styles, the castle's exterior remains virtually unchanged.

History and literature both figure prominently in an account of two great castles in the north of Zealand, Denmark's largest island. Frederiksborg, on three lakes in Hillerod, is now in fact the Museum of National History. Kronborg, which stands on the edge of the harbor of Helsingor (Elsinore) and overlooks the narrow body of water separating Denmark and southern Sweden, is the setting of Shakespeare's *Hamlet* and the scene of numerous productions of that drama. Each castle, moreover, has made history in its own right. The present Frederiksborg stands on the site of an earlier castle that was built about 1560 by King Frederick II. His son, Christian IV, was born in that structure in 1577. An international adventurer, Christian was hardly a sentimentalist at home, for he had the original castle pulled down and a new one in the Dutch Renaissance style erected on the site between 1602 and 1620. For more than two centuries Denmark's kings were crowned here, and the palace also served as their summer residence. In 1859 a disastrous fire swept through the vast edifice, sparing little in the central part except the chapel, with its early-seventeenth-century organ. Fortunately the building was restored with great care. Kronborg's strategic site and armed might dictated its early function as an instrument for collecting tolls on shipping passing through the Danish-controlled sound, the Oresund. Eric of Pomerania built the first castle here early in the fifteenth century, and parts of it are incorporated in the present one, which is another Dutch Renaissance structure; faced with gray sandstone, it was designed principally by Anton van Opbergen and erected between 1574 and 1585, also during the reign of Frederick II. Kronborg's interiors were destroyed by fire in 1629. The restored castle was sacked by Swedish forces in 1659; the period from 1785 to 1922, when it was Danish military barracks, was almost equally destructive to the interiors. The most recent restoration has attempted to make Kronborg resemble the royal residence that it, too, once was.

Frederiksborg (above) is now the Museum of National History; Kronborg is the setting of Shakespeare's Hamlet.

*Two modern Copenhagen landmarks are the har-
bor's mermaid sculpture and Tivoli (opposite).*

Landmarks achieve that status in a variety of ways, not all of which have to do
with historical events. So it is in Copenhagen with two that are probably
sought out by more travelers than all the city's other sites combined—and
that are familiar to many who have never set foot in Denmark's capital. Tivoli,
the twenty-acre amusement park and garden, and the bronze sculpture *Den
Lille Havfrue* (The Little Mermaid) in the harbor are as famous as they are
unpretentious. Tivoli stands in an area where once there were ramparts and
moats forming the fortifications along the southern boundary of the old city.
In 1843 a Danish architect and man of letters, Georg Carstensen, founded
this urban oasis, which has long outlived his own fame as a builder and writer
even among the Danes. Though the physical setting has changed somewhat
through the years, Tivoli retains the program that has made it appealing to an
unusually broad range of tastes. By day, from early May to mid-September,
it is a place in which to stroll, go boating, or relax amid pleasant surroundings.
By night, in various localities, it is a concert hall, theater, cabaret, and carnival
midway. Ballet, pantomime, and variety entertainment have long been other
staples. During the German occupation in World War II, the Glassalen, one
of Tivoli's best-known halls, was destroyed, but it has been rebuilt according
to original specifications. In the same period of unrest a bomb wrecked the
concert hall, but a new one was ready for use in 1956. With the restoration of
peace, such incidents gave way to traditional fireworks displays, and the only
military garb in evidence was that of the Tivoli Guard, a ceremonial company
of boys. The mermaid sculpture is one of the attractions along the Langelinie,
the waterside promenade of the harbor area north of Amalienborg. Edvard
Eriksen created the life-size figure, inspired by a Hans Christian Andersen
tale (or, according to some accounts, by a ballerina performing a work based
on the same story). In 1913 the sculpture was presented to the city by Carl
Jacobsen, of the family of brewers and philanthropists who have contributed
much besides beer to Copenhagen's life.

324

At right, a window in Andersen's first home looks out on one of Odense's most traveled streets. Opposite are two meccas for visitors in Copenhagen: the palace-museum Rosenborg (left) and the Børsen (stock exchange).

Odense, Denmark's third largest city, is an important center of industry and commerce, and it has a historic cathedral, Sankt Knuds Kirke, that is thought to contain the remains of the nation's patron saint, King Canute IV. To the world at large, however, the city's principal export is still the literary output of an ungainly native son who remains one of the patron saints of all who write for children; and the center of interest is the shrine established to that author, Hans Christian Andersen. The house on the Hans Jensensstraede that is now the principal building of the Andersen museum is believed to have been his birthplace (1805). It contains first editions of his writings, notably the *Fairy Tales* but including other works as well, for he was also a novelist, dramatist, poet, and writer of travel books. Frescoes by Niels Larsen Stevns depict scenes from Andersen's life. His actual belongings are represented by a top hat and an umbrella that became identified with him, and there are examples of his correspondence with Charles Dickens, who was Andersen's host in England, and Jenny Lind, one of the women with whom he cultivated a friendship that aspired to something more. The house at Munkemøllestraede 3, where Andersen spent his years from two to fourteen, is also maintained as a museum; from that abode he went to Copenhagen bent on a career in the theater. Odense's old church of Saint Hans, near Kongens Have, retains the medieval font at which Andersen was baptized.

Two of Copenhagen's monuments to the reign (1588–1648) of Christian IV now house the impressive collection of Danish crown jewels and the stock exchange. Between 1608 and 1617 Christian built the palace named Rosenborg as a country manor near the limits of Copenhagen (it is now well within the city boundaries in the western section of Kongens Have, or King's Garden). Until the nineteenth century it was a royal residence. Since 1858 it has been an important state museum, and it stands today little changed architecturally. Besides the crown jewels, Rosenborg contains the royal orb and sword, together with the belongings of individual sovereigns. If Rosenborg is the most charming of Christian IV's legacies to the capital, the Børsen (stock exchange) is the most durable. Constructed between 1619 and 1640, it is the oldest surviving commercial exchange in Europe, according to the Danes. There is a Bertel Thorvaldsen statue of Christian IV in the principal hall, but most visitors are attracted by an exterior feature that has made the Børsen a landmark: the green copper spire formed by the interlocking tails of four dragons.

Borreby Castle, which rose in 1556 and still retains its original form, is a monument to a period of great prosperity in Denmark.

The middle years of the sixteenth century, the period from which such Renaissance castles as Borreby and Egeskov date, were among Denmark's finest. Commerce thrived, and so did the Danes; Denmark was the dominant country of Scandinavia. All Norway was under its control, together with southern Sweden; every entrance to the Baltic Sea lay in Danish territory and was a source of revenue for the Danish Crown. At home all was relatively peaceful following the introduction of the Reformation and the suppression of a peasant uprising against the landed aristocracy during a three-year period (1534–36) of internal strife. From that crisis the Crown (in the person of Christian III), the nobility, and Lutheranism emerged triumphant, but not before many noble estates with their castles had been destroyed. Borreby, in southwestern Zealand just outside the Great Belt port of Skaelskor, is among the surviving castles that arose after the end of civil war. Built in 1556 by Chancellor Johan Friis, it stands today little changed from its original form. Within Skaelskor is a thirteenth-century church.

In their separate ways, Roskilde and Aarhus provide a panorama of Danish history from medieval times to the present. Roskilde, which lies on the fjord of that name in north-central Zealand, was a Viking stronghold — and since 1969 the new ship museum there has attracted thousands of visitors to its display of five restored Viking craft recently raised from the bottom of the town's busy harbor. From the last years of the Viking era to the Reformation Roskilde was also Denmark's most important bishopric. Of that aspect of its past, the most impressive monument is the Domkirke, the great cathedral of red brick begun shortly after 1170 by Archbishop Absalon as one of the successors of an original wooden church on the site built by King Harold Bluetooth about 960. The present structure's mixture of Romanesque and Gothic styles, and its many extensions in the form of chapels and porches, testify to the cathedral's continuing growth. Danish rulers from the Middle Ages to the very recent past are buried here, among them Queen Margaret, whose Kalmar Union of 1397 joined Denmark, Norway, and Sweden in a vast but uneasy alliance. At Aarhus, in Jutland, the open-air museum Den Gamle By, or Old Town, offers a cross-section of early Danish town life. Some fifty merchants' homes and workshops, assembled from throughout Denmark, are the core of this unique exhibit.

The cathedral in Roskilde (below), with its numerous extensions, houses the tombs of many Danish rulers. At Aarhus (below, right) stands a reconstructed early town.

A farm in Rjukan, Telemark (left), is near the scene of underground resistance in World War II. The Borgund stave church (opposite) bears the date 1150.

Norway

Norway's most impressive monuments are largely natural ones, which is scarcely a reflection on its people. Few lands are as spectacularly endowed scenically; historically the picture is less bright. The dream of a united Norway began at least as far back as the late ninth century, when Harold I, "the Fairhaired," deposed a band of petty rulers and drove them out of his kingdom. But the dream was only partially realized and did not outlive him: in the next four hundred years it was a reality only sporadically under a line of successors. From the time of the Kalmar Union of 1397, Norway spent the next four centuries, not very happily, under Danish rule. In 1814 Stockholm replaced Copenhagen as the seat of ultimate authority, and though another Norwegian goal, that of self-determination, became less elusive during a century of union with Sweden, it was not fully achieved until 1905. One important consequence of the long period of absentee rule is that much of Norway's history was determined elsewhere. The country is not without castles and cathedrals, but many of the most genuinely national landmarks after the Viking age are to be found outside the urban centers. Of these, perhaps none are more distinctively Scandinavian than the stave churches, which arose not long after Olaf II made Christianity the official religion of Norway. Of the hundreds built from 1050 to 1180, about twenty-five survive, the most famous one in the village of Borgund, north of Bergen. Its carved capitals and exterior portal decoration are outstanding examples of medieval art. The farms that dot this area, and others along the coasts and in deep valleys, are typically small, individually owned, and quite productive, even though less than 5 per cent of Norway's rugged and richly forested surface is under active cultivation.

OVERLEAF: *Geiranger Fjord, along the west coast, typifies Norway's scenic wonders.*
SHOSTAL

Oslo's Frogner Park (left) and Rådhus (city hall) contain work by leading contemporary artists of Norway. Much of Adolf Gustav Vigeland's career was devoted to the sculptures in Frogner Park.

Both officially and culturally, Oslo is Norway's capital, and there is a certain duality in its history as well. King Harold III, "Hard-Ruler," built a city near the present site about 1050; it thrived handsomely in the fourteenth century as the royal residence of Haakon V, who erected the fortress named Akershus in its harbor, and then as a port of the Hanseatic League. Union with Denmark brought a decline, and a fire in 1624 all but destroyed the city. With the blessing of Denmark's Christian IV, a new city arose beneath the walls of Akershus, a little to the west of the first site. (It was called Christiania after that king until 1877, then Kristiania until 1924, when the original name was reinstated.) Upon Norway's separation from Denmark in 1814, the city gained its capital status, and the nineteenth century brought both economic and cultural good fortune. The cultural legacy was largely due to Henrik Ibsen, who spent the years 1857–62 there as director of a predecessor of the present National Theater. It was not a fruitful period for Ibsen; but his plays are still a pillar of the National Theater and of all modern drama. A reconstruction of his study is one of the prized exhibits of the Folk Museum on nearby Bygdoy Peninsula. Akershus still stands. It is where Norwegian patriots were executed during the German occupation of World War II—and where, in 1945, the Nazi collaborator Vidkun Quisling was put to death. Across the harbor from this old fortress stands Oslo's newest monument, the Rådhus (City Hall), inaugurated in 1950. Its décor is decidedly historical in theme; in terms that tend toward gargantuan, Norway's contemporary artists and sculptors have sought to tell the story of the city and the nation from earliest times.

"You're not a Norwegian—you're from Bergen." That saying, not altogether appreciated by natives of the country's second city, is probably less than half true, but it does suggest something of Bergen's past, which was strongly influenced by outside forces. It also speaks well of the city's cosmopolitan air, which is not characteristic of this rugged land. Historically Bergen is very Norwegian. It was the principal residence of the country's rulers in the Middle Ages, when it was their largest city. Olaf III founded it about 1070 on the site of a bay and a splendid fjord, and at the turn of the century on the north side of the harbor there was a castle that survives to this day in altered form. About 1200 the castle was fortified; as Bergenhus, it became the hub of royal life, so it was not surprising that in the thirteenth century Haakon IV chose it to house the most lavish hall in medieval Norway. Håkonshall, as it became known, is the principal remnant of the old fort and is still one of the most visited landmarks in the country. Restored in the nineteenth century, it was rebuilt after the explosion of a German ship loaded with munitions in 1944. The sea was in other respects the lifeblood of Bergen and the source of its cosmopolitanism as well. Directly east of Bergenhus is the Hanseatic Museum, a restored part of an old quarter, formerly walled, that recalls the era from about 1300 to 1560 when the German mercantile alliance known as the Hanseatic League was Bergen's real ruler. The city's most famous church, Mariakirken, between these sites, is also associated with this "German period." Just south of the city limits is Troldhaugen, the estate of Edvard Grieg, whose music maintains Bergen's status as a summer festival center.

The picturesque waterfront of Bergen is also the most historic part of the city, formerly a port of the Hanseatic League.

Sweden

Stockholm got its start about 1250 as a trading center, with a small island, Staden, as its site and with a typical medieval fortress as its source of protection. Seven centuries and six great fires later, the city has long since outgrown the confines of the island and several adjacent ones that composed the original Stockholm. Now the capital of Sweden has the look of a very modern and well-planned metropolis, which has utilized enforced rebuilding wisely in the interest of social welfare. Fortunately the fires and urban renewal have not eradicated all traces of old Stockholm, "the city between bridges"; the network of waterways in the areas of expansion, moreover, preserved a geographical pattern that has caused Stockholm to be called the northern Venice. The original fortress (see page 339) burned in 1697 and was replaced by an equally imposing Royal Palace, where King Charles XVI Gustavus was invested in 1973. Just southeast of it is the cathedral called the Storkyrkan, which was the scene of coronations from the fourteenth century to modern times. Another landmark in Staden's northern part is the Riddarhuset, or House of Nobility, once the bastion of Swedish nobles in their struggle with the Crown for ultimate authority. And just across the bridge from Staden, on Riddarholm Island, stands Riddarholms Kyrkan, long the burial place of Swedish monarchs. A bridge just north of the Royal Palace leads to the Riksdagshuset, the seat of Sweden's bicameral Parliament.

Many of Stockholm's landmarks are part of its original island. Among them is the Royal Palace (foreground, right).

The lion insignia at upper right is from the restored man-of-war Vasa *on the Stockholm harbor. The historic marketplace Stortorget (above) witnessed a massacre in 1520.*

Vasa, a name long sacred to the Swedes, has special ties to Stockholm. The story of Scandinavian history from late medieval times to the seventeenth century was that of a struggle to upset Danish dominance. Unlike Norway, Sweden was able to make a successful early challenge, and the event that galvanized the country into action took place in Stortorget, the marketplace of old Stockholm, in 1520. This was the mass execution of more than a hundred Swedish nobles, clerics, and merchants, a grisly side show to the coronation of Denmark's Christian II as king of Sweden upon his conquest of the Swedes. A year later Sweden's Gustavus I (Gustavus Vasa) led an uprising that drove Christian from the country. In 1628 a Swedish man-of-war named the *Vasa*, after Gustavus, sank on her maiden voyage near the mouth of Stockholm harbor. Raised in 1961, she is now a prized exhibit on the city's waterfront.

337

Drottningholm, the stately palace on the island of Lovo in Lake Malar, just outside Stockholm, is the principal summer residence of the Swedish royal family, and its construction was a family project as well. Work was begun in 1662 by Nicodemus Tessin the elder, on the site of an earlier suburban palace dating from 1581; it was completed about 1700 by his son Nicodemus, principal baroque master of northern Europe. Both attained the post of royal architect, and the Royal Palace on Stockholm's original island is also the creation of the younger Tessin. Drottningholm's richly decorated interiors and its park and principal outbuilding, a rococo pavilion decorated in Chinese style, have caused it to be likened to Versailles. Sweden became an absolute monarchy during the reign of Charles XI (1660–97), but most of his successors in the century that followed found the job less than fully rewarding, owing principally to the intrigues of factions of nobles who, when they were not fighting among themselves along pro-Russian and anti-Russian lines, opposed their own kings. One exception to the rule, at least for a time, had particular ties to Drottningholm. Gustavus III, who proclaimed a new constitution in 1772 after surrounding the House of Nobility with loyal artillery, developed the court theater of the palace into the jewel it remains today. A poet and playwright himself, Gustavus founded the Swedish Academy and did much for the arts in general. A conspiracy of the aristocrats he opposed finally ended his life, but the story of his assassination in 1792 at a midnight masquerade lingers on as the plot of Verdi's opera A Masked Ball. Drottningholm's theater retains the stage machinery designed by Gustavus.

When it was finally destroyed by fire in 1697, Stockholm's original fortress-palace, Tre Kroner (Three Crowns), had been the center of Swedish affairs for almost four and a half centuries. By common consent its founder, Birger of Bjälbo, is today credited with having built the city as well. Certain it is that he was the ruler of Stockholm, and of all Sweden, throughout the years of a forceful regency (1250–66), during which the foundations of the nation's industry, commerce, and legal system were laid. Among Tre Kroner's most illustrious royal tenants thereafter were Gustavus I, founder of the Vasa dynasty, and his grandson Gustavus II (Gustavus Adolphus), under whom Sweden prospered at home while reaching the height of its ascendancy as a European power. Gustavus Adolphus was succeeded by his daughter Christina in 1632, and if the old palace did not shine as brightly as a center of international affairs during her reign, until 1654, it was far from dull in other respects. When she abdicated as a convert to Rome and Catholicism, she had established a Swedish precedent for royal patronage of the arts and sciences—and for a code of liberated womanhood that was at least three centuries ahead of its time.

Drottningholm (shown opposite), on Stockholm's outskirts, contains one of Scandinavia's most famous theaters. The painting above depicts Christina's entry into Rome following her abdication; the one below is of Stockholm's former fortress-palace.

Gotland, Sweden's main offshore possession in the Baltic Sea, has a maximum width of thirty-one miles and approximately four times that number of churches, many of which are still in active service. Since the island's population is just over fifty thousand, the statistics speak well both of the religious habits of its residents and of the workmanship of the builders, for virtually all these structures date from the Middle Ages. Gotland and its capital, Visby, are in many respects the essence of medieval Scandinavia, a fact that may explain their recent resurgence as tourist centers after centuries of neglect. The island was a gateway for trade between Russia and the north, and it is not surprising to find Visby among the principal outposts of the old Hanseatic League. Nor was it out of keeping with Scandinavian history that Sweden and Denmark quarreled over Gotland, which was nominally Swedish from the ninth to the fourteenth century and Danish until 1645, when the Swedes regained control of what was, by then, rich only in tradition. In one of its most colorful eras, the first half of the fifteenth century, the island was a pirate stronghold. Between 1439 and 1449 it was the base of Eric of Pomerania; having been deposed as king by Denmark, Sweden, and Norway in turn, he capped a remarkable career by becoming a freebooter without royal license.

Stånga Church (above) is one of the best examples of the religious structures that have made Sweden's island of Gotland famous. At right is Saint Katarina, one of the ruined churches of Visby, on Gotland.

340

Visby offers one of the best examples of medieval town atmosphere in all Sweden, notwithstanding its rediscovery by modern tourists. In the eternal contest between commercialization and historical integrity, Gotland's capital has managed to have much of the best of both worlds, new and old; it is thriving once more, after a long period of decline, but the prosperity has done no appreciable harm to its character. The old town, which first attracted international attention in the twelfth century when German merchants became aware of its commercial possibilities, is still surrounded on all but its harbor side by a stone wall with some forty towers. Within, timbered houses and old shops line the narrow streets; not surprisingly, in view of Visby's past as a Hanseatic center, many of the best-preserved buildings have mercantile associations. Christianity reached Gotland a century ahead of the Hansa traders (much earlier Visby had been a pagan religious center), and competing for interest with secular structures are more than a dozen churches in varying stages of disrepair. Still in use is the Domkyrkan, the cathedral of Saint Mary, founded in 1225. Among the most famous ruins are those of Saint Katarina, originally a Franciscan abbey; Saint Nikolai, part of a Dominican monastery; and Helgeandskyrkan, all from the thirteenth century. Nearby the Gotland Museum traces the island's past from the Stone Age to its medieval days of glory, when Visby was an independent republic, prior to the Hanseatic affiliation, and author of an early international code of maritime law. Coins minted by the former republic are among the exhibits of the museum.

Visby, Gotland's capital, is known as the city of ruins and roses. A medieval wall still surrounds the oldest section.

Three examples of churches in the more remote areas of Sweden are those at Kiruna (above); at Rattvik (below), in Dalarna, still surrounded by stables; and at Gothem (opposite), on Gotland. The famous clock that rises to the height of one wall in the medieval cathedral of Lund is depicted at right.

Sweden's conversion to Christianity came about between the ninth and eleventh centuries, principally through the work of German and English missionaries. Even then, especially in the more remote areas, the old Norse pagan deities retained their hold on large segments of the population, and it was not until 1529, during the reign of Gustavus I, that Lutheranism became the state doctrine. Uppsala and Visby, among the major centers of pre-Christian Sweden, still preserve many interesting relics of their pagan past. As in Norway, some of the most striking examples of Swedish Christian churches are to be found off the beaten track pursued by the rank and file of tourists. Many visitors to Gotland never get beyond Visby, but those who venture on to Gothem find a thirteenth-century place of worship with a valuable collection of paintings of that period. The great iron-mining center, Kiruna, in Sweden's mountainous north, has a Lapp church from the same century containing some rare examples of medieval sculpture. Local color also abounds in the central province of Dalarna, near the Norwegian border; old-world costume and customs are preserved, and peasant dress is still worn by many parishioners of the famous white church in Rattvik, whose murals tell much of Dalarna's history. (It was there that the Swedish revolt against the Danes, led by Gustavus I, originated in 1521.) Sweden's great cathedrals are to be found in the urban centers of Stockholm, Goteborg, Uppsala, Lund, and Linkoping, where in 1598 King Sigismund III was thwarted in his attempt to reintroduce Roman Catholicism into the country. Lund's thirteenth-century Romanesque structure contains an astronomical clock, rising to the height of one wall, which records the positions of heavenly bodies.

Alvsborg, represented above in a drawing of 1502, was one of the castles on Sweden's west coast that became targets of Danish invasions. The medieval castle in Kalmar (opposite, top) has been restored and is a museum; the one in Kungalv (opposite, bottom) survives as a ruin.

Sweden's castles stretch from Stockholm in the east to Goteborg in the west, dotting its coasts and serving as repositories of its history, to which they contributed much. Some are now museums; others are ruins that seem part of another world. Down the coast of the Baltic at Kalmar, in the southeast, stands one of the most historic of all, a handsome twelfth-century structure once known as the key of Sweden. Within is a hall thought to have been the site of the ratification of the Kalmar Union of 1397. This was the confederation of the three major Scandinavian powers, intended to guarantee "eternal and unbroken peace" among them but destined to maintain a shaky truce for little more than fifty years. The castle was the scene of more than twenty encounters between the Swedes and Danes. Gustavus I of Sweden rebuilt it in the sixteenth century; thereafter it housed a distillery, a granary, and then a prison. Since 1880 it has been one of Sweden's major historical museums. Offshore, on the nearby island of Oland, are the ruins of Borgholm Castle and Gråborg Fortress, both from the Middle Ages. To an even greater degree, the remaining castles of the west coast, facing Denmark, figure in the long history of the Danish-Swedish struggle for control of southern Sweden. Malmo's moated fortress, Malmohus, was begun in 1434 and rebuilt a century later. For many years it served as a prison as well; between 1567 and 1573, as a Danish possession, it was a place of confinement for the earl of Bothwell, third husband of Mary queen of Scots, after his flight to the Continent. Now Malmohus, too, is a museum. A citadel tower called Kärnan is all that remains of a famous twelfth-century fortified castle in Halsingborg, but the fortress New Alvsborg, erected about 1650, still stands at the port entrance of Goteborg. A short distance to the north, outside Kungalv, are the imposing remains of a fortress dating from 1307, when the site marked the frontiers of Sweden, Denmark, and Norway.

Germany, Austria, and Switzerland

*G*ermany and Austria are sometimes referred to, either separately or together, as the heartland of Europe. Both lands entered the pages of recorded history with the Roman invasions of the first century B.C. From the time of Augustus to that of Diocletian, Rome's natural line of defense in northern Europe followed the two great rivers that flow through Germany and Austria, the Rhine and the Danube. As Roman power declined, outlandish tribes from beyond those rivers overran virtually the entire Western empire and reshaped it to their own purposes. In the eighth century the great Charlemagne, from his Frankish headquarters at Aachen in what is now Germany, forged a new empire that comprised most of continental Europe and became known as the Holy Roman Empire. But his grandiose scheme for imperial unification died with him. Within a few generations after his death the huge empire he had so laboriously pieced together was already a shambles as contending factions strove to carve out of it separate and autonomous areas of power and influence. Ironically, Germany was one of the last of those areas to develop into a consolidated national state. It was not until 1871, following the Franco-Prussian War, that the German Empire was proclaimed in the Hall of Mirrors at Versailles, with William I as emperor. Since then, of course, Germany has been split asunder once again as an aftermath of World War II, with its western portion facing the Iron Curtain, which separates it from East Germany and the Communist world at large. As a result of that war, many of Germany's large cities with their historic monuments were left in ruins. Austria, Germany's German-speaking neighbor, was once a province of Charlemagne's realm. Two centuries later it was joined to a revivified Holy Roman Empire. Before the end of the thirteenth century Austria had come firmly under the control of the Hapsburgs, the ruling family of the nation from 1282 until 1918. This dynasty developed an empire (largely through shrewd intermarriages) that by the sixteenth century covered a large part of central and southern Europe—and indeed, under the Flemish-born Charles V, an empire that encircled the globe. Relatively small as the country was, Austria constituted the fulcrum of that vast multinational domain. In the eighteenth century it was still the dominating influence in the Confederation of German States, but Prussia then successfully challenged it and assumed that role. Today Austria remains a neutral buffer between the blocs of the Atlantic alliance and the Warsaw Pact. Switzerland was also introduced to recorded history by the Romans. Bordering both Germany and Austria, this mountainous land early had fallen to the Franks; in 1033 it was also brought within the Holy Roman Empire. However, it became a first-rate military power in its own right and by 1499 had won virtual independence, a matter that was formally settled in 1648. Subsequently, its policy of neutrality has served it well. It remains one of the most beautiful countries in the world—a picturesque land of long-settled tranquillity.

The fairy-tale mountaintop castle of Neuschwanstein, built for King Ludwig II of Bavaria

German Beginnings

East of the Rhine and north of the Danube the Roman Empire never held sway. This is probably the most important single fact in the history of German civilization. Yet it is oddly misleading. It suggests that Germany has become what it is because it knew nothing of Rome's laws or its decadent civilization. The truth is more subtle and more interesting. The fact is, the *idea* of the Roman Empire would prove more enthralling to the German people who never felt its rule than it ever would to those who had. From the moment they entered history, the barbaric German tribes defined themselves in essentially Roman terms. Perpetually at war with each other, the Germanic tribesmen recognized no common bond except the brute fact that they stood outside the empire. The very name of one of the greatest Germanic tribes, the Franks, simply meant "free of the Romans," while the word *deutsch*, the German word for things German, once meant non-Latin speech. Everywhere Rome's majestic presence was felt keenly, for even on its Germanic frontier Rome meant more than a thin line of fortifications. These in time the Germanic tribes would overrun and obliterate. What they did not obliterate, what they soon learned to cherish, were the Roman cities that the empire had established on what was soon to become Germanic soil. These cities, with their links to Rome's ancient glory, would exercise power in German affairs far beyond their wealth and size, suggesting how deeply the imperial idea had bitten into the German soul.

At Trier, once a Roman city, Emperor Constantine built the Porta Nigra (opposite). The figure of a wine ship (below) recalls the days when Roman galleys plied the Moselle. Trier's St. Matthias Church (bottom) holds the only tomb of an Apostle north of the Alps.

Among Germany's Roman cities, Trier, on the Moselle River, bears the deepest impress of ancient Rome. Founded by Augustus Caesar himself, it was known as Augusta Treverorum after a local Celtic tribe, the Treveri, whom Julius Caesar had vanquished. Trier was never a mere garrison town. With its forum, its amphitheater, and its baths — the third largest in the entire empire — Trier was like an arm of the Mediterranean world reaching into the transalpine heartland and bringing with it no less a Mediterranean sight than Roman galleys for shipping the wines of the Moselle. When he divided the Roman Empire into four administrative units in the third century, Diocletian made Trier the capital of the northern provinces and a partner of Rome itself in the rule of the Western empire. Not until Germanic tribes began to grow menacing early in the fourth century did Constantine the Great order Trier to erect a city wall. The wall's magnificent arcaded gateway, the Porta Nigra (so called because of the dark patina that has formed on its limestone blocks), still stands as the first Roman relic in all of Germany. It was Constantine who brought Christianity to Trier, which became the seat of a bishop as early as 314. Even when the Western empire collapsed and the Franks captured the city, Trier remained what it had always been — a city linked to empire. Under the later Holy Roman Empire, the archbishop of Trier was one of the seven powerful elector-princes who chose the German emperors for almost a millennium (along with the archbishop of Cologne, another Roman city, originally known as Colonia Agrippinensis in honor of Claudius's wife). Trier holds yet another link to the Mediterranean past. The reliquary of Saint Matthias Church contains the only tomb of an Apostle located north of the Alps. Not until Otto von Bismark forged a modern German nation under the hegemony of faraway Prussia did Germany's ancient Roman cities lose their long-lasting significance. Yet the mark of the Roman Empire still remains upon Germany. When Martin Luther's Protestant Reformation swept over Germany, it was precisely the old Romanized portions of the country that remained loyal to the Church of Rome.

A small 9th-century bronze statue (left) depicts Charlemagne in the garb of a Frankish king. Charlemagne's chapel at Aachen (opposite), capital of his empire, was consecrated by Pope Leo III in 805. It is alleged that Charlemagne's talisman (below) contains a fragment of the true cross.

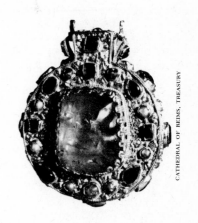

Of all the great men of European history only one is the hero of both the French and the Germans. That hero is Karl der Grosse, better known as Charlemagne, the Frankish king who singlehandedly established a civilized empire and a uniform government across a brutalized and war-torn Europe. Tall, handsome, eloquent, and genial, Charlemagne was the wonder of the age, a great military leader who sought not personal victory, but the triumph of civilization itself. During his forty-three-year reign, which began in 768, the intransigent Saxon chiefs were converted to Christianity, the Roman towns of the Rhineland were revived, schools were established, Latin learning promoted, and Germanic tribes rendered subservient, for the first time, to civil government. When Pope Leo III crowned Charlemagne "emperor of the Romans" in 800 and draped the purple cloak of the Caesars over his broad Frankish shoulders, he was merely giving formal recognition to what many had already recognized: that in Charlemagne the Western empire had found its second Augustus, and the Roman Church its second Constantine. To strengthen his links with ancient Rome Charlemagne made his capital at Aachen, or Aquis Granum, as its Roman founders called it. He modeled his imperial chapel after the octagonal Byzantine church at Ravenna, the imperial chapel of the last ancient emperors of the West, and even used marble from that church in its construction. Yet Charlemagne's imperium was essentially a personal tour de force. Forty years after his death in 814, the empire existed only as a cherished ideal. For the Germanic peoples especially it would stand out as a beacon of light for many long centuries to come. It is due to the influence of Charlemagne, bringer of law to the tribes of Germania, that the German word *reich* has the double meaning of "law" and "empire."

As long as Germanic kings sought the authority of Roman emperors, the tiny Rhineland town of Worms played an outsize role in the Germanic world. A Roman city as early as 16 B.C., Worms became, by turns, the capital of a short-lived Burgundian kingdom, the residence of Frankish kings, and the city whence Charlemagne launched his historic expedition against the pagan Saxons. When the Franks lost interest in empire, and one of those selfsame Saxons, Otto the Great, took up the imperial task—Otto was crowned in Rome in 962—Worms remained true to its past. Its bishops espoused the emperor's cause, not only against his lay enemies, but against the papacy as well, which gives to the name of Worms's cathedral, Saint Peter's, a somewhat ironic ring. In 1150 Worms reaped the reward for its fealty—the emperor Henry V made it the first free imperial city, free, that is, of vassalage to a feudal lord. Worms's bishops were given the rank of imperial princes and made territorial rulers in their own right, a privilege they enjoyed until Napoleon's armies finally put finis to the Holy Roman Empire. Above all, Worms was the site of some of the most critical events in the history of the Church. It was at Worms that the emperor in 1076 made his historic effort to depose a pope. It was at Worms that the great men of the age tried to determine once and for all the proper division of authority between the empire and the papacy. Finally it was at Worms that the unity of Christendom was sundered. The occasion was the Imperial Diet of Worms convened by Emperor Charles V in 1521 to hear Martin Luther publicly recant his doctrines. Before an assembly of the mighty, Luther spoke his immortal words: "Here I stand. I can act in no other way. God help me. Amen." When the emperor, sitting at Worms, ordered Luther banned from the empire and his works destroyed, the split between papacy and Protestantism was complete.

Worms

The Romanesque cathedral of Worms (opposite), begun in the year 1000, looms up like a forbidding citadel. The leonine sculpture at upper left sits on a window ledge of the cathedral. The detail above, from an altar by Lucas Cranach, shows Luther preaching with an open Bible in front of him.

Heidelberg, below, is Germany's oldest university town. Above is the students' mess hall. A 19th-century illustration, opposite, shows a group of students frolicking.

All the elements of the German university idyll can be found in various mixtures in the university towns of Göttingen, Tübingen, and Heidelberg. For the aristocratic element there is Göttingen, founded in 1737 by George II, king of England and Elector of Hanover, largely for the sons of English and Hanoverian aristocrats. Their academic interests are well attested by one of the university's early features — a vast riding academy for instruction in the equestrian arts. The student body notwithstanding, Göttingen's professor of astronomy after 1807 was Karl Friedrich Gauss, one of the supreme geniuses in the history of mathematics. For a rich medieval atmosphere there is Tübingen, whose narrow, crooked streets border the Neckar River, where students have been going rowing at night in lantern-lit boats since the university was founded in 1477. Some of Tübingen's students took their lectures seriously, for in the honor roll of the university's students stands Georg Hegel, one of the world's greatest philosophers. For roistering there is Heidelberg, downstream from Tübingen on the Neckar and, dating from 1386, the oldest of German universities. Until 1914 Heidelberg operated a special student jail for excessively boisterous scholars, who inevitably considered incarceration a badge of honor. With its superb ruined castle on a nearby knoll, its meandering country footpaths, and its compact old town, venerable Heidelberg is the ultimate source and model for the romantic idyll of university life that Germany's universities, austere in themselves, have given to the world.

University Towns

Compared to the universities of other European countries, those of Germany are comparatively new, yet in no other European country have the universities played so prominent a role or appealed so deeply to the popular imagination. The great thinkers of Germany were, to a notable extent, men who served as university professors. The fight for liberty and equality in Germany was led, to a remarkable degree, by Germany's nineteenth-century university students, rallying under the banner of "Freedom and the Fatherland." When Germany was still a mere geographic term, German science and scholarship were drawing a great stream of students from abroad to Germany's universities. But this is not all that the universities have meant to Germany. They have provided the culture with a certain picture, or model, of romantic happiness. The figures in the picture are young, clean-limbed students, well-born, as most German university students have been, or even members of the nobility, as so many of them were. The setting is a university town with narrow medieval streets, gabled houses, and deep, dim rathskellers. There are roistering, sweet comradeship and gay spirits — youth playing an enviable role in an idyll of carefree youth. The picture is, of course, idealized, but it is not a mere fancy. The university towns of Germany have been truly idyllic places for numberless generations of university students. German university life thus has two very sharply contrasted aspects. One is the university itself, with its lofty professors and its austere lecture system. On the other hand there is the student body, which "went to lectures, made notes and read textbooks, but never pretended to take their professors seriously," to quote Henry Adams, who attended a German university after being graduated from Harvard in 1858. "Within a day or two," Adams reported, "he was running around with the rest to beer-cellars and music halls and dance-rooms."

German Heartland

Below is Peddler on Horseback, *a 19th-century caricature of the house of Rothschild. The placard on the horse reads: "Traveling Salesman for Merchants, makes deals in all branches of commerce." Goethe's boyhood study is illustrated at the right, below.*

For centuries Germany's Holy Roman Emperors took the Italian half of their imperium more seriously than its Germanic half. Not until the fourteenth century, and then largely due to weakness, did they begin to resist the lure of Italy and become, in effect, more Germanic. That trend accounts, in part, for the historic luster of Frankfurt-am-Main, a riverside town that owed its vitality not to a Roman foundation but to its position as a center of trade and transport: the city's very name, "Frank's ford," reveals its strategic situation. In the reviving commerce between the cities of Italy and the Netherlands, Frankfurt became a way station, a place where local currencies were exchanged, merchandise stored, and trade fairs held. It is the mark of the burgher spirit of Frankfurt that when Frederick Barbarossa, one of the greatest of Germany's emperors, built an imperial palace in the town early in the twelfth century, the citizenry let it decay and then turned it into a house for Dutch clothing merchants. Frankfurt's historic indifference to the faction-ridden politics of empire and its lack of links to ancient Rome gave it a useful neutrality in the waning days of the empire. In 1356 the city was made the permanent site of imperial elections, the final choice taking place in the elector's chapel in the church of Saint Bartholomew, the city's cathedral. The honor—to which was later added the distinction of being the coronation city as well—never sapped Frankfurt's adamant spirit of municipal independence. When the powerful Count Palatine tried to usurp the city's liberties in the 1380's, the people of Frankfurt fought and defeated him in pitched battle without benefit of help from the emperor.

Only a small fragment of medieval Frankfurt can be seen in the city today. This is the tight cluster of gabled burghers' houses, some dating back to the fourteenth century, known collectively as the Romer. To the people of Frankfurt, the Romer is the true emblem of the city's historic glory, and when it was destroyed in World War II they meticulously reconstructed it. In his boyhood Frankfurt's greatest son and Germany's greatest poet, Johann von Goethe, used to prowl the lanes of the Romer so assiduously that he said it was "as familiar to him as a mousehole." The house where Goethe grew up lies a few hundred yards from the Romer and also has been meticulously restored since the war. Goethe was at the height of his fame in 1806, when the dissolution of the Holy Roman Empire rid his birthplace of its imperial incumbrance and Frankfurt began to fulfill its older, preimperial destiny. Under the aegis of one of its humblest families, that of Nathan Amschel Rothschild, the city became the leading banking center on the Continent. By order of the Congress of Vienna it became the capital of an independent republic and remained so until Prussia put a final end to its municipal liberties.

A group of burghers' homes, above, part of the Romer, in Frankfurt, are meticulous reconstructions replacing fourteenth-century houses destroyed in World War II. As an active medieval trading center, Frankfurt was served by the bordering River Main, shown below.

There was a time when Ulm, a smallish town on the upper Danube River, was the third largest city in Germany, its population surpassed only by ancient Cologne and energetic Lübeck, on the Baltic Sea. This was at the end of the fifteenth century, when the townspeople of Ulm ceased work forever on their vast unfinished Gothic cathedral and left its principal spire a squared-off ungainly trunk. The reason they did so goes to the heart of the history of the time. Cathedral building is an immense undertaking, which draws not only on vast quantities of municipal wealth, but on deep reservoirs of religious faith. In 1377, when the foundation stones of Ulm's cathedral were laid, the city plainly had an abundance of both, for its leaders designed their church on a scale surpassed in Germany only by Cologne's cathedral. As late as 1469 they commissioned the finest wood carver in the country, Jorg Syrkin the Elder, to furnish the cathedral with choir stalls that remain virtually without peer. Ulm was still prosperous in 1500—indeed it was still a common saying that Ulm's money ruled the world. What Ulm had lost, what Germany was fast losing as heresy and anticlericalism spread across the land late in the fifteenth century, was the other essential ingredient in cathedral building: a devotion to the glory of God matched by trust in His ecclesiastical agents.

Crowning Ulm's cathedral (right) is a 528-foot Gothic tower, the tallest church spire in the world. The choir stall of the church (opposite), with its figures of Christian saints and heroes from the Old Testament, is a masterpiece of fifteenth-century wood carving. The astronomical clock opposite adorns the city's town hall.

Politics, too, played a part in Ulm's decision to call a halt to cathedral building. If France by 1500 was rapidly becoming the "nation par excellence," then Germany was already the antination par excellence. The ruin of the empire was complete: its administrative offices had become hereditary fiefdoms, its writs mere pieces of paper ignored at will by the various dukes, landgraves, margraves, and other hereditary landed magnates, who divided the once-formidable German Empire into two hundred forty separate autonomous states. Anarchy and dissension had become the endemic condition of Germany as lords fought against lords while oppressing and virtually enslaving their peasants. Above all, the nobles menaced the wealth and independence of the sixty-six free imperial cities, including Ulm, which successive Holy Roman Emperors had by then created in their desperate search for allies to counterbalance the hereditary landowners. At the very moment when the rising monarchies of France and England had triumphed over feudalism, a debased feudalism in Germany had triumphed over monarchy. In the prevailing disorder, Germany's cities were islands of peace and safety, but only as long as they remained strong—their citizens united, their governments well conducted, and their civic patriotism keen. When they abandoned work on their great incomplete church, the townspeople of Ulm did not cease to build. At the beginning of the sixteenth century in fact, they erected a new Renaissance-style town hall, as if to provide visible proof to all that Ulm was determined to take care of itself in a world in which a once-mighty empire had collapsed and a once-unchallenged Church was tottering with rot. Not until 1890 was Ulm's cathedral completed, but it was a municipal project no longer. The cathedral's superb, soaring spire owes its existence almost entirely to the king of Prussia and the government of Bismarckian Germany.

Charity homes for the poor of Augsburg (above) were built in 1519 by Jakob Fugger the Rich. The exuberantly rococo loggia at top is part of Nymphenburg Palace, a former summer home of Bavaria's rulers. A cascade of water towers over the formal gardens of the Linderhof (opposite), the lavish Alpine retreat completed in 1879 by Bavaria's King Ludwig II, whose private hobby was the construction of dream palaces.

Germany has been either ahead of or behind its neighbors, but almost never in step. In 1519 Jakob Fugger, the great banking magnate of Augsburg, put Germany ahead. Out of compassion for the poor of the ancient city (Augsburg was founded by Rome in 15 B.C.), he built a residential enclosure of neat dwellings to house some of the city's needy. The first such charitable institution in the world, the Fuggerei is still administered according to its founder's rules, one of which is the residents' obligation to pray for the soul of Jakob Fugger the Rich. The poor peasants of the countryside were never so fortunate, for in the realms of Germany's princelings backwardness was a way of life. Just when absolutist monarchy was being called into question in France, the petty potentates of Germany began sedulously aping the worst aspects of the regime of Louis XIV—its extravagance, its parasitic court, its sheer indifference to the plight of the humble. When the ruler of Bavaria turned his Italianate summer villa, the Nymphenburg Palace, into a rococo imitation Versailles, he started a trend that soon swept across Germany. Despite the size of their tiny domains, virtually every German ruler began trying to duplicate the Sun King's splendor, quickly establishing a contrast between overprivileged rulers and their underprivileged subjects that was more cruelly conspicuous in Germany than anywhere else precisely because its kingdoms were so small. In Bavaria the aping of Louis XIV reached an apogee of sorts almost a hundred fifty years after the French king had died. At that time Bavaria's king Ludwig II began building extravagant palaces as a personal hobby. He built, by turns, a replica of a feudal castle, a replica of Versailles, and a rococo dream palace, the Linderhof, whose formal gardens form a superbly incongruous contrast to their wild alpine setting.

Nuremberg's greatest son, Albrecht Dürer (his house is at right), depicted the dancing peasants above in 1514. Below, a 1493 woodcut portrays Nuremberg during its heyday.

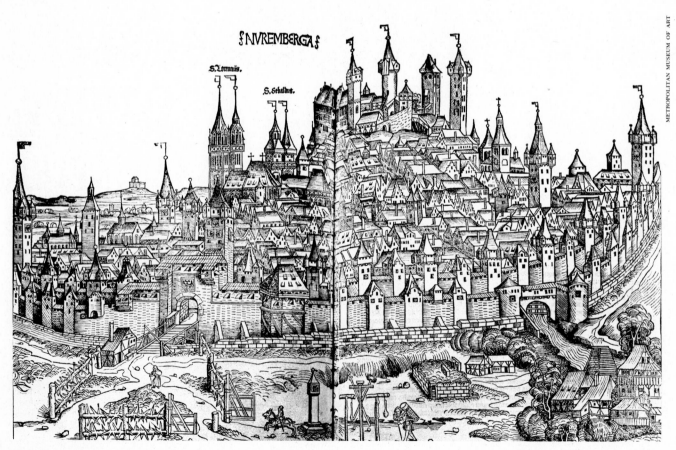

Of all the cities of medieval Germany, Nuremberg was the loveliest, and of all the cities of contemporary Germany, modern Nuremberg, with its venerable ramparts still standing, remains the most medieval. No ancient glory hallows the sandy plain on which it stands. The very name "Nuremberg" was not mentioned in an official document until 1050, making it an upstart among historic German cities. At that, what was mentioned was not the town but the then newly built imperial castle, or Kaiserburg, a towering citadel that still looks down domineeringly on the old medieval city center. The presence of that castle made Nuremberg one of those free imperial cities whose fealty to the emperor was more than nominal. It took true burgher tenacity to persuade Germany's emperors finally to surrender their claims on the city. The town fathers were not truly triumphant until 1415, when the emperor formally ceded the citadel to the town. After that, its independence secured, Nuremberg began to look more and more like a pearl ensconced in a crusty shell. The shell was the double line of ramparts, twenty-two feet high, that the town began building in 1345 and that, even after its completion in 1452, the citizenry kept on augmenting for two centuries more. To strengthen the city's defenses after the introduction of gunpowder into warfare, stone towers were erected to enable the city's defenders to enfilade an enemy bold enough to attempt an attack. With more than a hundred such towers piercing the sky, Nuremberg, by the end of the fifteenth century, had become a city of spiky stone spires. Yet within the fortresslike city a most unwarlike spirit prevailed, for Nuremberg was Germany's greatest cultural center. That was the pearl within the shell. Nuremberg, in a sense, was a manufacturing town, but what it chiefly manufactured were works of art. Nuremberg's bronze casters, its sculptors, its goldsmiths, its altar painters, and its cabinetmakers provided art and ornament for all Germany. Its great guild of mastersingers, led by Hans Sachs, provided music for all Germany. And when a Hungarian goldsmith decided to settle in Nuremberg, he gave the city its chance to raise, and one of the city's master artists the opportunity to train, the greatest artistic genius Germany has ever produced—Albrecht Dürer, who was born in the city in 1471 and set up his own studio there in 1494 as a member in good standing of Nuremberg's Society of Artists. When he returned to Germany from a long sojourn in Venice Dürer almost singlehandedly brought the Italian High Renaissance back with him. In doing so, ironically, he contributed to the rapid decline of painting in his native city. Other northern artists, more responsive to the new currents, would rob the guild-protected painters of Nuremberg of their former prominence. Yet Dürer himself spent the last twenty years of his life in the city, in a gabled house hard by the city walls. No major catastrophe ever shook Nuremberg to its core, but two great national calamities darkened the city's life. The horrors of the Thirty Years' War brought an end to the city's preeminence and initiated its slow decline during the eighteenth century. The second calamity was Hitler and his decision to make Nuremberg the site of the Nazi party's mammoth annual rallies. Perhaps it was the bitter memory of those rallies and the wish to preserve far better ones that inspired the people of Nuremberg, after World War II, to restore their war-torn medieval buildings more thoroughly and more extensively than any other German city has done.

The "Beautiful Fountain," right, at Nuremberg, built in the 14th century

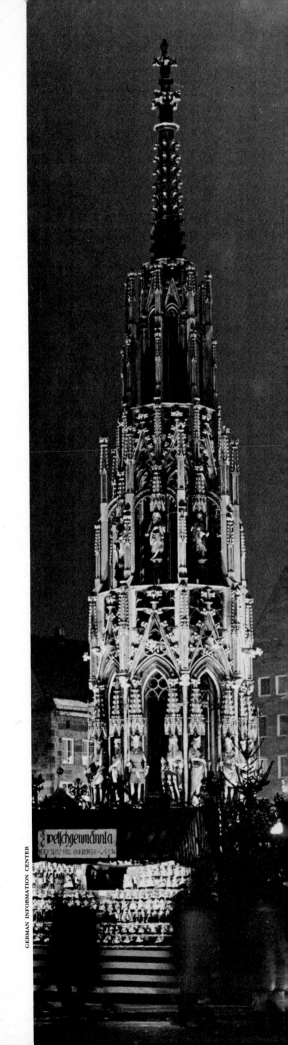

Aspects of Rothenburg: below, a blacksmith's house; right, the town hall's Gothic tower

Every year on Whitsunday and Monday the twelve thousand citizens of Rothenburg ob der Tauber celebrate the central event in the town's long but historically nugatory existence. The event thus memorialized is a perfect symbol of Rothenburg, for it concerns something that did not happen: the nonrazing of the town by the Imperial General Tilly, champion of the Catholic cause—a boon he granted the stout Protestants of the city after capturing it during the Thirty Years' War. Since then, when nothing happened, nothing else has happened in Rothenburg. It figured not at all in the plans of emperors, the strategies of warlords, the designs of industrial developers, or the targetings of aerial bombardiers. As a result, Rothenburg has become a priceless and enthralling historical relic. It is a town that looks today almost exactly as it did four hundred years ago—a chunk of sixteenth-century Germany, neither restored nor reconstructed but simply preserved through the general blessing of historical inconsequence and the particular mercy of the count of Tilly. Nature, too, conspired in Rothenburg's favor. Back in the eleventh century it was burdened with the perilous status of an imperial stronghold, with a mighty citadel consisting of the linked castles of an emperor and a count. In 1356, however, an earthquake leveled them both, leaving only a chapel and a gateway, which stand to this day, and erasing the town from the list of places that mattered. Breathing a great sigh of relief, the good people of the town set about their principal business, serving as a market for the local farmers. In 1540 the town joined the Protestant Reformation and there history ended for Rothenburg, snug behind its curving ramparts, which the citizenry had completed in the fourteenth century.

PHOTO RESEARCHERS – FRITZ HENLE

At left, Rothenburg's 600-year-old ramparts; below, a view of the town's tiled rooftops

PETER ARNOLD

Late in the eighteenth century French and English travelers grown weary of the rationalism of the age discovered the charms of backward, slumbering Germany, and what charmed them can still be seen in Rothenburg: a way of life resolutely resistant to straight lines, endless vistas, and rigid, mechanical rationality. The walls of Rothenburg are curved and describe the outline of a wine goblet. The streets are irregular and unpredictable; steep-roofed burgher homes have lined their edges since the Gothic age. Womblike, the town looks inward, intent upon its own communal life. Characteristically, Rothenburg's most prominent building is the town hall, and just as characteristically that building is a historical medley, consisting of a Gothic portion (with dungeons in the cellar) topped by a fourteenth-century belfry and supplemented by a Renaissance wing. With a fine sense of history and fine disregard for rigid consistency, Rothenburg has built its churches in the Gothic style—apogee of religious architecture—and its secular buildings in the Renaissance style—apogee of civic architecture. Treasuring its own continuity the people of Rothenburg have been preserving relics of its history almost from the beginning of its history. When they tore down the oldest city wall in the thirteenth century, for example, the town fathers saw fit to preserve a portion of it to keep its memory alive. The spirit of little Rothenburg actually lies at the heart of German thought even in its highest reaches. When German philosophers began elaborating a fundamental distinction between the aridity of civilization and the richness of community, it was the life of towns like Rothenburg—of which Rothenburg's alone now survives—which gave to that profoundly German contrast its content and its validity.

The fashionable spa at Baden-Baden is pictured below in a nineteenth-century print. A monument to Gutenberg, opposite, above, stands in Mainz. A page from the Latin Bible printed by Gutenberg at Mainz about 1455 is opposite, below.

Another kind of world preserves its spirit and its splendor at Baden-Baden. It is the fashionable world of the privileged, basking in the security of Europe's nineteenth-century heyday, when privilege still had a good conscience and lavishly displayed itself in public. In that world and time, a sort of summertime in modern history, Baden-Baden was the summer capital. The seat of an independent grand duchy with a genuine flavor of aristocracy about it, Baden-Baden was, pre-eminently, the place where the rich and the well-born repaired to gamble, to flirt, to promenade, and to dance while taking (or pretending to take) the city's famed mineral waters. Of the curative powers of Baden-Baden's spa there may be some doubt, although its reputation is venerable: the Roman emperor Caracalla visited Baden-Baden in the third century in hopes of curing his rheumatism. What is certainly not in doubt was Baden-Baden's power to cure ennui, for it gave to the privileged classes of Europe the supreme excitement of seeing each other and being seen in return. On the beautiful riverside promenade known as the Lichtentaler Allee they could vie with each other in displaying the fashionable cut of their clothes, the good looks of their mistresses, the splendor of their carriages, or the daring of their aristocratic insouciance. The duke of Hamilton once strolled down the promenade leading a calf on a blue ribbon in order to win a sporting bet, while England's Prince Edward rode down it draped in a white sheet en route to a ghost party. In the gambling casinos the privileged compared their luck. On the race course they pitted their horses, and in the Grand Salon of the vast, colonnaded Kurhourse they gave glittering balls to honor each other. And when balls and parties palled, Baden-Baden offered yet another splendid restorative: the vast sylvan preserve known as the Black Forest, which begins a few miles from the city. To the fortunate who summered at Baden-Baden it must have seemed as though Europe's summertime would never come to an end. From Baden-Baden to Mainz is a long spiritual journey. The spa is a modern playground and Mainz one of the venerated cities of Germany, one of the four whose archbishops served as electors of Germany's emperors. Yet there is a tenuous link between the modern world's playground and the ancient imperial city, for Mainz is one of the sources of that modern world which danced at Baden-Baden. Its greatest son is Johann Gutenberg, inventor of movable type, who altered the course of European history with a printing press that can still be seen in the city of his birth.

Like Germany's emperors, its medieval cathedral builders also dreamed dreams too vast for fulfillment. Nowhere were the dream and its apparent failure more stunning than in Cologne, the richest, largest, and proudest city of medieval Germany. Inspired by the rise of Amiens Cathedral, the townspeople in 1248 began to build a second and yet more grandiose Amiens, befitting Cologne's greatness. A century later work ceased on the still towerless, roofless, half-built cathedral. Any real hope that it would one day be finished the people of Cologne abandoned, although they worked on it halfheartedly from time to time, putting up a temporary roof, for example, in the sixteenth century. By 1800 the cathedral was a dilapidated, melancholy ruin, a blighted dream whose incompleteness Goethe himself bemoaned. Yet the original plans for the cathedral survived through the ages like a nagging conscience, and in 1842 the king of Prussia initiated the work of completing what had been begun six centuries before. Since 1880 Cologne's cathedral has been all that its first builders had hoped it would be — the most awesome Gothic church in the world. If dreaming outsized dreams has been the German rule, then the little town of Freiburg is the rule's exception. Founded in the twelfth century, Freiburg set about almost at once to build itself a fitting cathedral. A century later it was done. Manageable aims get their reward. Not only is the lacy Gothic spire of the Freiburg Cathedral the loveliest in Germany, it is one of the very few German Gothic towers actually completed in the Gothic age.

Freiburg's partly Romanesque cathedral (right) was begun in 1200 and finished in 1252. Cologne's cathedral (arch, opposite) took 632 years to complete.

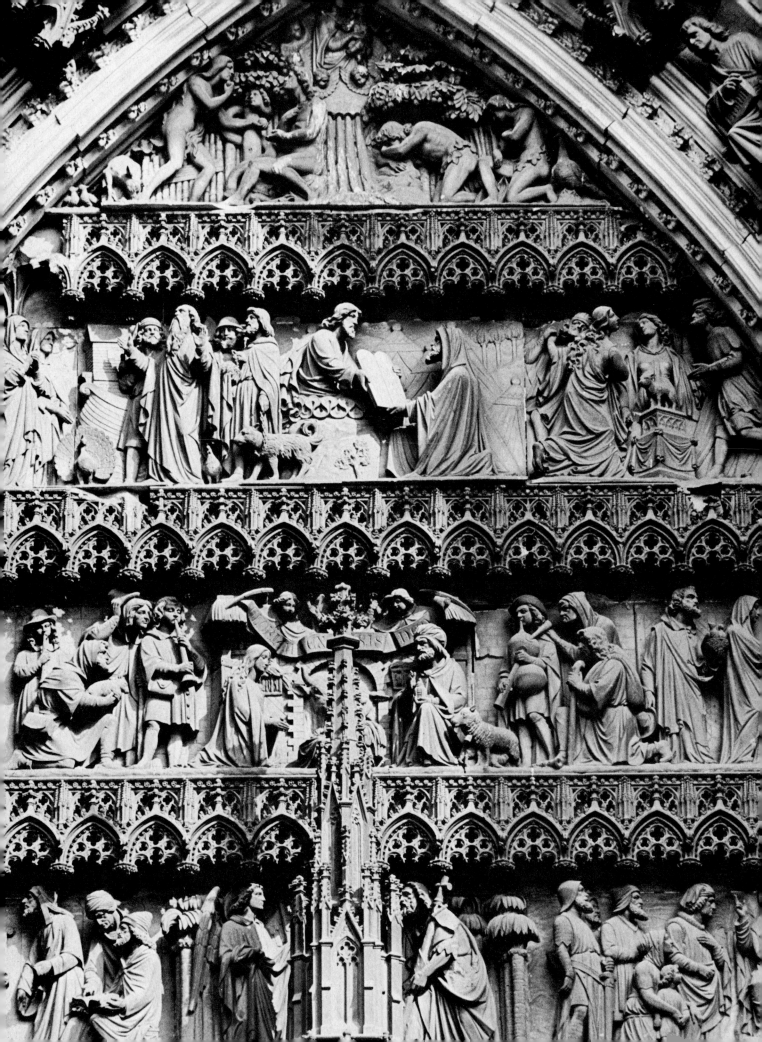

Hanseatic Towns

The medieval walls of Bremen (below) are now green walks, but they still sharply outline the old city.

In the eleventh and twelfth centuries, in the remote northern portions of Germany, far away from the seats of empire, small maritime trading villages began enjoying a hard-won prosperity as trade began to grow in the Baltic and North seas. Beset by pirates, pillaged by mounted brigands, perpetually threatened by the feudal nobility, the towns not only lived at hazard but had only themselves to rely upon. In 1241 two of those towns, Lübeck, on the Baltic Sea, and Hamburg, on the River Elbe, made a compact for the mutual protection of their trade. Their agreement soon made history. With canal-girded Lübeck as its capital, the association of "hanse" grew rapidly as seaports as far away as Amsterdam entered the confederation. By the time Bremen, a port on the River Weser, joined it in 1358, the Hanseatic League, as it then became known, was a power in the land, with formidable fleets of its own and citizen-armies to deploy. Independent of the emperor, independent of the feudal nobility, far from reverent toward the higher clergy, the towns of the Hanse were peopled by men imbued with civic pride and governed by mayors who, as often as not, were formidable military leaders. Hamburg for centuries bore the proud title "free and Hanseatic," while Lübeck in 1370 defeated the armies of the king of Denmark and for one hundred fifty years thereafter held the right to confirm Denmark's kings. The Hanse towns were genuine city-states — Hamburg was officially called a city-state — powerful little republics rising out of the ruins of a disintegrating empire powerless to help or to harm them.

The Hanseatic League died out in the sixteenth century, but its principal cities did not. Bremen and Hamburg today are two of the busiest ports in Europe, and even Lübeck, though far less rich, has long since overflowed its medieval girdle of canals. Yet in these Hanse cities something of the Hanseatic civic spirit remains visible and intact. In Bremen and Lübeck, the old town halls still stand in their dominating positions in the center of the old city districts, overlooking their ancient market squares. Although the town hall of Hamburg was built in 1897, its sheer imposing size and its soaring campanile demonstrate the determination of Hamburg's town fathers to keep the city's civic institutions at the forefront even in a sprawling metropolis. The atmosphere of the Hanseatic era remains strongest in Lübeck, whose old city contains such revealing relics of the old days as tiny courtyards set back from the streets. These Lübeck's seventeenth-century patricians donated to the city as public amenities for their fellow citizens. Inevitably in an age of nation-states, what remains of the old Hanse spirit of civic patriotism and republican virtue is more a flavor than a reality. To one authoritative observer, the great German novelist Thomas Mann, the flavor alone was sadly inadequate. Mann's celebrated novel *Buddenbrooks*, which traces the moral decline of a ruling family of Lübeck, is fundamentally the history of the decay of the Hanseatic spirit.

At Bremen's town hall (top), ship models commemorate the days when Bremen's square-riggers plied the North Sea. Hamburg's lordly town hall (center) stands near the Alster River, tributary of the Elbe and original site of the city. The twin turrets of Koming overlook the center of Lübeck, former Hanseatic League capital.

Berlin

The famous Brandenburg Gate (below), designed in the classical style by C. G. Langhans from 1788 to 1793, stands near the concrete and barbed-wire wall that divides Berlin into eastern and western zones. Remains of the Romanesque Revival Kaiser Wilhelm Memorial Church, opposite, are incorporated into a modern campanile and church built in 1961.

The landmarks that are preserved in Germany today are found for the most part in remote and often obscure areas. Such large cities as Berlin, with their wealth of historic monuments, were virtually razed in the destruction that attended the fall of the Third Reich. Berlin itself is of relatively recent origin, having developed from two medieval villages that merged in 1307 and serving, from the fifteenth century, as the seat of the electors of Brandenburg. Frederick William, "the Great Elector," who reigned from 1640 to 1688, established the basis for Berlin's modern importance by encouraging Dutch Calvinists, French Huguenots, and other foreigners to settle there and engage in industry, commerce, and artistic enterprise. Succeeding monarchs extended Berlin's boundaries and enriched their capital with elegant edifices. The city's progress was only temporarily impeded when it fell to the Austrians and Russians during the Seven Years' War and later was occupied by French troops during the Napoleonic campaigns. Early in the nineteenth century Berlin became the focal point of German nationalist aspirations. With the coronation of William I in 1871, the metropolis, as capital of the German Empire, entered its most remarkable period of growth and prosperity. And between the world wars, continental Europe's second largest city reached its cultural zenith as an avant-garde center of the arts, literature, and music. At the outset of World War II Berlin presented a curious architectural mélange of heavy Prussian splendor and Bauhaus functionalism. All this was obliterated by bombardment and artillery fire when the Russians attacked the city from April to May of 1945. Among the few public buildings to survive the holocaust were the undamaged Brandenburg Gate of 1793, which now stands in the Communist-held eastern sector of Berlin, and the ruins of the Kaiser Wilhelm Memorial Church of 1895, which have been incorporated into a modern church.

Austria

PHOTO RESEARCHERS – FRITZ HENLE

St. Stephen's Cathedral (below)—"Der Alte Steffel," or Old Stevie, as it is affectionately called—stands at the center of Vienna's inner city, displaying on its roof the two-headed eagle of the Hapsburgs (right). The painting opposite, top, shows the city in 1683, under siege by the Turks, the crowned head shown below it being that first of Austria's many Hapsburg rulers, Emperor Rudolf I.

RAPHO-GUILLUMETTE PICTURES – BERNARD G. SILBERSTEIN

Vienna

Austria and the Hapsburgs, W. J. G. KNOCH

Vienna, Austria's capital and only metropolis, is, or was until recently, one of the world's most cosmopolitan cities—for reasons rooted in history. And its history is rooted, in turn, in geography, in its situation athwart a major crossroads of central Europe: straddling the ancient north-south trade route between the Baltic and the Adriatic, Vienna stands, too, at the eastern end of the Alps, on the verge of the immense Hungarian plain. So its citizens, though linked by blood and language to the German peoples west and northwest of them, have down the centuries also looked east and southeast, to the Balkan lands drained by the Danube River. Vienna started as a settlement, Vindobona, where Roman legionaries set up a frontier fortress and where the emperor Marcus Aurelius is believed to have died in A.D. 180; overrun by Ostrogoths in the fifth century, it was mentioned again in documents as Venia in 880 and in 1030 as Wienne. During the early Middle Ages the town was a center of trade and a staging post for Crusades to the Holy Land. Given a charter as a city in 1137, Vienna became in 1156 the capital of the dukes of Austria, the Babenbergs, but in 1251 Ottokar of Bohemia took possession of the duchy and city; it was he who in 1258 began to build Saint Stephen's Cathedral. In 1278 Ottokar was defeated by Rudolf von Hapsburg, and Vienna became the seat of the Hapsburg dynasty, which it was to remain until 1918. During the fourteenth through the sixteenth centuries Romanesque Saint Stephen's Cathedral was transformed into Austria's most important Gothic edifice. But Vienna's finest hour came in 1683, when for the second time (the first was in 1529) its defenders stood fast against a vast Turkish army invading from the east, and so saved Western Europe for Christianity. After the siege was lifted, the Viennese found bags of coffee left behind by the fleeing Turks; from this discovery evolved the café life that has since been a distinctive feature of the Vienna scene.

375

As rulers of Austria, the Hapsburgs wielded power so adroitly that within three centuries they could adopt as their device the motto "A.E.I.O.U."—*Austriae est imperare orbi universo*, or "Austria shall rule the world." By the time they were made archdukes in 1453 they were already emperors, for after 1440 the theoretically elective post of Holy Roman Emperor was, in fact, a hereditary Hapsburg perquisite; when the empire was finally dissolved in 1806, the incumbent simply became emperor of Austria. Generation after generation they added to their holdings through marriage—giving rise to the saying *Bella gerant alii; tu, felix Austria, nube* ("Let others wage war; thou, happy Austria, marry")—until by 1519 their domain reached from the Carpathians to Peru, Emperor Charles V having inherited from his mother, Juana of Castile, Spain's entire empire in the New World. Throughout this period—indeed, throughout the whole of the Hapsburgs' long ascendancy—their headquarters continued to be the Hofburg, a town of imperial residences and offices within Vienna. And as Austria grew so did the Hofburg, one notable legacy of Hapsburg rule in Spain, for instance, being the celebrated Spanish Riding School there, where white Lippizaner stallions go through a complicated dressage centuries old. In the eighteenth century the Hofburg had, for the first and only time, an imperial mistress, the redoubtable Maria Theresa, and after the defeat of Austria's enemy, Napoleon, in 1814, it welcomed the great powers of Europe at the Congress of Vienna. Following Francis Joseph's long reign (1848–1916) and his successor Charles I's brief one (1916–18), the Hapsburgs faded into history; but their memory continues to pervade Vienna, more than any other place at the Hofburg.

The Hofburg, an imperial town within Vienna, took seven centuries to build. Its treasures include the regalia of the Holy Roman Emperors. Opposite is the imposing entrance of the Neue Hofburg; left, Maria Theresa Square; and below, the interior of the famous Spanish Riding School.

No other city in Europe—or even, perhaps, in the world—can match Vienna in the richness of its musical heritage. Its association with music began early: soon after the Babenbergs established themselves in Vienna in 1156, their court became a resort of minnesingers, and it was there that Walther von der Vogelweide, "the finest lyric poet of the Middle Ages," learned to "sing and say." The Hapsburgs, in turn, also supported music: Maximilian I founded the court choir to further church music, and Leopold I was a composer in his own right. But not until the eighteenth century did the city enter upon its golden age of music. In 1750 C. W. Gluck came to Vienna, there to conduct the imperial opera for a decade and to write, in 1762, *Orpheus and Euridyce*, the first opera in the new, as distinct from the Italian, style. Joseph Haydn, having received his musical education in Vienna and gone elsewhere, returned in 1790; in 1797 he composed Austria's national anthem, and in the next few years his noble oratorios *The Creation* and *The Seasons*. Wolfgang Amadeus Mozart, born in Salzburg, spent the last ten years of his short life in Vienna, where he composed his great operas, including *The Magic Flute;* his last work, *The Requiem,* is performed annually in the Hofburg chapel. Ludwig von Beethoven, born in Bonn, came to Vienna as a youth to learn music from Haydn, among others; it was there that he composed almost all his major works, including the Sixth Symphony (1808), the great Ninth (1817–23), and the *Missa Solemnis* (1818–22). Like Gluck, Haydn, and Mozart, Beethoven died in Vienna. Franz Schubert, by contrast, was born in that music-drenched city, and his joyful, melodic airs give authentic voice to the Viennese spirit. It was during the so-called Biedermeier period (1815–50) that the Viennese waltz came into its own in the works of Josef Lanner, and, most memorably, Johann Strauss, whose son and namesake wrote the classic Viennese operetta *Die Fledermaus.* Among more recent notable composers who lived and worked in Vienna were Johannes Brahms, Anton Bruckner, Gustav Mahler, and Richard Strauss; the last two served as directors of Vienna's opera house.

Erected in the 1860's, Vienna's Opera House, below, stands on the broad Ringstrasse, the city's pride. Its interior, as the grand staircase, opposite, attests, is sumptuously decorated.

Prince Eugene of Savoy's two Belvedere palaces now house art collections. At left, a rampant stone horse guards the Upper Belvedere, wherein the prince, opposite, allegorically defeats the Turks.

While Vienna has, in Saint Stephen's Cathedral and other old churches, a few notable Gothic buildings, more typical of the city—and more suited to the taste of its lighthearted citizens—are its vastly more numerous structures in the post-medieval manner called baroque. Outstanding among these are two buildings, set one above the other on a gentle slope, that are together known as the Belvedere: this graceful garden-palace was constructed between 1714 and 1723 by the master architect Lukas von Hildebrandt for one of Austria's greatest military heroes, Prince Eugene of Savoy. As a young man the prince, the son of a niece of Cardinal Mazarin, was refused a commission in the French army by Louis XIV, whereupon, in 1683, he entered the service of Emperor Leopold I. After participating in the relief of Vienna, he fought in Hungary, helped to capture Belgrade, and in 1697 annihilated an entire Turkish army at Senta. During the War of the Spanish Succession (1701–14) he made the aged Louis XIV pay dearly for his earlier rebuff: after defeating the French in Italy, he joined England's duke of Marlborough in Bavaria, and the two won the brilliant victory of Blenheim (1704); four years later he again cooperated with Marlborough in Flanders, helping him rout the French at Oudenaarde (1708) and Malplaquet (1709). After the war-weary French sued for peace in 1714, Eugene served as governor of the Austrian Netherlands and as imperial vicar in Italy; in 1716–18 he again fought the Turks successfully in Serbia. At last he retired, covered with honors, only to return to the field of battle in the War of the Polish Succession (1733–35). He died in 1736 at the age of seventy-three. Sixteen years later his palace, the Belvedere, became the property of the imperial family.

It was, the story goes, the early-seventeenth-century emperor Matthias I who discovered the beautiful fountain (*schöner brunnen*) that was to give its name to a pleasant elevated district of southwest Vienna—and before that area became urban, to the Schönbrunn Palace, pictured below in an eighteenth-century view by Bernardo Belotto. Matthias's successors were kept busy by the Thirty Years' War (1618–48), then by imperial wars against France's King Louis XIV—and by the Turkish menace. In 1683 a hunting lodge on the site of the future palace was destroyed by the Turks, but in 1694, with the Turks on the run, Emperor Leopold I conceived the idea of erecting at Schönbrunn an imperial residence that would outshine that of his archrival, Louis, at Versailles. He entrusted the task to the greatest Austrian architect of that or perhaps any day, Johann Bernhard Fischer von Erlach. The architect drew up grandiose plans and began to supervise construction, but before long Austria became enmeshed in the War of the Spanish Succession (1701–14), and the huge project was left unfinished; it was completed later in the century under Empress Maria Theresa—once she had established her right to rule in the War of the Austrian Succession (1740–48)—and her son Joseph II. Though it failed to surpass Versailles, Schönbrunn was an architectural success, particularly when viewed in the setting of its splendid park; and its scale (1,441 rooms, 139 kitchens among its various accommodations) made it roomy enough even for Hapsburgs.

To Schönbrunn Palace, below, Empress Maria Theresa welcomed, among many others, the precocious boy Mozart, opposite, at right.

Schönbrunn Palace is rich in historical associations. In Maria Theresa's time it was the summer residence of the court and the empress's favorite home: there, when not attending to state business, she delighted in playing with her thirteen children by her husband, Francis Stephen of Lorraine. (One of them, Marie Antoinette, was to become queen of France and fall victim to the French Revolution, for Maria Theresa carried on the traditional Hapsburg policy of international matchmaking, the consequences of which could never be known in advance.) When the remarkable Mozart family came to Vienna the empress welcomed them to Schönbrunn, where they gave recitals, as in the engraving at right; the six-year-old prodigy Wolfgang Amadeus, seen here at the keyboard, astonished everyone with his virtuosity. In 1805 and 1809 Austria's temporary nemesis, Napoleon, set up his headquarters at Schönbrunn; the next year he too married a Hapsburg princess, Marie-Louise, but four years later his vanquishers, at the Congress of Vienna, gave fancy balls at Schönbrunn. ("The Congress doesn't advance; it dances," said the old prince de Ligne.) At Schönbrunn Emperor Francis Joseph was born and died; there lived his heir apparent, Francis Ferdinand, whose assassination touched off World War I; and there Emperor Charles I relinquished his authority.

Melk

The town and abbey of Melk, situated respectively on and above the Danube at a point fifty miles west of Vienna, occupy a unique place in Austrian history. Formerly the Roman stronghold of Namare, Melk (which is incidentally mentioned in the *Nibelungenlied* as Medelike) was captured toward the end of the tenth century by Leopold I von Babenberg, who fixed his seat there. The Babenbergs, natives of Bavaria, were the first rulers of Austria, then called the Ostmark, or eastern border tract. Melk remained their capital for more than a hundred years, until the beginning of the twelfth century, when (recalling the fate of the Nibelungs) they followed the Danube Valley eastward, to establish their court first at Tulln, and finally, in 1156, at Vienna—where, after less than a century, they died out. In 1101, before leaving Melk, Margrave Leopold III turned over his castle there to the Benedictines, who converted it into a fortified abbey. The abbey prospered, becoming famous throughout the region as a center of learning and spiritual ardor. The onset of the Reformation early in the sixteenth century, however, confronted the monastic orders with a new and serious challenge; in 1525 the Peasants' War spread to Austria from Germany, and although the suppression of the uprising in Germany also destroyed the movement in Austria, Lutheranism found powerful support among the Austrian nobles. Not until early in the seventeenth century did Austria's rulers become vigorously and militantly Catholic. In 1683 the invading Turks ravaged Melk Abbey's estates; the abbey was gutted by fire, but after 1702 it was rebuilt.

Melk Abbey, below, had to be rebuilt in the 18th century on a trapeze-shaped site; its architects clearly succeeded. This Benedictine monastery is treasured as a gem of Austrian late baroque. The interior of its church, at right, gives an impression of great lightness.

"Austria," the English essayist Sacheverell Sitwell has written, "is essentially a land of the Counter Reformation." During the turbulent sixteenth century, while Europe was gradually polarized between a Protestant north and a Catholic south, Austria was often a battleground of the contesting creeds; its rulers, though committed as Holy Roman Emperors to all-out defense of the Church, were forced by circumstances to pursue a policy of accommodation. Thus in 1567, in order to win the support of powerful nobles in his struggle against the Turks, Emperor Maximilian II made concessions to the Protestants in the exercise of their faith. His precursor Ferdinand I had, however, already introduced the Counter Reformation into Austria by summoning the Jesuits to Vienna and Prague; and when at the century's end the Protestant peasants of Upper Austria rebelled, their suppression resulted in the complete restoration of Catholicism. This development found concrete expression in such buildings as Melk Abbey, rebuilt between 1702 and 1749 in the baroque style from plans by Jakob Prandauer. Thus the triumph of the Counter Reformation, one of the most decisive events of Austrian history, became permanently memorialized in the country's architecture and in the characteristic appearance of its towns.

385

Waterways, once vital arteries of commerce, add greatly to the charm of rural Austria, drawing visitors to towns like Hallstatt, below, on the Hallstättersee, and Waidhofen an der Ybbs, above, on a tributary of the Danube. Opposite, a 9th-century castle in that river's Wachau region attests to the insecurity of life in bygone days.

Austria, a landlocked and largely mountainous country, is traversed by numerous rivers, many if not most of which flow into the Danube (whose basin, comprising the federal provinces of Upper and Lower Austria, formed the core of "Osterreich," the easternmost realm of Charlemagne's empire, and is consequently known as the cradle of Austria). It was in the wide, fertile river valleys and beside the lakes that the first permanent settlements arose in what was to become a potent nation; these prehistoric communities were mostly given over to subsistence farming, but in a number of areas mining was the principal activity, as the mountains were—and are—rich in minerals. In historical times the extraction and exploitation of various metals was to play an important part in Austria's national economy: in the sixteenth century, for instance, the ironworks at Waidhofen an der Ybbs brought great prosperity to that town. Another mineral resource, salt, long dominated the economy of the Salzkammergut (literally, "salt exchequer property"). At lakeside Hallstatt (Salt Town), archaeological excavations have laid bare the remains of an important settlement of the first Iron Age, whose Celtic inhabitants mined salt in deep shafts that can still be explored and fashioned varied cultural and art objects in bronze and iron, ingeniously worked and of great beauty.

Waterways

The Danube, with a total course of 1,776 miles from its source in the Black Forest to its mouth on the Black Sea, is, after the Volga (2,293 miles), Europe's longest river. Running past or through eight countries, it has three national capitals on its banks — Vienna, Budapest, and Belgrade — and although it crosses Austria for only 224 miles, or one eighth of its length, it is a vital artery for the economy of that country. But if the river, which is navigable for its entire course within Austria, has long played a crucial role in commerce, its chief importance historically has been strategic: in the Roman era, it first protected the barbarians against the Romans' advance, and then, after Trajan crossed it and subdued the Dacians, it acted as a barrier against them. Many centuries later the valley of the Danube was the route chosen by the Turks for their abortive invasions of Austria in 1529 and 1683. But the river has played a cultural role too, for the forests and other beauties of nature along its banks have inspired many painters, notably the early-fifteenth-century masters Albrecht Altdorfer, Hans Burgkmair, Jörg Breu, and Lucas Cranach the Elder. Today the Danube's lower reaches in Austria remain rural, just as the Rhine was before industrialization.

In the view of Salzburg at left —the view enjoyed by successive prince-archbishops from their stronghold, the Hohensalzburg— the 17th-century cathedral dominates the foreground. Opposite, a gallimaufry of ornate signs in the Old Town beguiles visitors.

Salzburg

"All the beauty of Nature that I have seen elsewhere is, in my opinion, nothing compared to that of Salzburg." So wrote that city's most famous son, Wolfgang Amadeus Mozart. Situated on the Salzach River a few miles below the point at which it enters Austria from Germany, Salzburg has a long history: the area was inhabited as far back as the Stone Age, and during the Bronze and Iron ages its Celtic settlers worked its salt deposits and mined its copper and gold, carrying on a trade in artifacts that extended as far north as the Baltic. In the last years before Christ, the Romans conquered the region and set up a commercial center, Juvavum, there; about A.D. 470 Juvavum's leading citizens fled the barbarian incursions, but in 690 Bishop Hruodbert (Saint Rupert) founded the present Saint Peter's Monastery on the site of the ruined town. In 798, under Charlemagne, Salzburg became the see of an archbishop charged with converting Carinthia, Styria, and western Hungary to Christianity; the archbishopric steadily grew in importance, and in 1278 Austria's new ruler, Rudolf von Hapsburg, who was also Holy Roman Emperor, named the archbishops imperial princes. Thereafter Salzburg and its surrounding lands were to maintain a separate identity as an ecclesiastical state for more than half a millennium, becoming fully absorbed, at last, into Austria only in 1805. As a rule, Salzburg's prince-archbishops wielded their almost unlimited power with great severity, expelling the Jews late in the fifteenth century and persecuting the local Protestants early in the eighteenth century so rigorously that in 1723 thirty thousand of them emigrated to Prussia; late in the sixteenth and early in the seventeenth centuries, however, three of them (Wolf Dietrich von Raitenau, Marcus Sitticus, and Paris Lodron) demonstrated a talent for building worthy of Renaissance princes, and in little more than fifty years they transformed Salzburg, with its medieval maze of narrow streets, into a town resembling the great cities of Italy, with palaces and open spaces. During the Napoleonic Wars, Salzburg was secularized (1802) and annexed by Austria (1805); by the Peace of Schönbrunn (1809) it was awarded to Bavaria, but in 1815 the Congress of Vienna restored it in toto to Austria.

PHOTO RESEARCHERS – ANITA M. BEER

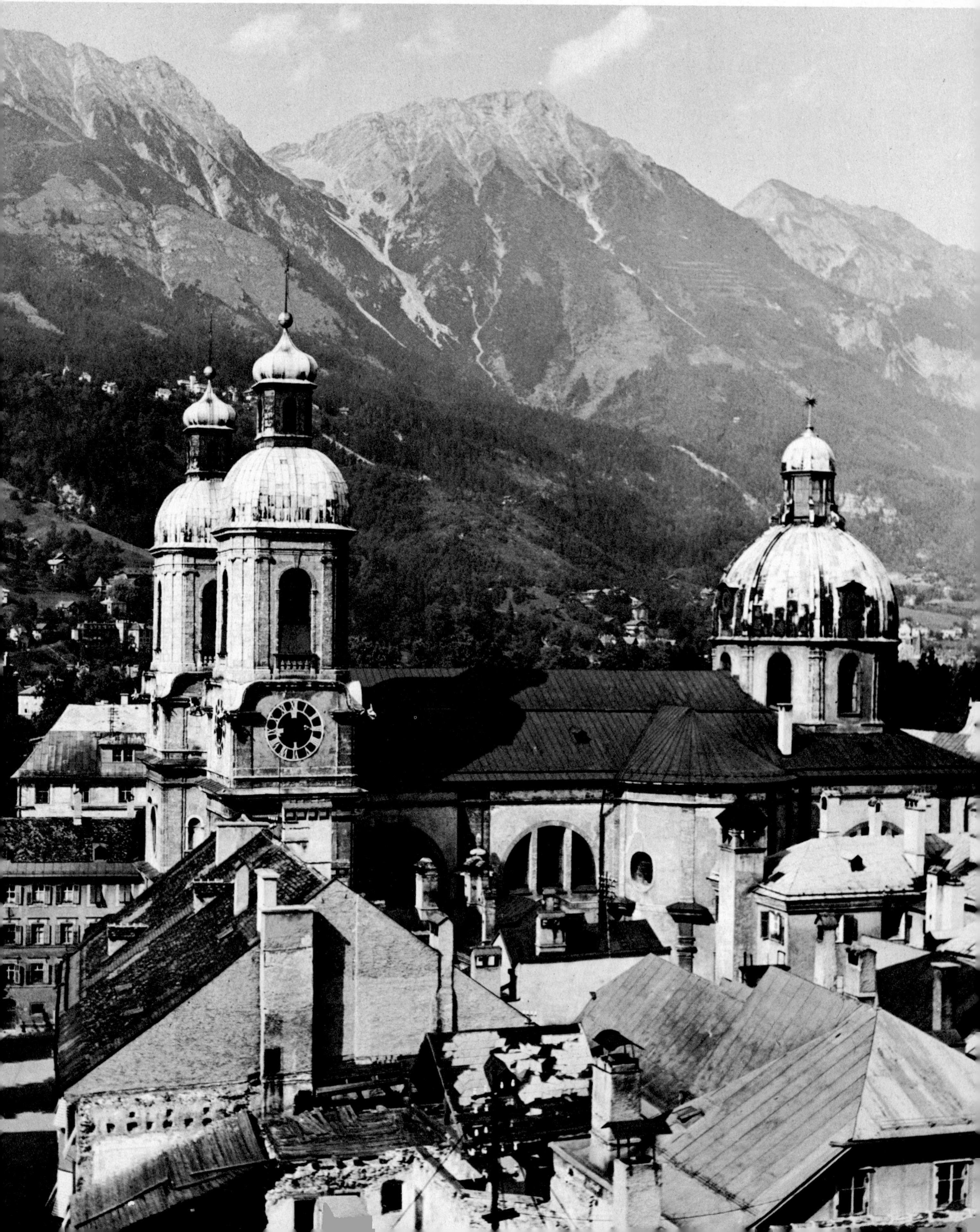

The Tyrol, a western province of Austria, is actually the northern part of an Alpine region of that name, whose southern part is in Italy. Conquered by the Romans in 15 B.C., the Tyrol was overrun in the sixth century by Teutonic tribesmen and later by the Franks, who by the eighth century held it all. After the eleventh century much of the South Tyrol was ruled by the bishops of Trent and of Brixen; the North Tyrol was united under the counts of Tyrol, but in 1363 it passed to the Hapsburgs, and in 1420 its chief center, Innsbruck, supplanted the more southerly Merano as capital of the region. Innsbruck, on the site of Roman Veldelina, was first mentioned in 1187 and received the rights of a city in 1233, but it attained true prominence only at the close of the Middle Ages, in the reign of Emperor Maximilian I (1493–1519), whose marriage to Mary of Burgundy greatly enlarged the Hapsburg realm. "The Last Knight," as he is affectionately remembered, preferred Innsbruck above all his other towns: there in 1494 he married his second wife, Bianca Maria Sforza; there he set off on many a hunt after Alpine game; and there he chose to be buried. (He was, in fact, interred at his birthplace, Wiener Neustadt, but the sumptuous Hofkirche he ordered as his tomb was duly built and remains one of Innsbruck's chief glories.) In 1765 the town was celebrating the wedding of Prince Leopold (later Leopold II) to the Spanish Infanta, and had erected a triumphal arch, when word came that Maria Theresa's consort, Emperor Francis, had died: one face of the arch was altered to show scenes of mourning. At the start of the nineteenth century Austria acquired all of the Tyrol, but after World War I, by the Treaty of Saint Germain, the South Tyrol was awarded to Italy. Today Innsbruck remains a lively city in a setting of breathtaking grandeur.

Opposite, Innsbruck's main street, with Alps beyond. Above, left, the triumphal arch. Above, 2 of the 28 statues of Maximilian I's forebears in the Hofkirche.

Innsbruck

The Saint Gotthard Pass (above) had a historic role in Switzerland's early fight for union and independence. In Zug (below) the Zytturm (clock tower) remains from medieval fortifications. Opposite is Chur, which also has a medieval quarter.

OVERLEAF: *Fribourg, a center of Swiss Catholicism*

Switzerland

Just as Switzerland is a confederation of cantons, its history has much of the character of a mosaic. The pattern of that history is almost as intricate as the mechanism of one of the watches for which the country is famous. Yet in aggregate the first four sites represented on these pages reveal the start of a recognizable outline. In the beginning there were the Helvetii, a Celtic tribe that succumbed to Julius Caesar's invasion in 58 B.C., the first milestone along a tortuous trail. The Romans remained until the fifth century. The Saint Gotthard Pass through the Lepontine Alps of south-central Switzerland was known to the Romans, but there is much firmer evidence of their colonization in other present-day localities, including Zug, the historic town fourteen miles south of Zurich. (Zug's Prehistoric Museum, in fact, contains remnants of the area's past tracing back to 2000 B.C.) Germanic tribes, the Burgundians and Alemanni, succeeded the Romans and were in turn ousted by the Franks in the sixth century. Important links with that era, during which Switzerland was part of Charlemagne's realm, are to be found in Chur, an ancient town near the Austrian border. Chur's bishops were princes of the Holy Roman Empire, whose groundwork had been laid by Charlemagne and whose fief Switzerland was to be for two and a half centuries. It was in the vicinity of Zug that the Swiss finally asserted themselves — and there that their history began to assume the pattern of national identity. In 1291, when the Hapsburgs of Austria had become the overlords of much of the country, three central cantons banded together in the archetype of the modern confederation. In 1315 they routed a Hapsburg army at Morgarten, just south of Zug, in a pioneer test of strength through union. And in the two centuries that followed, the Saint Gotthard Pass became a vital communications link for the confederates, including Fribourg in the west.

Switzerland's late-medieval period, during which the goals of federation and freedom began to be realized, also produced something very material in the form of architectural landmarks. Although the histories of Zug and Chur considerably antedate that period, the appeal of those towns now resides in their medieval flavor. Most of the ecclesiastical structures that symbolize Fribourg's position as the early center of Swiss Catholicism date from the twelfth and thirteenth centuries. By 1481, when Fribourg was admitted to the growing confederation, membership already numbered eight Swiss cantons; Fribourg had qualified for admission by participating in the union's successful war (1474–77) against another foreigner with designs on its territory—Charles the Bold, last duke of Burgundy. Throughout the confederation's early years, the rural cantons' fear of being outnumbered by cities limited the growth of this union. Bickering over the admission of Fribourg and Solothurn as city cantons almost provoked civil war, but a religious hermit, Nicholas of Flüe, made a dramatically successful plea for union at the Diet of Stans in 1481, ensuring both the continuing life of the confederation and his own place in Swiss history as patron saint (he was canonized in 1872). Among many rural areas that have preserved old-world atmosphere, the valley known as the Lower Engadine is justly famous. Stretching to the Italian and Austrian borders in the extreme east, it contains villages, like Ardez, whose homes still bear the mottoes and heraldic emblems of early settlers in the form of incised graffito decoration. Another such picturesque area is the north shore of the Lake of Thun. In Oberhofen, just southeast of Thun, stands one of Switzerland's finest castles, built in the twelfth century and subsequently enlarged. It is now a museum. The castle and a surrounding park face the lake.

Incised graffito decoration is a characteristic of the Swiss rural houses in towns like Ardez (below). At right is the castle in Oberhofen, on the Lake of Thun.

The Kapellbrücke (Chapel Bridge) and the Wasserturm (water tower) identify present-day Lucerne and recall the city's medieval past.

Lucerne, famous for the bridges that connect its old and modern sections perched on opposite sides of the Reuss River, is itself an important link in the early history of Switzerland. The city developed around an eighth-century Benedictine monastery. About 1220, when the construction of a road made the Saint Gotthard Pass usable as a commercial route, Lucerne became a thriving center for trade passing between the upper Rhine and Lombardy. The prosperity did not go unnoticed: in 1291 Rudolf I of Hapsburg bought both town and monastery, a practice with substantial precedent in that period of Swiss history but one not always favored by the populace thus affected. In 1332 Lucerne joined the three cantons (Uri, Schwyz, and Unterwalden) of the original confederation of 1291 and had a hand in the second major victory of the independence-minded Swiss over their Hapsburg overlords. The scene of that action was Sempach, seven miles northwest of Lucerne, where in 1386 an Austrian army under the Hapsburg duke Leopold III was routed by a force only a quarter of its own size. Of the seven bridges at present spanning the Reuss in the area of Lucerne, the two that are roofed have particular claim to interest. The Kapellbrücke (Chapel Bridge), completed in 1333, adjoins the even older Wasserturm (water tower), which was in turn a torture chamber and prison, a treasury building, and a place for storing archives. The Spreuerbrücke (Mills Bridge) dates from 1407. The panels of both bridges are decorated with seventeenth-century paintings. Most of the other historic sites are located on the right bank in the old town. Rising above them, to the north, are the remains of fourteenth- and fifteenth-century town walls. Nine watchtowers survive from these early fortifications.

The illustration below, from a St. Gall manuscript, depicts Carolingian warfare. Bellinzona's walled castles are shown at right; opposite is the medieval castle in Aigle.

Although Saint Gall and Ticino did not become full-fledged cantons of the Swiss Confederation until 1803, the history of their capitals can be traced to the early years of the Middle Ages. Saint Gall, in the German-speaking northeast of Switzerland near the Lake of Constance, takes its name from the capital city, which in turn derived the name from Gallus, a Celtic missionary who established a hermitage on the site about 612. From that beginning there grew an eighth-century Benedictine abbey and a town, forerunner of the present capital of the canton. The abbey of Saint Gall was one of the great centers of medieval Europe; before the beginning of the eleventh century its school was the foremost educational institution north of the Alps. The coming of the Reformation in the sixteenth century signaled the eclipse of the abbey in both religious and temporal respects, but its rebuilt structures are still the center of interest for visitors to present-day Saint Gall. Moreover, the abbey library, with its precious manuscripts, retains the city's most palpable link to its illustrious past as a center of learning. Far to the south, in Italian-speaking Ticino, the capital city, Bellinzona, has even more tangible historical ties in the form of three imposing castles, rebuilt most recently by the dukes of Milan in the fifteenth century, and the remains of a fourteenth-century wall, constructed to bar entry to the Ticino valley. Bellinzona became the property of the original cantons of the Swiss Confederation in 1503.

Switzerland, which abounds in spectacular scenery and national languages, also has its share of gently picturesque sites. Aigle, for example, is a quiet town amid the vineyards and orchards of the Rhone valley of Vaud, the country's westernmost canton. Aigle's claim to historical interest rests largely on a castle constructed in the twelfth century for one of the dukes of Savoy and rebuilt three centuries later. Until the eighteenth century it was the residence of Bernese bailiffs; more recently it has served as a prison. Vaud came under Roman control in 58 B.C. and subsequently was the possession of the Franks and Burgundians. The dominant language here is French, one of three tongues given official sanction by the constitution of 1874. (Since 1938 French, German, and Italian have been joined as national languages by Romansch, which is confined largely to the easternmost canton, Grisons.) Vaud, like Saint Gall and Ticino, was one of six new units admitted to the confederation in 1803. From the original three cantons of the first union of 1291, the figure rose to eight by 1353 and to thirteen by 1501. There it remained until 1803—but Switzerland meanwhile was far from stable in other respects. Its reputation as a military power, bolstered in the fifteenth century by victories over Charles the Bold of Burgundy and then over Maximilian I, who had tried to reassert the claims of the Holy Roman Empire, suffered a severe blow at the hands of the French in northern Italy in 1515. Thereafter Switzerland was neutral internationally. At home it was a different story. In 1519 the first of a series of sermons in Zurich by Ulrich Zwingli marked the introduction of the Reformation. With it came three centuries of internal strife, which split the country both religiously and politically: Catholics were aligned against Protestants, city cantons (predominantly pro-Zwingli) against rural ones. Zwingli himself died in 1531 during the religious warfare.

The Zähringer fountain, with its figure of a bear in armor, stands before an even more historic Bern landmark, the Zeitglockenturm (clock tower), from the original town walls. Opposite is another view of the old quarter.

One of the most familiar landmarks in Bern's old section embodies something of the start and spirit of the capital city of the Swiss Confederation. The Zähringer fountain, named for Bern's founder, stands near the main crossroads, surmounted by the figure of a bear in armor. From earliest times the bear has been the heraldic symbol of the city — appropriately enough in light of its history — and nearby there is a pit where bears have been on view since 1513. Bern got its start in 1191, when Duke Berchtold V of Zähringen established a military post on its site. By 1218 Bern had been made a free imperial city by the Holy Roman Emperor Frederick II; by 1353, as an independent state with ever-increasing surrounding territory won from Austrian and Burgundian overlords and the local nobility, Bern had become a member of the Swiss Confederation, in which it played a leading role. Several of the remaining landmarks of the old city date from the fifteenth century, including the Gothic Münster (cathedral) and Rathaus (city hall). The famous Zeitglockenturm (clock tower) was once a part of the town walls. Even before Geneva, Bern had become a stronghold of the Reformation, and in the eighteenth century its aggressive oligarchy dominated more than fifty territories. Uprisings threatened to topple this rule on three occasions, but it took a much mightier revolt, to the west, to accomplish the task. In 1798, as an aftermath of the French Revolution, French troops marched into Switzerland and occupied Bern on March 5. That year saw the suspension of the confederation and the formation of a dependent Helvetic Republic, whose five-year existence was one of turmoil for the Swiss. Restored and enlarged in 1803, the confederation managed to escape the remaining Napoleonic Wars; in 1815 its territorial integrity was guaranteed.

Two of Zurich's great landmarks are churches: the Grossmünster (left), with its twin towers, and the Fraumünster (opposite). Stein am Rhein (below) retains eighteenth-century houses and older religious remains.

By any arrangement other than an alphabetical one, Zurich ranks in the forefront of Swiss sites. It is the country's largest city and its first city economically. Historically, Zurich commands a top position by either of two yardsticks: it is on one of the most ancient sites in Switzerland, and along the way to its present eminence the city became the center of the Swiss Reformation, which threatened to split the confederation two centuries before Napoleon's forces arrived in 1798 to put an abrupt though temporary end to the union of cantons. The Reformation was a continuing source of both religious and political strife, for even after the confederation had been restored and a course of perpetual independence and neutrality had been set for Switzerland by the Congress of Vienna in 1815, the cantons revived their old differences and fought a brief civil war in 1847. If it is possible to pinpoint the site of the Reformation's start in Switzerland, Zurich's old cathedral, the Grossmünster, has a good claim to that distinction. It was there, in 1519, that the pastor Ulrich Zwingli began to preach his revolutionary doctrine. The Romanesque structure, begun in the eleventh century, still stands on the right bank of the Limmat River. On the stream's other side are the Fraumünster, which was begun in the thirteenth century, and the Lindenhof, a mound that marks the early settlements of the Helvetii and their conquerors, the Romans. The Celtic Helvetii arrived long after Zurich's locale had been the residence of prehistoric lake dwellers. Zurich became a free imperial city in 1218, and it was admitted to the confederation in 1351. Northeast of it, near the German border, stands Stein am Rhein, a picturesque town whose existing medieval buildings also have strong religious ties. There are the remains of a monastery dating from the eleventh century, and on a nearby island in the Rhine, a fifteenth-century chapel that once was the destination of processions of pilgrims. The town's houses are noted for their decorations.

What the Matterhorn and the almost equally famous Castle of Chillon have in common is romance. For millions who have never set foot in Switzerland they exist as symbols of a fanciful realm of high adventure, and each has a solid claim to historic significance. From the time that man first had the urge to ascend distant peaks, the Matterhorn seems to have been high on the list of places to be conquered. It towers 14,700 feet above nearby Zermatt, the sports center in the Pennine Alps along the Swiss-Italian border from which it is now often climbed. A little more than a century ago, however, the Matterhorn was still the unattainable "mountain of all mountains," and even after the British explorer Edward Whymper finally reached the top on July 14, 1865, traveling along the Swiss ridge after six unsuccessful attempts from the Italian side, four members of his party fell to their death during the descent. Zermatt's museum contains mementos of the earliest ascents, and the graveyard of its parish church has a memorial to the four whose lives the Matterhorn claimed that day in 1865 as if by a stroke of revenge. Lord Byron's poem "The Prisoner of Chillon" memorializes both the castle, just south of Montreux, and the Genevan patriot François de Bonnivard, who was its most famous occupant. Although Byron's portrait of Bonnivard incorporates a large measure of fiction, the broad outline of his account is historically sound. The thirteenth-century castle, now a museum, is on the site of Roman fortifications and took its present form when it was the property of the dukes of Savoy. Bonnivard, a clergyman and Humanist, stoutly opposed the attempts of Duke Charles III to control Geneva; he was twice imprisoned by Charles, the second time at Chillon. Visitors to the castle can see the dungeon where Bonnivard was chained from 1532 to 1536, when the forces of Bern, coming to Geneva's aid in the struggle against Savoy, captured Chillon and liberated him. Vaudois patriots took the castle in 1798, during the period when Bern's empire was being dismantled; since 1803 it has been the property of the canton of Vaud. Byron's famous visit took place in 1816. In this century an association was formed to preserve and maintain one of the most famous landmarks in all Switzerland, which has the status of a national monument.

The Matterhorn (opposite) towers high over tiny Zermatt. Above is the Castle of Chillon near Montreux.

Index

Den Gamle By (Old Town), Aarhus, 329, **329**
Denis, Saint, 206–7, **207**
Denmark, 257, 302, 315, **316**, 317, 318, 319, 320–29, 331, 334, 337, 340, 342, 344, 370
Detaille, Édouard, painting, **215**
Diaz, Narcisse V., 186; painting of Fontainebleau, **187**
Dickens, Charles, 326
Dinant, Belgium, 232, **234–35**
Diocletian, emperor, 347, 349
Dionysus, god, 32; House of, Delos, mosaic, **35**
Dives sur Mer, France, **201**
Divine Comedy (Dante), 91
Doge's Palace, Venice, 98, **99**
Domesday Book, 270
Dominican order, 341
Domitian, circus of, Rome, 68, **68**
Domkirke, Roskilde, 329, **329**
Domkyrkan, Visby, 341
Domnall, of Tara, 311
Donatello, 82
Don Quixote (Cervantes), 132, **133**
Dordogne valley, France, **161**
Doric style, 21, 49, **49**, 51
Dover, England, cliffs, **256**, 257
Drottningholm, Stockholm, 338, **338**
Druids, 301
Dryburgh Abbey, Scotland, 301, **301**
Du Barry, Madame, 211
Dublin, Ireland, 308–9, **308**
Duccio de Buoninsegna, 78
Dufy, Raoul, 204
Dumas, Alexandre, 163
Duncairn, Edward Carson, baron of, 309
Duncan I, of Scotland, 299
Duomo di Santa Maria del Fiore, Florence, 79, 82, **83**; bronze doors, 82, **83**; campanile, **83**
Dürer, Albrecht, 363; house, **362**; painting by, **362**
Dutch. *See* Netherlands

E

Eastern Orthodox Church, 27, 38, 42
Edam, Netherlands, 252
Edinburgh, Scotland, 296–97, **296–97**
Edward I, of England, 301, 305
Edward III, of England, 222, 255
Edward V, of England, 287
Edwin, of Northumbria, 297
Egeskov, Kvaerndrup, 322, **322**, 328
Egmont, Lamoral, count of, 227
Egypt, 11, 35, 72, 95, 211
Eiffel Tower, Paris, 206, 212, **212**
Eighty Years' War, 246
Elbe River, Germany, 370, 371
Eleanor of Aquitaine, 178, 183; tomb, 183, **183**

Eleusis, Greece, 31, **31**
Eliot, T. S., 264
Elizabeth I, of England, 228, 257, 270, 273, 308
Elsinore. *See* Helsingor
Ely, England, 269
England, 86, 100, 122, 147, 156, 221, 231, 237, 241, 252, 257–95, 315, 316, 317, 342, 354, 359, 363, 367; civil war, 270; influence in: France, 181, 183, 184, 195, 196, 201, 203, 204, 232, Low Countries, 222, 233, 252, Scotland, 297, 300, 301, 302
English Channel, 184, 196, 204, 219, 257, 263
Enkhuizen, Netherlands, 237
Epidaurus, Greece, theater, 32, **33**
Erasmus, Desiderius, 252
Erechtheum, Athens, 22, **23**, 27
Eretria, Greece, 18
Eric of Pomerania, 323, 340
Eriksen, Edvard, 324
Erlach, Johann Bernhard Fischer von, 382
Erlandsen, Jacob, 320
Ermesinde, countess of Luxembourg, 254
Esch-sur-Sûre, Luxembourg, 254, **254–55**
Eschwege, Baron, 157
Escorial, Spain, 122, **122**, 123, 128, 153
Este, Ippolito II d', 73
Estrées, Gabrielle d', **187**
Estrith dynasty, 320
Etna, Mount, Sicily, 50
Etretat, France, 204, **204**
Etruria, Italy, 60
Etruscans, 60–61, **61**, **63**, 88; tombs, 60, **60**, **61**, 76
Euboea, Greece, 18
Eugene, prince of Savoy, 380, **381**
Eugénie, empress, 204
Euripides, 32, 33, 49
Eurotas plain, Greece, 38
Evans, Sir Arthur, 11
Evelyn, John, 243, 288
Eyck, Jan van, 56, 221

F

Ferdinand I, of Austria, 385
Ferdinand II, of Aragon. *See* Ferdinand V
Ferdinand II, of Portugal, 157
Ferdinand III, of Castile, 117, 141
Ferdinand V, of Castile, 109, 120, 143
Field of the Cloth of Gold, 274, **274**
Fitzherbert, Maria Anne, 285
Flamboyant Gothic style, 171, **221**, 227, **230**, 231
Flanders, 129, 171, 219, 221, 222, **222**, 223, 227, 231, 232, 233, 380
Florence, Italy, 79, 82–87, 91, 233
Floris V, count of Holland, 244
Foix, Gaston de, 91, **91**

Fontainebleau, France, 186, **186**, 187, **187**
Fontana del Moro, Rome, **68**
Fontevrault, France, church, 183, **183**
Forum, Rome, 66, **67**, 68
Foscari, Francesco, 98, **98**
Fougères, France, 196, **197**
Fountain of Vaucluse, Avignon, **168**, 169
"Four Tetrarchs," Venice, 97, **97**
France, 42, 53, 84, 86, 87, 106, 109, 110, 112, 122, 136, 146, 148, **158–217**, 219, 221, 224, 232, 233, 241, 248, 257, 264, 266, 278, 291, 297, 302, 315, 317, 351, 359, 360, 372, 380, 399, 400; influence in: Italy, 57, 91, 107, Low Countries, 221, 222, 227, 245, 255
Francis I, of France, 163, 182, 184–85, 186, 187, 196, 274
Francis II, of France, 297
Franciscan order, 76, 121, 341
Francis Ferdinand, of Austria, 383
Francis Joseph I, of Austria, 377, 383
Francis of Assisi, Saint, 76, **77**
Francis Stephen, duke of Lorraine, 383, 391
Franco-Prussian War, 191, 193, 347
Frankfurt-am-Main, Germany, **356**, 356–57, **357**
Franks, 38, 42, 112, 170, 176, 196, 219, 321, 347, 348, 349, 351, 352, 383, 391, 392, 399
Fraumünster, Zurich, 402, **403**
Frederick I Barbarossa, 356
Frederick II, of Denmark, 323
Frederick II, emperor, 400
Frederick William (the Great Elector), 372
Frederiksborg, Hillerod, 315, 323, **323**
Freiburg, Germany, cathedral, 368, **368**
Fribourg, Switzerland, 392, **394–95**, 396
Friday Market, Ghent, 222, **222**
Frideswide, Saint, 270
Friesland, Netherlands, 236
Friis, Johan, 328
Frisia, Netherlands, 240
Frogner Park, Oslo, **344**
Fugger, Jakob, 360
Fyn, Denmark, 317, 322
Fyrkat, Denmark, 319

G

Gabriel, Jacques Ange, 211
Gaddi, Taddeo, 86
Gaius Marius, 169
Galileo Galilei, 74, **74**
Galla·Placidia, 91
Gallus, missionary, 398
Gama, Vasco da, **152**, 153, 157
Gandoglia, Italy, 105

M

DATE DUE

MR 25 '82			